Tantric Temples

Tantric Temples

Eros and Magic in Java

Peter Levenda

Ibis Press
Lake Worth, FL

Published in 2011 by Ibis Press
An imprint of Nicolas-Hays, Inc.
P. O. Box 540206
Lake Worth, FL 33454-0206
www.ibispress.net

Distributed to the trade by
Red Wheel/Weiser, LLC
65 Parker St. • Ste. 7
Newburyport, MA 01950
www.redwheelweiser.com

ISBN 978-089254-169-0

Library of Congress Cataloging-in-Publication Data

Levenda, Peter.
Tantric temples : eros and magic in Java / Peter Levenda.
p. cm.
Includes bibliographical references and index.
Summary: "A history of tantra in Java and its origin and practice and how it has influenced and interacted with Tibetan Tantra, Hindu mysticism and Sufi Islam and Western sexual magical practices. Illustrated with full color photos of old and newly excavated and uncovered temples, along with with statues and iconography dedicated to practices in shrines, cemeteries and secret schools."--Publisher's description.
ISBN 978-0-89254-169-0 (alk. paper)
1. Tantrism—Indonesia—Java--History. 2. Tantric Buddhism—Indonesia—Java—History. 3.—Sex--Religious aspects—Tantrism. 4. Hindu temples—Indonesia—Java. 5. Buddhist temples—Indonesia—Java. 6. Java (Indonesia)—Religion. I. Title.
BL1283.835.I52J335 2011
204'.46--dc23 2011033581

Book design by Studio 31.
www.studio31.com

Printed in China

FRONTISPIECE: *This is a view of the volcanic eruption that struck Merapi in 2010 as the author was completing this book. The building in the foreground is the Universitas Gadjah Mada (UGM), the "Harvard of Indonesia." Many of the Temples shown in this book were damaged by being covered in volcanic ash. Experts grieve over the setback to their efforts in uncovering and preserving these ancient treasures. The White Temple at Candi Kimpulan was uncovered in late 2009 just before the latest eruption and has since been covered again. Borobudur has also been damaged.*

Magic is merely eroticism applied,
directed, and aroused by its performer.

Ioan Couliano[1]

1 Ioan P. Couliano, *Eros and Magic in the Renaissance* (Chicago: University of Chicago Press, 1987), p. xviii.

Acknowledgments

This is always the trickiest part of any book. So many people have influenced the process of writing a book that it is impossible to credit all of them. Like most writers, I always credit family and friends ... and then realize that I have enlarged my social sphere in the act of creating a book to the extent that new friends are made and new families formed, all while I wasn't looking.

With that in mind, then, I happily acknowledge the impact made on this project by Donald Weiser and Yvonne Paglia, who recognized the value in such a study very early on and encouraged me to write what would become an investigation of Tantra as well as of the amazing Tantric temples of Java; and by James Wasserman, whom I have known for more decades than either of us cares to count, and whose unerring eye for the aesthetics of book publishing has contributed to this volume in an immediately obvious way.

To Nina Rojas, for her early and steady support.

To Sophie Anderson, for the same.

To my two Indonesian colleagues, without whom I would have never known that there were such things as "Tantric temples" in Java and who kindly and patiently led me by the hand to visit them and photograph them: Sita Hidayah and Wilis Rengganiasih Endah Ekowati, the former a brilliant professor of anthropology and the latter an expert in the very strange and wonderful dance I describe in chapter eight. *Semangat*!

To Jean-Pascal Elbaz, of Sangam Restaurant (easily the best Indian restaurant in Yogyakarta), who co-authored a remarkable trilingual guidebook to the temples and who suggested that I visit Candi Ijo ... which I'm glad he did, since it contributed some very strange experiences to this study.

To Mr. and Mrs. Brian Geubtner, of the Pittsburgh and Brooklyn Geubtners.

To Monstracita and her faithful if snide companion, Pit Pitico.

To the Luce Foundation, which financed my first academic trip to Indonesia in 2007, and to the (sometimes) embattled Religious Studies Department of Florida International University: *¡Venceremos!*

And, in the same spirit, to Universitas Gadjah Mada—the "Harvard of Indonesia"—which tolerates the intrusion of many dazed and inquiring minds from abroad such as my own.

And finally to the people of Yogyakarta, Indonesia who suffered so much during the devastating eruption of Mount Merapi that took place in October 2010 while I was finishing this book, I dedicate this humble endeavor and hope that it will encourage more foreigners to visit Indonesia and especially Yogyakarta.

Contents

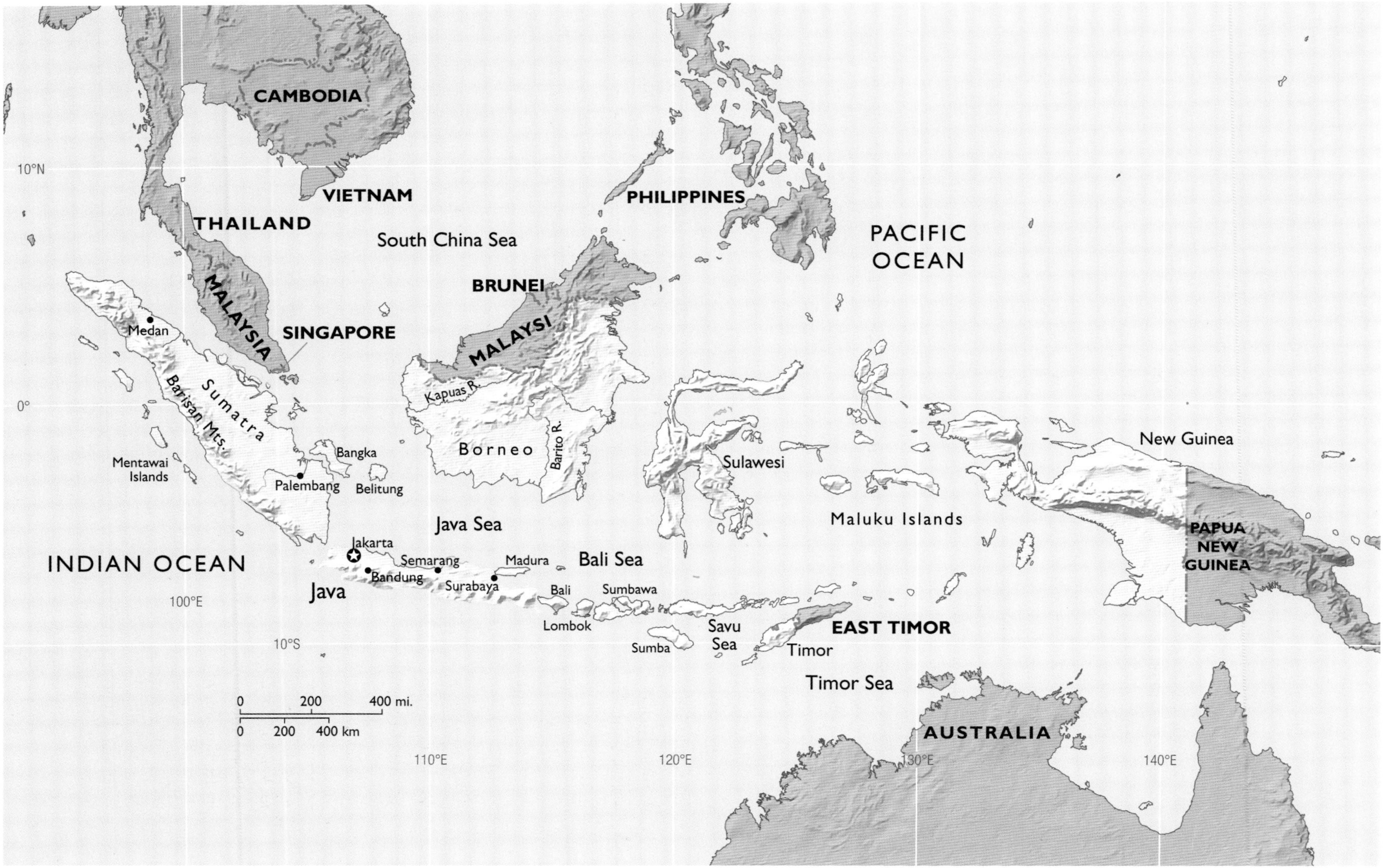
CAMBODIA
VIETNAM
THAILAND
PHILIPPINES
South China Sea
PACIFIC
OCEAN
BRUNEI
MALAYSIA
SINGAPORE
MALAYSI
Medan
Kapuas R.
Sumatra
Barisan Mts.
Borneo
Barito R.
Sulawesi
New Guinea
Bangka
Mentawai
Islands
Palembang
Belitung
Java Sea
Maluku Islands
PAPUA
NEW
GUINEA
Jakarta
Semarang
Madura
Bali Sea
INDIAN OCEAN
Bandung
Surabaya
Java
Bali
Sumbawa
Lombok
Savu
Sea
EAST TIMOR
Sumba
Timor
Timor Sea
AUSTRALIA
0
200
400 mi.
0
200
400 km
10°N
0°
10°S
100°E
110°E
120°E
130°E
140°E

Introduction

In his *Essential Tibetan Buddhism*, renowned Tibetan scholar and chair of the Religion Department at Columbia University Robert A. F. Thurman made several references to the fact that Atisha Dipamkara Shrijnana (982–1054), the Lord Master and one of the Three Most Gracious Living Buddhas in Tibetan Buddhist religion and legend, actually lived for a number of years in Java before returning to Tibet to revitalize the teaching there and overcome a period of spiritual stagnation at the hands of secular rulers and misinformed or malicious teachers.

There is some controversy over the allegation that Atisha spent time in Java, however, and this is an example of the type of historical ambiguity we will encounter from time to time in this study of Tantra in Asia. Until recently, most historians were of the opinion that Atisha never made it as far as Java, but studied in Sumatra at the feet of a Buddhist sage in the capital of the kingdom of Survarnadvipa, most likely today's city of Palembang. Sumatra is another large island in what is now the Indonesian archipelago, but that is culturally and linguistically rather distinct from Java. Recent scholarship, however, tends to accept that the kingdom where Atisha lived during his sojourn in Indonesia was in the region of Kalasa, an ancient capital of Survarnadvipa, which itself may have comprised all of Sumatra, parts of Java, and parts of other islands in the archipelago. There is a temple called Candi Kalasa in the Sultanate of Yogyakarta, and an inscription linking it to the worship of the Goddess Tara. This—along with other textual and archaeological evidence—tends to support a Javanese locus for Atisha's instruction and initiation.[2]

This may seem like nit-picking, but since no Indonesian would mistake a Javanese for a Sumatran, it is worthwhile to point this out. Thurman makes that statement concerning Atisha's stay in Java several times in his excellent introduction to Tibetan Buddhism.[3] Moreover, while he rightfully mentions Atisha's crucial role in the renaissance of Tibetan Buddhism in the 11th century CE, he does not go into any detail about Atisha's Indonesian master nor, indeed, does Thurman assign any

2 Roy E. Jordaan, "Tara and Nyai Lara Kidul: images of the divine feminine in Java," *Asian Folklore Studies*, Vol. 56, No. 2, October 1997, pp. 285–312.

3 Robert Thurman, *Essential Tibetan Buddhism* (New York: Castle Books, 1995), p. 3, 11. For a more in-depth treatment of this critical subject, see John R. Newman, "A Brief History of the Kalachakra" in *The Wheel of Time: the Kalachakra in Context*, Geshe Lhundub Sopa, Roger Jackson, and John Newman, with a Foreword by HH The Dalai Lama (Madison, WI: Deer Park Books, 1985), pp. 51–90. Here Newman makes the case that Atisha's teacher was the same man as Naropa's teacher, Kalachakrapada the Elder, and that he lived in Java in the 11th century CE. The implication is that the Kalachakra initiations originated—at least in the relatively modern era—in Java.

serious importance to Atisha's twelve-year sojourn in that country.[4] It was Atisha's intensive period of meditation and study in Java that enabled him to bring not only the genuine teachings of Tantric Buddhism back to Tibet—including the seven-step meditation practice known as Tong Len—but also the worship of the Green Goddess, Tara.

I point this out because of the importance of the Tibet-Indonesia nexus to our story. Indonesia is well-known as the fourth-largest country in the world, and the world's most populous Muslim nation, with more than 200 million inhabitants living on perhaps 2000 of the country's more than 17,000 islands. It is notorious due to the famous Bali bombings of October 12, 2002, and as the headquarters of Jemaah Islamiyyah, a radical organization and known terrorist operation with ties to Al-Qaeda. It is also famous as the country where a future American president—Barack Obama—spent four years of his life as a child. Indeed, in 1982, the present Dalai Lama visited Indonesia to consecrate the Buddhist shrine of Borobudur, thereby firmly putting his stamp to the idea that this magnificent ninth-century CE monument is representative of the influence of Vajrayana, or Tibetan Tantric, Buddhism.

Yet, with all of this publicity in the world press, most foreigners are unaware of the role that Tantric Hinduism and Tantric Buddhism (and, perhaps, "Tantric" Sufism) have played in Indonesia, particularly in Java. And they continue to play this role, albeit in an esoteric and very quiet manner when compared to their Tantric counterparts in India and Tibet.

Thus, what we will do in the pages that follow is uncover layers of Tantric ritual and belief in this romantic and exotic land. We will gradually come to the realization that a form of Tantra (perhaps several forms) has been practiced there for centuries, and that its Tantric institutions are at least as robust as—if less well-known than—their Indian counterparts. Hopefully, in the process, we will discover a bit of the truth about Tantra itself and scrape away the accumulated detritus of well-meaning but badly-informed "neo-Tantra" practitioners in the West, continuing that journey with an examination of this esoteric practice's most blatant and informative evidence: Indonesia's Tantric temples.

Peter Levenda
Yogyakarta 2010

4 Twelve years is assumed to be a symbolic period of time, as it is used to refer to the study of many other Buddhist sages and monks. It could as easily have been a few years or a few decades, but in this case twelve years may be close to the mark.

A Note on Languages

The sources consulted for this work utilize Sanskrit, Pali, Hindi, Arabic, Chinese, Japanese, Bahasa Indonesia, and Bahasa Malaysia (the former Bahasa Melayu), as well as Javanese terms. In the case of Bahasa Indonesia and Bahasa Malaysia, there are no diacritical marks to consider, since these languages use the Roman alphabet (albeit with some pronunciation differences). With the other languages, however, methods of transliterating foreign alphabets or characters vary from text to text, and from scholar to scholar.

In order not to overburden the reader, I have reduced as much as possible the use of diacritical marks and printed each foreign term in a way as close as possible to its pronunciation. In Chinese, for instance, the Pinyin system for transliterating Mandarin has become quite familiar to Western readers over the years (*Beijing* instead of *Peking*), so I will use that system when it comes to Chinese. When it comes to Sanskrit, however, I had to make a decision—one that may not be comfortable for many scholars, but that will make the text more readable. Śiva and Śakti, for instance, will be printed phonetically as Shiva and Shakti. A term like *jñāna* will appear simply as jnana.

Similarly, for Arabic words I will use transliterations that most closely approximate general usage, understanding that some sounds do not travel well from the Arabic alphabet to the Roman.

Unless otherwise noted, all translations of foreign language texts are my own, so I am responsible for any errors that may appear.

Section I

The Tantric Context

Chapter 1

An Introduction to Tantra

Almost every study of Tantrism begins by apologizing.

Robert L. Brown[5]

The reason for the apology is simple, and points us in the direction we want to go: there is no consensus among scholars as to what the term *Tantra* actually refers. It is, in fact, a Western concept (as is Hinduism). Tantra is the result of more than a century of colonial scholars visiting India and seeing a discrepancy between normative Vedic Brahmanism and some shocking antinomian practices that we, in the West, would probably term "magic," or that equally slippery concept, "shamanism." Tantra became identified as a separate philosophy and was divided into Hindu Tantra and Buddhist Tantra—which is a misleading distinction that will get us nowhere in the end and which, logically, makes no sense if Tantra really is a separate philosophy.

In fact, according to André Padoux, one of the leading scholars of Tantra in the world today:

> Neither in traditional India nor in Sanskrit texts is there a term for Tantrism; no description or definition of such a category is to be found anywhere. We know also that, more often than not, Tantric texts are not called Tantra.[6]

Part of the problem lies in the West's reliance on the written word—on textuality and on textual analysis. Scholars have discovered books called Tantras that were written by Buddhists and still others that were written by Hindus—i.e., non-Buddhist Indians. This seems to indicate that there is some fundamental difference between the two practices. In fact, on the level of theory, there are differences, even important ones. On the level of practice, however, they are much the same. And Tantra is all about the practice.

And this is the point I want to make, and the direction in which we want to go.

5 Brown and Harper, eds., "Introduction," *The Roots of Tantra* (Albany, NY: State University of New York, 2002).

6 Andre Padoux, "What Do We Mean By Tantrism?" *The Roots of Tantra,* p. 17.

There are two main religious currents that gave rise to the phenomenon known as Tantra: Hinduism and Buddhism. Hinduism is a catch-all term for what may better be described as "Hindu religious traditions," for there is no single religious faith that can be described as Hinduism. Rather Hinduism is a wide variety of religious and spiritual experiences encountered on the sub-continent of India. While we will continue to use the term Hinduism for the sake of convenience, it should be noted that we do that primarily to distinguish the indigenous religions of India from Buddhism, which came much later.

There are scriptures that are considered Hindu; these include the Vedas, the Upanishads, and the Puranas, among others. There are also the famous epic poems the *Ramayana* and the *Mahabharata* that are just as important to the Indian people and that also were introduced into Indonesia at an early date. These epics were embraced by the population there as well, finding one manifestation in the famous *wayang kulit*, the shadow puppet theater that has tremendous cultural, social, and religious importance for the Javanese.

It was Vedic Hinduism that provided the rigid social structure known as the caste system. No one really knows how old the Vedas are, but they can be reliably dated to sometime in the second millennium BCE. Written in Sanskrit, they may be considered the core texts of Indian culture and faith. They contain instructions for the various rituals that should be performed, but they also contain medical knowledge, astronomical lore, and—in the case of the Atharva Veda, the so-called "fourth Veda"—occult texts as well.

One of the primary rituals of Vedic Hinduism is the *Homa,* or fire ritual, sometimes also called the *Agnihotra* (*agni* is the Sanskrit word for "fire"; *hotra* means "healing") when used to refer to the twice-daily fire offering, the most basic form of the ritual. This rite is reminiscent of the fire rituals of the Zoroastrians and has many variations, depending on their purpose. It is considered quite ancient and probably pre-Vedic. Basically, a fire is created in a special device using consecrated material—often *ghee* (clarified butter), as well as milk, honey, or other substances specific to the purpose. These form the basis of offerings, which are accompanied by the relevant prayers and meditations. The device or fire pit is often in the shape of an upside-down pyramid that allows the fire to burn quite hot. The cardinal direction practitioners face during the Homa ritual is of great importance, as are the number of Brahmins who are performing it and the purpose for which it is being performed.[7] Even in the relatively staid Vedic practice of the Homa ritual, the symbolism is often interpreted quite deliberately in a sexual manner, with the

7 For a complete description, with photographs, of this important rite see Tachikawa, Babulkar, and Kolhatkar, *Indian Fire Ritual* (New Delhi: Motilal Banarsidass, 2001).

fire representing the *yoni,* or sexual organs, of a goddess.[8] The Homa ritual eventually found a place in Tibetan Buddhist practice, as well as in Japanese Shingon ritual. Its practice is amply represented in the Tantric temples of Java.

Buddhism, of course, owes its origins to its founder, Siddhartha Gautama, who it is said was a prince living in northeast India sometime in the sixth century BCE, or perhaps a little later. While not much is known definitively about his life, most sources agree that he was born to a family of privilege and he is usually referred to as Prince Siddhartha. At the age of twenty-nine, he decided to end his life of ease and isolation from the rest of the world and ventured outside the palace walls to see real human existence as it is.

According to canonical Buddhist sources, he was astonished and saddened by the sights of sickness, death, and misery that were everywhere in the world, and he devoted himself to finding a solution to the human condition. After years of false starts with a variety of gurus and ascetic disciplines, he chose silent meditation. During the course of this practice, he realized that the root of all suffering was attachment: to things, to people, to ideas, and particularly to the concept of an individual self. The solution, he claimed, was non-attachment, even to the self, even to the gods. Because humans were attached to objects that gave them no real joy or happiness, he came to the conclusion that these objects did not really exist in any kind of absolute sense, but were illusions and impediments to spiritual liberation—here understood as freedom from the endless cycle of birth and rebirth. By grasping after things, we remain unsettled spiritually. In fact, by assuming that we have a soul at all (or an ego, a self, a personality), we identify with the ephemeral, with a string of events that we believe constitute individuality.[9] By withdrawing from the world—or, at least, from lusting after the things of the world—we begin to find a well of inner peace.

While accepting that we are making a much longer and more detailed story too short, we can say that the Buddha attained an exalted state of consciousness—illumination, or enlightenment, the ultimate stage—and then proceeded to teach others how to reach the same stage. The methods utilized by Buddhists involve intellectual study, meditation, and a kind of psycho-spiritual practice of negation in order to reach a perfect state of non-attachment. Among the Eastern Orthodox monks of the Christian world, this is sometimes called *apophatism.* It is a way of

8 For more information on this aspect of the Homa, see Richard K. Payne, "Tongues of Flame: Homologies in the Tantric *Homa,*" *The Roots of Tantra,* Harper & Brown, eds. (Albany, NY: State University of New York Press, 2002), pp. 193–210.

9 The concept of *anatta,* or "no-soul," is perhaps one of the most difficult of the Buddhist ideas to understand, especially for Westerners.

knowing God by saying what God is *not,* as opposed to what God *is*, since God is essentially unknowable. To a Buddhist, however, there is no God at all. God is perhaps the supreme illusion, the last obstacle on the way to perfect illumination. The end result of Buddhist apophatism is the realization that there is only a kind of absolute, albeit blissful, Void.

Buddhism is non-dualist for obvious reasons.[10] In Buddhism, there is no "this" and "that." The multiplicity of things perceived is an illusion, a kind of magic theater that distracts the spirit from true understanding. The goal of Buddhist practice is to achieve perfect Unity, a state where there is no "I" and "you" and "it," but only pure essential Being. However, one cannot arrive at that destination overnight, or merely by thinking very hard about it. It requires a program of phased initiations involving strenuous forms of meditation and ritual practice, and these vary from school to school, from sect to sect.

The oldest form of Buddhism, known as Theravada, is found today primarily in Southeast Asia, especially in Thailand and Sri Lanka. Mahayana Buddhism, a later form, is discovered in northern Asia: in China, Japan, and Korea. In Tibet, however, there is a third form, known as Vajrayana Buddhism, that is virtually indistinguishable from Tantra, but that has roots in Mahayana Buddhism as well as in the indigenous religion of Tibet.

Theravadin Buddhist scriptures include the Pali Canon, the oldest known Buddhist writings, which contain a variety of what are known as *suttas* (or, in non-Pali usage, the more familiar *sutras*). These include instructions for Buddhist disciples and discipline, as well as deeper articulations of Buddhist thought. One of the most famous of these is the *Dhammapada*, which has undergone several translations (including that by Max Muller in his *Sacred Books of the East* series), and the *Brahmajala Sutta*.

Mahayana scriptures are of later creation, but are based—to a certain extent—on some of the earlier Theravadin suttas. The origins of Mahayana Buddhism are in dispute, but the earliest Mahayana writings date from about the first century CE and are largely known from their Chinese- and Tibetan-language originals. While Theravada is thought to represent a pure form of Buddhism, Mahayana is sometimes characterized as a "popular" form of the same belief system. Perhaps the most famous of the Mahayana scriptures are the Diamond Sutra, the Lotus Sutra, and the Heart Sutra, the latter of which is only sixteen sentences long and contains the famous phrase: "Form itself is emptiness; emptiness itself is form."

In India, Buddhism reached an early crescendo, but had lost a great deal of its influence by the beginning of the medieval period. The Hindu religious tradition,

10 We may say that *advaita,* or non-duality, is a concept parallel to *anatta*, or no-soul.

however, continued and became stronger. As India moved out of its Buddhist period, Tantra grew quickly and may be said to have come into its own.

As mentioned, there are actual texts known as Tantras. These are largely in the form of dialogues between the Indian God Shiva and his female consort. This consort can be identified variously as Parvati, as Uma, as any one of dozens of other goddesses, or simply as Shakti. In any case, the female consort represents power: spiritual power. The whole focus of Tantra is on this power, which is believed to pervade every aspect, every particle, of the universe. By aligning oneself with this power, one can also effect material ends. For that reason, Tantra has had a following among those who find the traditional methods of worship, the caste system, and the Brahminical hierarchies stifling or inefficient, and among those who wish to have direct experience of the divine. The motivation for this may be purely spiritual—enlightenment or *nirvana*—or it may be purely mundane—for instance, obtaining a lover, wealth, or health. Or it may be both at the same time. In this, Tantra is virtually identical to Western forms of ceremonial magic and, indeed, the two systems have a great deal in common.

Tantra cuts across denominational boundaries, as does Western magic. One can be Jewish, Catholic, or Protestant—or anything else, for that matter—and still be a magician in the Western sense. Magic is a practice, as opposed to a coherent, carefully articulated philosophy, although it is predicated on a certain view of the interconnectedness of the universe, the doctrine of correspondences, and the idea that knowledge of the inner workings of the universe can give a person the ability to effect change at a distance using methods that seem to defy normal concepts of cause and effect. It is also based on a belief that you can become "as a god." Indeed, some magicians are drawn to the practice because they believe it enables them to commune directly with the divine, without the encumbrance of a high priest or other middle-man. It is a practice that is available to anyone, from clergyman to commoner, as is Tantra. And it is a threat to the status quo—politically, religiously, and culturally.

As is Tantra.

Like magic, Tantra is a technology. It is a means to an end. It involves the manipulation of consciousness through ritual, the end result of which has been pre-determined by the practitioner. And, as a technology, it makes use of all available materials. The tools of Tantra are the tools of consciousness—the five senses. Virtually anything can be employed in a Tantric ritual, from food and wine, to drugs, icons, incense, music, and sex, but always with a concentration on the physical body itself. While many of the texts called Tantras are deeply profound in their explanations of how reality is structured—using either dualist or non-dualist approaches—the attraction of Tantra is found mainly in the practices that permit devotees access to altered states of consciousness and the elevation of the mind to spiritual realms—i.e., to illumination.

Without these practices, the texts themselves are virtually useless. The texts are methodologies that are meant to be applied, instruction manuals intended to be used. They are recipe books, in a sense—and imagine how useless a recipe book is in the hands of someone who does not cook. This is the distinction that can be made between normative scripture-based religions like Christianity and Tantra. In Christianity, the Bible is the ultimate spiritual authority and, for many fundamentalist Christians, the only authority. Reading the Bible and preaching the Bible constitutes the core experience. (Conversely, a mystic may observe that those who can, do; while those who can't, preach.) A *Tantrika* (a practitioner of Tantra) may well ask: How can we use the Bible to attain altered states of consciousness? How can we use the Bible to come directly into the presence of the divine? Is the Bible a manual of operation? Does the Bible teach how to breathe, how to chant, how to visualize?

That the Bible does none of these things is obvious. However, there were groups of believers—both Jewish and Christian—who analyzed Biblical writings to derive physical and spiritual practices from them. These were the Kabbalists, the mystics, the magicians. Their role models were Ezekiel, Moses, and Solomon (and, for Christian Kabbalists, the Book of Revelation). They wrote their own texts, their own "Tantras": the *grimoires*. In Asia, the Tantrikas based their ritual syntax on their own spiritual culture—the Vedas, the *Ramayana*, the *Mahabharata*—and eventually developed the wider and more specific field of texts known as the Agamas, the Samhitas, and of course the Tantras themselves. Thus, there would be greater communication between a medieval European magician or sorcerer and a medieval Indian Tantrika than there would be between a Catholic priest and a Brahmin. Indeed, there are respected scholars in this field who have promoted the idea that there was actual contact between Kabbalists and Tantrikas centuries ago, with a resulting cross-fertilization of ideas and practices. We will come to that later.

It is my intention to demonstrate that the practice of Tantra, in some sense, takes place outside the philosophical or theological structures that have been imposed on it, either by adherents of the different religions through which Tantric texts have appeared over the centuries (most notably Indian religions, but also Chinese and Japanese faith systems) or by foreign observers such as English colonial scholars and commentators. Indonesia is a useful laboratory for this investigation, because many of the religions of the world have had an impact on its culture—especially in Java—from the Hindu religious traditions and Buddhism (in all its forms) to Islam and Christianity, and even including such modern-day spiritual movements as Theosophy. With all that, however, certain indigenous practices and beliefs have survived the imposition of foreign dogmas and faith systems ever since the beginning of Java's recorded history. From this perspective, Javanese mysticism has as much to say to us about how Tantra not only survives but thrives in a multi-religious, multi-cultural environment as does any study of Tantra in its indigenous land, the Indian sub-continent.

In order to accomplish this, we will look first at the history of Tantra and even offer some ideas concerning its origins. Using this as a roadmap, we will then approach Javanese mysticism—*kejawen* and *kebatinan*—and then Java's Tantric temples themselves to understand why they were designed the way they were. We will look at present-day Javanese practices that bear striking similarity to Tantra as traditionally understood. Then we will use what we have learned from this fusion of theory and practice, text and ritual, to take a look at modern Western ideas of Tantra, as enshrined in the rituals and concepts of modern esoteric and hermetic societies, Western and Eastern.

During this investigation, we will reveal some of the most closely guarded secrets of these groups, secrets that are well-known to privileged spiritual elites and suspected by interested non-initiates. We will see how European alchemy was influenced by concepts familiar to the Tantrikas, and even how Chinese alchemy can help us understand both the European and Indian versions. We will even find ourselves startled to learn that Jewish mysticism also has a great deal in common with Indian Tantra, and that some aspects of Tantra—like the idea of Kundalini—may have had their origins in the ancient Near East.

Tantra as Action

> The ideological aspect of the Tantric vision is the cosmos as permeated by power (or powers), a vision wherein energy (sakti) is both cosmic and human and where microcosm and macrocosm correspond and interact.[11]

In the West, a common distinction is made between two forms of esoteric spirituality: magic and mysticism. While this distinction is purely arbitrary and not applicable in any kind of absolute sense, it provides a helpful introduction to the question of where Tantra should be located within the general field of religion or the more specific area of esotericism.

11 Harper and Brown, eds. *The Roots of Tantra*, p. 19.

This distinction also asks us to think about two forms of religious experience and expression: the exoteric and the esoteric. When most people profess a religious affiliation, they are referring to an exoteric form of spirituality—for example, Christianity, Islam, Judaism, or Buddhism. These are often scriptural denominations with religious "specialists" or "professionals" like priests, rabbis, imams, or monks. The average person is conscious of their faith in rudimentary ways, in terms of what behavior is proper and acceptable, or what duties their religion prescribes. There is often a specific place used for the performance of religious obligations and rituals—a mosque, synagogue, church, or other physical location. In addition to all of this, there is also a religious calendar with days or periods that are more sacred or meaningful than others. Thus, there is sacred time, sacred space, and a text—whether written or oral—embodying the precepts of the faith as well as religious professionals who interpret the scriptures, perform rituals, lead prayers, and whose opinion in matters of law and practice is considered authoritative.[12]

Esotericism, on the other hand, is intensely individualistic. Where exoteric spirituality often relies on the society of like-minded individuals who are members of the same faith and thus can be expected to share identical beliefs and loyalties, esoteric spirituality is conscious of being apart from society at large and estranged in some essential ways from the base or root religion, the exoteric form. Thus, there are esoteric forms of most of the world's major religions. Kabbalah, for example, can be considered an esoteric form of its exoteric root, Judaism. Sufism can be considered an esoteric form of Islam. Indeed, Islam recognizes two different manifestations of its faith: *lahir*, the exoteric form, and *batin*, the inner or esoteric form.

Esotericism finds its expression in non-canonical texts, in beliefs that are refinements of or extrapolations on the base or root belief of a faith, and most especially in acts that would be considered questionable by orthodox believers, if not actually forbidden or tabu. Esoteric practices may take place according to different structures of sacred space and time, and they may be under the control of an alternate hierarchy of specialists. Tantra is, itself, an esoteric practice and may represent one of the oldest forms of esotericism in the world, if we are to accept a pre-Aryan origin for some of its most cherished characteristics, like worship of a divine Mother and the concept of sacred sexuality.

As mentioned above, scholars are divided as to the definition of Tantra, the date of its first emergence as a coherent practice, and even whether Tantra arose

12 The exception to this would be orthodox Islam, which recognizes no ultimate human authority and places all authority in the text; yet, in practice, there are many religious authority figures in Islam and there is a mutable, if unofficial, hierarchy among certain groups that attracts attention and loyalty from believers.

out of Buddhism first and then became adapted to Hinduism, or the other way around. While these are all compelling questions, and the answers would do much to illuminate the history of the sub-continent, they need not concern us much at this point. We will come back to them again and again over the course of this work, and maybe we will obtain a clearer picture as we go along.

Tantra is primarily a practice, and can be considered an esoteric, rather than an exoteric, one. It is a means of attaining altered states of consciousness, spiritual illumination, and even occult powers and abilities known as *siddhas*. It involves the identification of the human practitioner with a god or goddess and the partner with a deity of the opposite gender—but that comes later. In the beginning, a Tantrika—that is, a person who belongs to any one of a variety of Tantric sects or who has received initiation from a Tantric guru—spends a great deal of time in meditation, doing physical exercises that are familiar to us from yoga (pranayama, asana, etc.), and performing a range of *puja,* or ceremonies and rituals. Most authorities agree that mantras (specific words of power, recited over and over), mudras (ritual gestures), and yantras (mystical diagrams) are main features of Tantric ritual. Because the practice of Tantra takes place within a specific context—usually Buddhist or Hindu—the prayers, meditations, mandalas, and rituals will all be developed within that context, and based on that particular philosophy. The end result, however, will be the same.

The two main philosophies found in any scholarly description of Tantra are dualism and non-dualism. Non-duality, or *advaita,* is the basic philosophy associated with Buddhism. A Buddhist believes there is no real polarization of male/female, god/human, reality/unreality, but that these concepts and their divisions are all illusions and the source of sorrow and discontent. A dualist belief, on the other hand, is one in which the "polarities" of creation are acknowledged and celebrated. To a Tantrika, both of these philosophies are, in a sense, true.

A Tantrika understands that the duality being employed in Tantric ritual is a means to an end: union with the Divine. In other words, we might say that a Tantrika uses dualist ritual to attain a non-dualist end.

Buddhists can be accused of the same thing. A visit to any Buddhist temple will introduce the seeker to a variety of statues of different aspects of the Buddha and even, depending on the type of Buddhism and the location of the temple, various other deities specific to that location. For instance, a Chinese Buddhist temple will be filled with statues, not only of the Buddha, but of other Chinese saints and even of the famous goddess Guan Yin, the Goddess of Mercy who is identified with the Indian god Avalokitesvara (of whom it is said the Dalai Lama is an incarnation). All of this certainly seems like a lot of unnecessary duplication in a belief system that emphasizes non-duality, but it is understood that people in general require these images in order to approach the esoteric, inner truth of Buddhism that all is illusion and that the only refuge we can take is in the Buddha. From that point of view, a scholar may interpret these religious trappings as mnemonic devices or even as a kind of memory palace, enabling Buddhists to navigate the terrain of their own culture and consciousness in a somewhat orderly way in order to become divested of the useless accoutrements of conventional religion.

Yet, as we shall see, the entire field of Tibetan Buddhism (as an example) is basically Tantric Buddhism, the form known as Vajrayana Buddhism. The famous Tibetan Tantric texts, like the Kalachakra Tantra, are veritable treasure troves of Tantric information and instructions for practice. There is no way to understand this apparent dichotomy between the non-dualist, basically anti-theist approach of orthodox Buddhism on the one hand and these arcane and complex ritual procedures on the other, unless we accept that Tantra is a technology, a tool for reaching the state of consciousness necessary for directly experiencing the bliss of advaita, and that the philosophies that seem embedded in Tantric texts refer more to the method itself than to an overarching philosophy of life or religion. Even this statement, however, can be hotly contested by specialists in the field who place more emphasis on the philosophy—what I choose to call the theory—of Buddhism than on the practice.

With the type of Tantra we encounter in a non-Buddhist context, however, we are on familiar ground. The emphasis on the dualities of male/female, god/goddess, etc. are clear and unequivocal; but the union of these opposites is just as clear and important. To a Tantrika, everything in creation is basically sexual; everything we see, touch, feel is the result of a cosmic sexual reproductive act. The human act of sexual intercourse is a reenactment of the original, divine intercourse. By becoming totally aware and spiritually prepared prior to consummating a sex act with a similarly trained partner, one is able to experience that moment when all existence came into being or, perhaps, the moment a split second before. This suggests that, in common with many forms of mysticism, the *transcendence* of the divine may be experienced in its *immanence* in all things—that the route from the microcosm to the macrocosm is through the one act that is common to both, the sex act. This act is a tangential point between the two forms of consciousness.

The challenge, especially for a Westerner with a great deal of baggage when it comes to sexuality, is in reducing the prurient aspect of Tantra as much as possible. Tantra does indeed sacralize sexuality, but the reverse is also true. Sexuality itself becomes a sacred act that should not be abused for the sake of immediate gratification. Instead, sexuality sacralizes the universe. Tantra is a way of understanding a sacred *process*. In this way, Tantra has been used to understand chemical as well as biological reactions and to formulate psychological theories. It can even be applied to Western alchemy and Jewish mysticism.

The tremendously colorful and complex images of gods and goddesses in ecstatic embrace that we encounter in Tantra are not meant to titillate, but to instruct. But how do we use blatantly sexual images—a kind of religious pornography—to instruct us in spiritual matters?

The Body as Tantric Laboratory

> I believe that precisely at the bottom of all our mystical states there are body techniques which we have not studied, but which were studied in China and India, even in very remote periods. I think that there are necessarily biological means of entering into "communication with God."[13]

The core tension of Indian spiritual practice—and, indeed, of many religions around the world—is found in the ambiguous relationship between the spirit and the body, or between the invisible and the visible. In many religious cultures, the body is conceived as a source of sorrow, of attachment to physical desires, of ignoble yearnings, of pollution. It is a locus of danger that needs to be controlled by the mind of its owner. The desires of the body are virtually all expressions of what are considered negative forces—lust, hunger, thirst, sleep, etc.—as if the body were a Sherman tank with a pacifist as its driver. The tank is all metal and armor and munitions, with a giant cannon, mindless but lethal; in the hands of a trained soldier, it will cause terrible damage to the community. Thus, there is a need for a pacifist at the controls who will use the tank for other purposes, perhaps to plow the earth for crops. And one can only be sure that the people at the controls are pacifists if they are checked on a constant basis to insure that their purity is intact and to prove that their hands are where they are supposed to be at all times.

The imposition of celibacy by the Roman Catholic Church (a relatively late development in Church history) is one example of this discomfort with the body and the assumption that bodily needs are an obstacle to union with God. In addition to celibacy, other controls of the body include fasting (particularly during Lent) and prolonged periods of prayer in sometimes uncomfortable positions. In

13 Marcel Mauss, *Sociology and Psychology: Essays* (London: Routledge, 1979), p. 122.

extreme cases, self-flagellation and other methods are used to emphasize the inherent sinfulness of the human body and the need to dominate it through brute force. The French postmodern philosopher Michel Foucault has had a great deal to say concerning the control of the body by governments, churches, the medical profession, the penal system, and others. We do not need to revisit those arguments here, except to point out that a Foucaldian interpretation of our theme—sacred sexuality—would be a welcome addition to this field of study.[14]

The Catholic approach to the body has been to suppress sexual desire as much as possible, not only among its clergy, but also in its commands to the faithful to avoid all forms of birth control (save the rhythm method) and to engage in sex only if procreation is possible, thus ruling out not only birth control, but also forms of sexual expression that do not lead to conception. This is an attitude that has made its way into many other Christian denominations as well. There are strains of Gnosticism in this position: the idea that matter itself is evil, a creation of the Demi-Urge, and that only spirit is good and clean and pure.

In the Tantric tradition, however, every effort is made to address this problem rather than simply suppress it. There are two general schools of thought concerning the human body that may be discerned in a review of both Hindu and Buddhist Tantra. The body can be conceived as a vehicle to liberation and enlightenment in both schools, but the utilization of the body is problematic. One approach is to "spiritualize" the body and the sexual act to such an extent that the body's natural urges are transcended through intensive physical and mental practices, sublimating the sexual urge and transforming it into an engine of spiritual force. This is a form of denial that would be consistent with Catholic ideas, were it not for the active involvement of the Tantrika in the contemplation of detailed depictions of gods and goddesses in sexual embrace, the study of descriptions of the sexual act that could be construed as lascivious to Western sensibilities, and ritual enactments of sexual liaison with spiritual forces.

In some forms of Tantra, one is expected to transcend normal physical sexuality by confronting it head-on, albeit symbolically. In other forms, however, we detect a decidedly "hands-on" approach in which sexuality is considered a vehicle for liberation (just as in the former example). There is an important difference, however. In these forms, the sex act is made part of an elaborate ritual (the most famous—or infamous—of which is the Ritual of the Five Ms, or *pancatattva*). This practice involves meditation, mantras, yantras, mudras, and spiritual initiation, as

14 Actually, there has already been some activity in that direction. See, for instance, Romain Bertrand, "Penser le Java mystique de l'âge modern avec Foucault: peut-on écrire une histoire 'non-intentionaliste' du politique?" *Sociétés politiques comparées*, no. 2, February 2008.

well as—or as integral elements of—actual intercourse. While the symbolic aspect is very much part of the ritual and essential to its success, the active participation of sexual partners provides another level of engagement through full investment of the psycho-biological instruments of two, very human, partners.

In fact, it may be a requirement that these acts are carried out, not only symbolically, but in actuality.

According to authorities on the Vedic fire ritual (the Homa), for instance, we are told that one may perform the Homa symbolically (the Inner Homa, a meditative rite) if there are no "requisite offerings" at hand. However, if the offerings are available, it is not permitted to perform the Inner Homa only; the Outer Homa (i.e., the full ritual) *must* be performed.[15]

Logically, then, if the offerings are available in the Tantric ritual known as the *pancatattva* or *pancamakara* (the famous "five Ms"), which requires the breaking of five Vedic tabus—drinking wine (*madya*), eating meat (*mamsa*), eating fish (*matsya*), eating grain (*mudra*), and sexual intercourse with a partner who may not be married to you (*maithuna)*—then it follows that they should be part of the rite, not only in a symbolic sense, but in an actual sense as well. Bear in mind, however, that the "inner" part of the ritual must also be performed and not only the outer observance.

How Old Is Tantra?

Again, we enter the realm of apology. We simply don't know. Some important Tantric texts can be dated reliably to the seventh century CE, but Tantric practices are certainly much older than that.[16] One of the four Vedic scriptures, the Atharva Veda, is sometimes considered a Tantric text because of its focus on magic and occult powers, which leads some to think that Tantra can be dated to the Atharva Veda. Unfortunately, however, that is not the case, since scholars are divided as to whether the Atharva Veda represents a scripture that was composed after the first three Vedas and is therefore relatively late, or if, in fact, the Atharva Veda represents a tradition that is older than all four! Regardless, however, the Vedas as a group are quite ancient, with some estimates placing their origin sometime in the

15 Richard K. Payne, "Tongues of Flame: Homologies in the Tantric Homa," *The Roots of Tantra*, p. 202.

16 See David N. Lorenzen, "Early Evidence for Tantric Religion," *The Roots of Tantra*, pp. 25–36 for a discussion of the earliest epigraphic evidence circa 423 CE, and the earliest textual evidence, circa seventh century CE.

second millennium BCE. The written Tantras, with their emphasis on the esoteric aspects of Vedic religion, must therefore be considerably newer.

Generally speaking, the Vedas represent an entire body of knowledge, from astronomy to architecture and medicine, and from history to public policy. The rituals associated with the Vedas are performed by a priestly caste, the Brahmins. Vedic society was divided into four basic castes, or *varnas*, with the Brahmins at the top of the pyramid, followed by the Kshatriyas (the warriors and rulers), the Vaishyas (merchants, traders; Gandhi was a member of this caste), and the Sudras (laborers). Outside the system is the class of Untouchables, the Dalits, who number roughly 170 million people in India, or 13 percent of the total population—in contrast to the Brahmins, who represent only roughly 5 percent. In actuality, there are many sub-castes as well, so we are talking about a massive stratification of society that includes 3000 actual castes and about ten times that number of sub-castes. Since Independence, however, much of the caste system has been overhauled so that members of different castes may marry, for instance, but the plight of many of the lowest castes—and especially of the Untouchables—remains a serious problem in India. This is pointed out so that the reader may better appreciate the role of Tantra in this country of strongly divided social roles.

The caste of Brahmins is purity-obsessed. Brahmins may not eat food unless it has been prepared by other Brahmins, for example. They may only marry other Brahmins. Indeed, no one may even look at a Brahmin (or a fire) while urinating or defecating. For the Brahmins, the body itself is the vehicle for purity and for divinity. The care of religion and ritual is their province, their sacred responsibility. They cannot carry out their duties if they are in a state of ritual impurity. For Brahminical priests, purity of the body is analogous to purity of the soul; in a very real sense, "cleanliness is next to godliness."

Purity is a hallmark of many religious practices around the globe, of course. Ritual purity is important in Judaism, for instance, as well as in Islam. The Qumran sect that gave us the Dead Sea Scrolls was also fanatically interested in questions of ritual purity. Thus this idea that bodily impurity is an obstacle to full participation in the rites of the community is very old, and relatively widespread. Yet, the idea of willful transgression of the purity laws is also old and widespread, and that is where Tantra comes in.

From Tantra to Tantroid— Transcendence through Transgression

For our purposes, I suggest we occasionally make use of a term that has gained some ground in academic circles owing to the difficulty of accurately defining what is, and is not, Tantra. This word, "tantroid," will enable us to discuss this subject in a provisional way without committing ourselves to a narrow interpretation, especially when we come to discuss Javanese practices in particular. According to Bruce M. Sullivan, we can characterize a practice as tantroid if it has the following three characteristics: fierce goddesses, transgressive sacrality, and identification with a deity.[17]

With some modification, we can apply this scheme to what we will see of Javanese practices, especially those concerning the temples under review. Goddesses in Java tend to be rather fierce or, at the very least, powerful and unforgiving. (The case of the famous Goddess of the Southern Ocean is one firm example, and we will discuss her shortly.) In Java, the idea of "transgressive sacrality" applies not only to the Indian perspective on examples of ritual marriage, sex in cemeteries, and sacred prostitution, but also to the Islamic perspective; both cultures consider them equally transgressive. It is the third characteristic—identification with a deity—that will give us the most problems in present-day Java, however, since that "deity" should be the God of Islam and identification with that God is normally understood as heresy or blasphemy. Yet, if we redefine "deity" in this instance as referring to other spiritual identities—like that of the Sultan of Yogyakarta in his role as husband of the Goddess of the Southern Ocean—then we may be closer to the mark.

We will not try to fit Javanese mystical or esoteric practices—those falling under our general rubric of "tantroid"—into a pre-formed template, or assume that what we are calling Javanese Tantrism is perfectly consistent with other forms of Tantra. The Javanese spiritual experience is unique, but it does demonstrate influences from other cultures, as we will see from their sacred architecture. In my own personal quest to understand what I call "the technology of spirituality," I focus more on the practice than the theory without attempting to extrapolate a philosophy or an ideology.

By starting from the body and its functions, I realize that I am in danger of developing a universalist point of view concerning spirituality, but that is a danger

17 Bruce M. Sullivan, "Tantroid Phenomena in Early Indic Literature: An Essay in Honor of Jim Sanford," *Pacific World Journal of the Institute of Buddhist Studies*, Third Series, Number 8, Fall 2006, pp. 9–20.

I have to accept. We all share the same biology and experience the same biological functions, at least at the basic level of the five senses and the nervous and reproductive systems. When the body is perceived as an instrument in the spiritual toolbox, then we are constrained by its constraints. Altered states of consciousness may be induced through fasting, meditation, or breath control, and we may interpret these states differently, depending on our culture and environment. But the states will be altered and these states will be valued as visions, as communications from spiritual sources, or as evidence of occult powers. The individuals who voluntarily undergo these rigors are the religious specialists of their respective cultures. They may not be the priests or religious hierarchs necessarily, but they will be revered for their direct experience of the Other. By transgressing the normal functions of the body, they also transgress the natural order of the community; they break tabus, they cross over the liminal divide that demarcates safety from danger. To breathe naturally, to eat when hungry, to sleep when tired—these are all natural functions of the human animal and society is arranged around them. To violate these functions—to control breathing through pranayama, for instance, or to fast, to remain awake for days without sleeping—is to break the body's own tabu system and, by extension, the tabu system of the community. The idea of transgression, then, seems to be at the heart of esoteric practice and, in particular, the practice we call Tantra.

There are statements in some Tantric literature that the practices considered the most transgressive and scandalous should not be performed, but rather should be interiorized—i.e., meditated upon in symbolic form only and not "acted out." The problem with this view is that it is not consistent with orthodox Vedic belief regarding ritual performance, as we have seen. More important, it is virtually impossible to read some of the more blatant Tantric texts—those with a long and distinguished pedigree—and see them as anything other than precise instructions for carrying out these rituals in actual form with living partners. While one may make the argument that, on some plane of understanding, to visualize transgression is the same as acting on that impulse—"committing adultery in the heart"—we may agree that actually committing the transgression in the mundane world while simultaneously visualizing it is to ensure that the transgressive act has been performed on all levels of awareness.

As Tantric scholar Harunaga Isaacson points out, even in the Buddhist form of Tantra:

> Having been instructed by the guru what he must do and on what he must concentrate, the initiand, uniting with the consort, must

> mark that moment of blissful experience that ... offers an at least apparent absence of all duality ... This experience is said to occur in the brief interval between the moment in which the initiand's *bodhicitta*, that is his semen, is in the center of the *mani*, that is the glans of the penis, and the moment of emission ...[18]

There are several important points made in the above excerpt. First, actual sexual union occurs, not merely a symbolic version. Second, emission also occurs (rather than the retention or internalization of the ejaculate). Third, one approaches advaita—the Buddhist sense of non-duality—at the moment of orgasm. And perhaps a fourth point can be made as well: There is a peculiar power in concentration. In fact, without concentration—the single-minded focus of consciousness—the ritual, or any ritual, cannot succeed. Thus mind and body must become fused around a very specific goal, and in order to reach that state, a great deal of preparation must be made that includes training the body as well as the mind.

Twilight Language

> All things are concealed in all.
>
> Paracelsus, *Coelum Philosophorum*

One of the essential characteristics of esotericism generally, and of the traditions that come out of Tantra specifically, is the implementation of a special language that is used to conceal and reveal secrets simultaneously. In the Western esoteric tradition, this is called the Language of the Birds or, more commonly today, the Green Language.[19] The enigmatic European alchemist Fulcanelli referred to this language as the *argotique*, a play on the term *ars gotique* or "Gothic art"—a reference to Gothic architecture, which is widely believed to represent an esoteric tradition written in stone.[20] To Fulcanelli, this argot was the means by which alchemists and adepts communicated with each other and selected members of the mundane world who could interpret the symbols. Like a kind of sacred rebus, the messages of the Green Language can be read on different levels of meaning simultane-

18 Harunaga Isaacson, "Tantric Buddhism in India (From c. A.D. 800 to c. A.D. 1200)," *Buddhismus in Geschichte und Gegenwart*. Band II. Hamburg, pp. 23–49.

19 See, for instance, David Ovason, *The Secrets of Nostradamus* (New York: HarperCollins, 2002), pp.121–160, 411–424.

20 Fulcanelli, *Le Mystère des Cathédrales* (Las Vegas: Brotherhood of Life, 2000), pp. 41–49.

ously, thus concealing sacred mysteries in plain sight. A famous example of this is Chartres Cathedral, whose strange sculptures and carvings have stimulated the imaginations of thousands of visitors and contributed to a cottage industry based in their interpretation.

In India, this sacred language is called *sandhya-bhasa*, or the "twilight language."[21] The word *sandhya* is particularly relevant to our case, because it means quite literally the "time of union." The time of union is considered to be both dawn and dusk—thus the union of night and day. Noon is sometimes also considered a "time of union," as it is the point where morning meets afternoon. An important Vedic ritual, the *sandhya vandanam,* is performed thrice daily—at high noon, and when the sun is on the horizon, either at sunrise or sunset. We should note that the sandhya vandanam ritual is focused on the concept of *amrita*, the nectar of immortality, which is a core element of Tantric ritual in general and which is emphasized at Candi Sukuh and Candi Ceto in Java.

The word *bhasa* means "language," so we can interpret sandhya-bhasa as the "language of the time of union," which has a perfectly Tantric ring. It is interesting that the term *sandhya* is also taken to mean "perfection," and is a common girl's name in India. Sandhya is the daughter of Brahma, who created her and then fell in love with her, in the process creating Kama, the god of desire. Thus, as a deity, she is often also considered the wife of Brahma as well as his daughter and, in other texts (like the *Siva Purana*), the wife of Shiva (which makes her the equivalent of Parvati or Uma). Catherine Benton raises the possibility that we can see this story as a way of understanding the nature of human love and desire.[22] It is, she claims, a projection of inner conflicts on an available object, just as Brahma fell in love with his own creation, Sandhya, even as he was aware that she was nothing more than his creation. Desire (Kama) born of this type of conflict is stronger than our conscious understanding, which sees it as ephemeral and perhaps even self-destructive. Tantra, which addresses desire and love head-on, may be an ancient form of psychotherapy, one in which psychological conflicts are used as energy sources to promote spiritual progress and illumination.

The usual complicated Indian theological structures, therefore, give rise to several possible interpretations of the role of Sandhya in a Tantric context. Throughout the rest of this work, we will focus mainly on her manifestations as Parvati and Uma, with further references to Kali and Durga.

---

21 Georg Feuerstein, *Tantra: The Path of Ecstasy* (Boston: Shambhala, 1998), pp. 132–134.

22 Catherine Benton, *God of Desire: Tales of Kamadeva in Sanskrit Story Literature* (New York: SUNY, 2005), p. 26.

The twilight language is an allegorical word game, with double and triple meanings for each term. For instance, in this language—which, after all, is the language extensively used in the Tantras—the Sanskrit term *vajra* can mean "thunderbolt," "power," *linga*, "penis," even *shunya* ("void")—all terms cognate with ideas of masculine energy and creative (and destructive) power.[23] While this example may seem obvious to a casual reader, the complexity increases with more specific terminology and references. We encounter the same thing in Western alchemical texts, which are replete with terms like "the white eagle," "the red lion," etc.—all in a seemingly metallurgical context. In his many works on alchemy, Jung made the claim that these terms had psychological significance, and I make the case that the terminology can be employed as well in metallurgical, chemical, biological, neurological, psychological, and sexual contexts, to name but a few.

The twilight language is employed to convey information about the world. It is a cosmological language and the processes it describes can be understood on a variety of levels, at times interchangeably. What this implies is that an alchemical text can be interpreted as a manual of Tantra just as easily as a Tantric text can be interpreted psychologically. The benefit to researchers is that the Tantric texts are almost blatant in their description of actual sexual processes—processes that have spiritual change and transformation as their purpose. This enables us to apply that interpretation to a variety of other texts in the "twilight" or "green" language. Using these texts to interpret each other suddenly opens up a rich field of information. In actuality, this concept was enshrined in the Vedas from the beginning, since the Vedas are considered *thrayi*—in other words, statements in the Vedas have three meanings: an exoteric meaning, an esoteric meaning, and a "philosophical" meaning. A parallel case can be seen in alchemical literature, which can have a purely chemical meaning, an inner or psychological or psycho-biological meaning, and a purely spiritual meaning.

One of the ways in which "green" or twilight language is employed is in the field of symbols. In the West, these symbols take the form of the images on tarot cards, the carvings on Gothic cathedrals, and the strange illustrations in books on alchemy, Kabbalah, and magic. Freud understood dream images to represent psychological states, many with a sexual component; Jung codified these symbols even further, finding a structure peopled with mythic ideas and concepts.

In Tantra, these symbols also can be found in architecture. Similar to the way images are used to convey esoteric information on Gothic cathedrals, like the well-known example of Chartres, carvings on Tantric temples are used to suggest various psycho-spiritual states and are illustrative of the means to achieve them.

23 Benton, *God of Desire*, p.133.

These carvings may be statues of the various deities of the Indian religions—each with specific qualities, aspects, and powers, just as Catholic saints are interpreted in the Afro-Caribbean religions of Santeria and Voudon—or they may be of scenes from the great Indian epics like the *Ramayana* and the *Mahabharata,* which have as much resonance for an Indian devotee as Biblical stories do for Westerners, with corresponding psychological relevance and depth. Some temples are explicit in sexual terms and depict actual sexual acts and positions. To the non-initiate, these may be interpreted at face value; an initiated view holds that the acts and positions have psycho-spiritual components and refer to altered spiritual states, some of which may be achieved by the application of these very acts and positions.

In Java, the temples of Candi Sukuh and Candi Ceto have the most blatant sexual imagery, as we will see. However, such massive and famous edifices as Borobudur and Prambanan can also be identified as Tantric temples. Borobudur itself has been acknowledged as an example of the Vajrayana Buddhism of Tibet, a Tantric denomination. Other temples and shrines may not boast as much iconography as Candi Sukuh, but they may be utilized as centers of Tantric practice just the same—like the shrine and cemetery at Gunung Kemukus, not far from Candi Sukuh. In this case, the twilight language is employed, not in images or allegorical language *per se,* but in the performance of ritual (what we may call "twilight action"), where the ritual itself is an allegory—in this case, the peculiar type of temporary marriage that is solemnized at Kemukus. Marriage has been understood allegorically all over the world and in many eras. In 17th-century Europe, we have the *Chymical Wedding of Christian Rosenkreutz*, which is considered to be an alchemical allegory. In the Gnostic texts discovered at Nag Hammadi, we read that the Holy of Holies of Solomon's Temple was interpreted as a bridal chamber. We will look at these examples in the last section of this work.

The Schools of Tantra

There are two main and distinct "schools" of Hindu Tantra, the Shiva and the Shakti schools. The Shiva school obviously places Shiva in the position of the High God and the focus is on him, with a somewhat lesser emphasis on his consort, Shakti. In the Shakti sects, however, this polarity is reversed, with the emphasis placed on the feminine aspect of the two. Both Shiva and Shakti represent forms of power, but Shakti is power by definition. Shiva is understood as the principle that directs this power, but it is Shakti who personifies the type of occult, esoteric force that is at the heart of the practices we call Tantra. During the course of this study, we may have occasion to refer to these differences from time to time, so it is wise to point them out now.

It is entirely possible that the first form of Tantra was Shakti in nature. An epigraphic reference to the *Matrikas*—the seven Mothers—that dates from 423 CE may be the earliest known Tantric mention anywhere.[24] According to the *Devi-Mahatmya*, a sixth-century CE Shakta text, the Matrikas are fierce goddesses who were summoned by Durga to help her in a battle with demons. They are the female forms of male deities, and are sometimes confused with the ten *Mahavidyas*, who are, themselves, rather frightening in appearance and who have some odd preferences (sex with corpses, a goddess who cuts off her own head, etc.).[25]

As mentioned, fierce goddesses are a staple of Tantric practice. The most famous of these is Kali, who is often depicted with a lolling red tongue, a necklace of human skulls, various weapons, and a skull cup full of human blood. Kali is in her element in a charnel ground or cemetery. She can sometimes be seen standing on the prone body of Shiva. In this manifestation, she can be interpreted as energy or power, without which Shiva is helpless.

The cult of Kali represents a Shakti version of Tantra, with its emphasis on the feminine as the dominant and supreme deity. Other forms of the fierce feminine include Durga—whom we will come across in Java—and Chinnamasta, the goddess who cuts off her own head. Even Tara, the gentle goddess of Tibetan Buddhism, is a blood-thirsty deity in the Hindu tradition.[26] In India, Tara resides in the cremation ground and is often depicted standing on a corpse, virtually identical in every respect to Kali. Blood sacrifices are made to her by her devotees.

We may well ask why it is that a belief system that holds the feminine to be the supreme deity would depict its goddess in this brutal, bloody, and altogether hideous fashion. We should remember that these goddesses are also often described as lustful, even rapacious. Are these stereotypically male qualities, projected onto a female object of adoration, meant to legitimize male tendencies toward the violent in death and sex? Is it a kind of Zen koan, requiring devotees to make a leap of consciousness from the idea of a nurturing, wholesome feminine to this outrageous caricature of death and destruction, putting two contradictory images side by side and forcing a psychic resolution?

24 See Lorenzen, "Early Evidence for Tantric Religion."

25 See, for instance, David Kinsley, *Tantric Visions of the Divine Feminine: the Ten Mahavidyas* (Berkeley: University of California Press, 1997) for a thorough discussion of this subject.

26 See Kinsley, *Tantric Visions of the Divine Feminine,* pp. 98–107.

Perhaps there is another way to understand the wrathful and bestial goddesses of Tantra. Kali and the Hindu Tara are both shown standing on motionless, prone corpses of men. Often, these are understood to represent Shiva, and sometimes the corpse is shown with an erect penis. We know that the principle of Shakti—psycho-spiritual power, or cosmic power, depending on how you interpret it—is feminine. A prone Shiva, a corpse-like Shiva, may imply a post-orgasmic Shiva and the image of Kali or Tara standing over him may signify the release of that energy. Why, then, the accompanying images of death?[27] Why the worship in a cremation ground?

How are sex and death related, particularly in the context of Tantric practice? This is a question to which we will return as we investigate some of the tantroid practices we will encounter in the mountains of Java.

Excursus: A Brief Summary of Indonesian History

Many readers who are familiar with Asian religions and knowledgeable about the cultures and histories of India and China may remain relatively unsure about Indonesia and its history and religious traditions. Because this history is so important to any intelligent discussion of Tantra in Java, it is necessary to offer a very brief summary of the subject before devoting ourselves to an investigation of Javanese mysticism itself.

The Javanese Dynasties

Indonesia is the name given to a huge territory in Southeast Asia that stretches across three time zones along the equator. It has the fourth-largest population in the world after China, India, and the United States. It is also the largest Muslim country in the world, with over 200 million citizens professing the Islamic faith. It consists of more than 17,000 separate islands, of which Java is the largest.

Since the nation's independence from the Dutch after World War II, the Javanese have dominated Indonesian government, culture, and politics. As the largest ethnic group, their language and customs have influenced the development of all that we think of as "typically Indonesian." We must remember, however, that "Indonesia" as a concept did not exist until about the 1920s, when the indepen-

27 The French refer to orgasm (or the immediate post-orgasmic phase) as *le petit mort*, the "little death," which is suggestive. The famous (unattributable) Latin phrase *Post coitum omne animal triste est, sive gallus et mulier* (After coitus all animals are sad, except the rooster and woman) may also be relevant!

dence movement began. Until then, Indonesia had been colonized by a succession of Asian and European powers.

We will not attempt a comprehensive account of Indonesian history, as colorful as it is with its tales of sultans and monks, colonialists and traders, Arab sailors and Chinese Buddhists. Much of what we know of early Indonesian history, however, comes to us (with some notable exceptions) from its foreign visitors. Manuscripts in Java and Sumatra were written on palm leaves and so were prone to early destruction and decay. It is, however, safe to say that the first Indonesian kingdoms of which we have any information are those that have their origins in India and elsewhere in Southeast Asia. The earliest, the kingdom of Tarumanagara, lasted from 358 to 669 CE and was located in the northwestern part of Java, near present-day Jakarta, in the Sundanese region. This was a Hindu kingdom, as epigraphic and other evidence—including some Chinese sources—attest. The earliest surviving written records in Java are stone inscriptions in Sanskrit using the Pallawa script, which is a form of writing that originated in the Tamil Nadu area of southern India. Thus, we can safely say that Hinduism was present in Java from at least the fourth century CE.

The Srivijaya empire, based in Sumatra with its center in Palembang, began in the late seventh century CE. It continued on through the 13th century and had a significant influence not only in Java, but also in the Malay peninsula, Cambodia, Thailand, and Vietnam. Oddly, very little remains of this once-powerful kingdom, which was not even known to have existed until foreign scholars began to uncover evidence of it in the 1920s. It, too, was heavily influenced by Indian religious traditions and was a veritable intellectual center of Vajrayana Buddhism by the seventh century.

Chinese Buddhist scholars went to Sumatra to study and, as we mentioned at the beginning of this book, the famous Buddhist teacher and saint Atisha lived in the Srivijayan kingdom for some years before bringing Vajrayana (Tantra) teachings back to India and Tibet. There is some debate as to where Atisha actually wound up, however, for by that time—the 11th century CE—Srivijaya extended to Java as well as to what is present-day Borneo, and its capital moved to Java for a period of time during the eighth century, when the massive Buddhist edifice at Borobudur was built. Another problem in locating important geographical sites lies in the ease with which foreign travelers and armchair tourists writing 1000 years ago used terminology and place names with only the barest first-hand knowledge of what they were talking about. Thus, there is some confusion as to the precise location of Srivijaya at certain critical periods in its history.

Other kingdoms existed alongside the Srivijayan empire, including the Sailendra and Sunda kingdoms as well as the famous Mataram kingdom. The Sailendra dynasty is often associated with Srivijaya for a variety of reasons, including the intermarriage of its rulers. Thus some scholars attribute the building of Borobudur to the Sailendras themselves. It is interesting that the earliest record of the Sailendras is a stone inscription that mentions the erection of a shrine to the goddess Tara that dates to 778 CE. The Sailendras, however, seem to have disappeared in the ninth century shortly after the completion of Borobudur and their defeat by a ruler from the short-lived Sanjaya dynasty who later moved back to Sumatra. In fact, there is still some debate as to whether the Sailendras were really Buddhists or Hindus—or both.

The Sunda kingdom, as its name implies, was located in western Java in the area now known by the same name. It represents one of the longest and most continuous of the Javanese regimes, lasting from 669 to 1579 CE. This also was a mixed Buddhist and Hindu kingdom, but with a strong element of indigenous ("animist" or "shamanistic") practices as well. Unlike the still somewhat mysterious Srivijaya and Sailendra cultures, the Sundanese have kept the memory of their greatness alive in a strong oral tradition that has passed down historical information—as well as its indigenous, pre-Buddhist beliefs and practices—through the centuries.

The Mataram kingdom (not to be confused with the Islamic Mataram Sultanate of the 13th to 16th centuries) lasted from the eighth to the 11th century CE, and its power centers were in present-day Yogyakarta and Surakarta (Solo). Some scholars attribute the origins of this dynasty to the Sanjayas, while others claim that the building of Borobudur and the equally impressive Hindu complex at Prambanan occurred thanks to the Mataram kings. In the 10th century, or possibly earlier, the kingdom moved its capital farther east to Central Java. This was possibly due to an eruption of Mount Merapi at that time that covered Borobudur in volcanic ash from which it was only rescued in the 19th century.

Perhaps the single most important dynasty—in terms of both our subject and of Indonesia as a whole—was the Majapahit kingdom, which lasted from 1293 to 1500 and disappeared with the ascension of Islam in the archipelago. Prior to the Majapahit, there were several other dynasties of greater or lesser importance, the most notable of which was the Singhasari kingdom (1222–1292) that gave rise to the Majapahit, and the Kediri kingdom (1045–1221) in Java, which was ruled by a series of kings who considered themselves incarnations of Hindu gods like Vishnu and Ganesha. The second king of Kediri was believed to be the incarnation of Kamajaya, the God of Love known in Sanskrit as Kamadeva; his queen was believed to be Kamaratih, the Goddess of Lust and Passion known in Sanskrit as Rati. Thus it can be seen that the Hindu religious tradition was quite strong in Java and remained that way until the advent of Islam.

By this time, the stresses imposed by foreign visitors and alien cultures was already beginning to strain the Javanese worldview. Java is an island, and the trade along its coasts was brisk, with ships arriving from India and all of Asia regularly. The entire Malay and Indonesian archipelago was famous worldwide for gold and spices. Muslim traders from India and other countries brought, not only their wares to sell, but also their religion. Slowly, Islam began making inroads from the coastal communities to deeper within the interior where the great Javanese palaces and temples were located. The riches and influence of the Javanese kingdoms were so well-known that the great Mongol emperor and warlord Kublai Khan (a contemporary of Marco Polo) sent an army of more than 20,000 troops to attack them, but was defeated in 1292 by forces under what would become the Majapahit dynasty.

Oddly enough, it was Dutch perfidy that almost lost the world the historical texts that revealed the existence of this magnificent kingdom—and a Dutch official who saved the texts from the flames. The story is illustrative of the how the people of Indonesia had lost virtually all memory of their greatness before the arrival of the colonial powers, save for legends passed down from generation to generation and, of course, the mute but insistent testimony of the stones—the temples, monuments, petroglyphs, and other artifacts found everywhere on the islands. The manuscript in question is the *Deshawarnana*, perhaps better known as the *Nagarakrtagama*, written in 1365 as a description of the court of Hayam Wuruk, Majapahit's most famous king, who reigned from 1350 to 1389. In the year 1894, the Dutch sent a small army to raze the palace of a ruler on the island of Lombok. Among the priceless treasures that were nearly consigned to the flames were the only written records known of the Majapahit empire. They were saved by an official attached to the Dutch expedition.

However, there was another text that was preserved as well. A set of six copper plates roughly the size of an A4 sheet of paper (or about 8" x 12") were discovered buried in the ground in East Java in the year 1780. Luckily, the inscribed plates were copied onto manuscript, because the originals were lost and never seen again. The copy itself disappeared, until it was rediscovered in 1888 in Leiden. Thus it was not until 1888 that the world learned how Majapahit came to be, for the copper plates told the story of its founder, King Wijaya. The manuscript from Lombok told the story of Hayam Wuruk. From these two core documents we have been able to piece together the history of this empire, assisted by an ever-growing body of other evidence, some of it from Chinese and other foreign sources who had been visiting Java and trading with it during that period.

All available evidence describes Majapahit as an empire that embraced the diverse religious and cultural interests of its people. Both Hindu—in this case,

Shiva worshippers—and Buddhist leaders lived at the palace, and indigenous religious leaders also enjoyed a great deal of autonomy. Vishnu worshippers were also in attendance during this period, although their influence at the court was not as great as that of the Shiva cult. During this period, we can see that Hindu and Buddhist deities were identified with local Javanese gods and goddesses, and the Javanese belief system was brought into line with Hindu and Buddhist practices—or vice versa. Also, Hayam Wuruk claimed the title of *chakravartin*, a peculiarly Indian title that means "the one through whom the wheel of Dharma turns." The implication, of course, is that the political ruler of the kingdom was also its spiritual leader, in the sense that he or she embodied the soul of the country and was the channel for the Dharma. Depending on the context, Dharma can mean the Law (as in religious law, analogous to the Torah for the Jews), or duty in the sense of spiritual responsibility. Both Buddhists and Hindus use the term, albeit with slightly different connotations. For those who live in accordance with the Dharma, life proceeds as it should; if a king rules in accordance with the Dharma, the entire nation prospers. In this way, it is also similar to the Chinese concept of the Dao.

There was more to regal authority than adherence to the Way, however. Power was also a prerequisite and, in the Majapahit empire—as in the previous Indian-style empires of Java and Sumatra—power was *shakti*. We must remember that these were Tantric kingdoms, whether nominally Buddhist or Hindu. The rituals, temples, and statuary all attest to a Tantric view of the world. Indonesia was so important to the preservation and transmission of Tantric doctrine and methods that one of Tibet's three most important teachers, the aforementioned Atisha, came to the Srivijayan kingdom to learn its teachings first-hand. Tantra fit in well with the indigenous spiritual beliefs of a people who identified themselves with the land: its volcanoes, its rugged coastline, its rice and tea fields, its breathtaking interior. Sexual prowess was respected as a manifestation of shakti, and a king was expected to have an abundance of it. The king was expected to be fertile, for that meant the land would be fertile.

> Sexual activity was also one way to obtain and direct power; mystic sexual union enveloped partners in cosmic energy and increased their power.[28]

---

28 See Kenneth R. Hall, "Ritual Networks and Royal Power in Majapahit Java," *Archipel*. Volume 52, 1996, p. 101, fn. 9.

In other words, this concept was not restricted to those who had a religious vocation. It was not the sole province of monks or ascetics. Tantra was practiced by monarchs in ancient Java and, to a certain extent, still is.

> In Javanese Tantric Buddhism there were three methods: *mantra*, the repetition of a formula endless times; *yantra*, a magical symbol which had to be drawn correctly; and *Tara*, energy possessing goddesses. Rituals, magic circles and diagrams, drunkenness, sexual union with a "*Tara*" and sacrifices of animals and even human beings were common to Javanese Tantric ritual ...[29]

The question of human sacrifice in Java is a controversial one. Human remains have been found at some temple sites, buried beneath the stones. The practice of human sacrifice as a ritual during the construction of an especially important building is one of which both circumstantial as well as some textual evidence exists, and in fact it is believed to have continued to this day in some parts of Asia.[30]

That a king should be so intimately involved with these seemingly bizarre practices may surprise those who have come to Tantra through the New Age, which usually frames Tantra in a personal way, as an individual's approach to a kind of spiritual ecstasy through sex. On the contrary, Tantra is first and foremost about power, shakti; those in society who are most concerned with getting power and keeping it are its rulers. Ronald M. Davidson has emphasized this aspect of Tantra, what he calls its "imperial metaphor," which revolves around the consecration of a king and, by extension, the exercise of royal power.[31] If we accept this as true, then it should come as no surprise that an actual king would see in Tantric practice rituals of legitimacy and the assurance of continued power.

---

29 Hall, "Ritual Networks and Royal Power," p. 106, fn. 31. Here, Hall refers to the 10th-century *Sanghyang Kamahayanikan*, the "Venerable Great Vehicle," a text of Vajrayana Buddhism that references the *Mahavairocana* Tantra, which contains the statement: "There is nothing which is prohibited for him who has attained the highest wisdom."

30 See, for instance, the work by Roy E. Jordaan and Robert Wessing on this subject, such as "Human Sacrifice of Prambanan," *Bijdragen tot de Taal-, Land-, en Volkenkunde*, 152:45–73 and "Construction Sacrifice in India: 'seen from the east,'" Jan E. M. Houben and Karel R. van Kooij (eds), *Violence Denied: Violence, non-violence, and the rationalization of violence in South Asian cultural history* (Leiden: Brill, 2002), as well as their "Death at the building-site: Construction sacrifice in Southeast Asia," *History of Religions*, 37:101–21.

31 Ronald M. Davidson, *Indian Esoteric Buddhism: A Social History of the Tantric Movement* (New York: Columbia University Press, 2002).

The mindset of a Tantric practitioner is such that he or she enters a realm where identification with a deity is required, at least during the course of the ritual. In the mundane world, kings occupy that sort of position as intermediaries between heaven and earth, and the Tantrika aspires to a similar state. That is one of the reasons why Tantra was considered such a threat to the established order. It wasn't due only to their antinomian practices and beliefs, but the idea that a Tantrika, of whatever caste—whatever position in society or even a total outcaste, a Dalit—could, through brute force it would seem, aquire direct contact with the divine forces that inform the monarchy and, by extension, the kingdom. Such a feat put the Tantrika on a par with the king.

In Java, however, the rulers dominated this type of activity for at least 1000 years—from the earliest beginnings of Indian religion in Java to the advent of Islam, and beyond. The people themselves had their own avenues to spiritual power, of course. Those who did not follow either the Buddhist or Hindu Tantric path could avail themselves of their indigenous methods and beliefs. During the Majapahit era, Buddhism, Shaivism (Shiva worshippers), Vaisnavism (Vishnu worshippers), and the indigenous faith all had their place at the court assured. There were, however, other personalities and cults in Java that did not necessarily enjoy the privileges of the court. Today, they would be considered "animists" or "shamans," but neither of these antique designations really communicates the genuine nature of these individuals and groups. Their rituals, their sacred spaces, their deities all changed with the territory. In Java, it seems that every mountain is sacred; every volcano is an *axis mundi*. There were (and are) spirits of the forests, of the rivers, of the mountains, of the fields, and of the sea. Sometimes, these take on human, or humanoid, form; at other times, they are perceived as snakes, monkeys, or other fauna. A seemingly innocent scene of a young woman walking alone down a road under a full moon can take on a hideous aspect, for that woman may not be a woman at all, but a fierce goddess, a Durga, or some other dangerous local spirit.

In Java today, you will find all of these beliefs represented, along with Islam and elements of Christianity and even Theosophy. The development of a truly unique form of mysticism is still taking place on the island, one that has accepted the best parts of all traditions—local and foreign—to create a methodology, a program of action, and what we may call "active spirituality" that is peculiar to Java. While African religions survived in somewhat different form among the slave populations of the Caribbean (for instance) and became today's Voudon, Santeria, Candomble, and Palo Mayombe, these are still essentially African religions that adopted a veneer of Catholicism. They were never truly "syncretic," as has been supposed. The Javanese, on the other hand, remained connected to their land even during long centuries of colonial interference and rule. Their very lives depend on maintaining a harmonious relationship with their environment, troubled as it is with dangerous volcanoes and monsoons. They never lost that connection and, with each succeeding wave of immigrant and colonist, invader and trader, they seem to have incorporated whatever seemed consistent with their own needs and beliefs. Even today, the slogan of the New Order in Indonesia is "Unity in Diversity" and, although there have been attempts by special interests to impose a unity upon the diversity, Indonesia has remained committed to maintaining its own unique culture while simultaneously embracing Islam, modernization, and democracy.

The Coming of Islam

The Majapahit dynasty was the last "Indian" kingdom in Java, and the last purely Tantric one. Tantra survived beneath the Islamic surface of its sultanates and managed to become absorbed to some extent in cultural practices and beliefs, as we shall see. As a formal recognized practice, it was never really suppressed or denied. This may be due to the fact that Sufism, the strain of Islamic teaching and influence that first came to Java, was itself mystical in origin. It was perhaps this confrontation of Tantra and Sufism that allowed the growth of what is known today as *kebatinan*, a peculiarly Javanese form of mysticism.

The origins of Sufism, like the origins of Tantra, are shrouded in mystery. Traditionally, Sufism is considered the secret or esoteric side of Islam that was taught by the Prophet to his disciples. Thus it may be considered a form of Islamic Gnosticism. The outer form of Islam is called *lahir*; its inner, or esoteric form is known as *batin*. This Arabic word has given us the Javanese term *kebatinan*. One of the central practices of Sufism—the constant repetition of the name of God—is called *dhikr* in Arabic. Its parallel with the Indian practice of mantra is obvious. It is believed that the constant repetition of the name of God will bring one into a state of spiritual ecstasy. Since the practice of mantra was well-known to the Javanese for a millennium, it is assumed that, when the Sufi sheikhs arrived with their version, it was readily understood in an Indian and Javanese context.

More important, just as Tantra was sometimes seen as an unorthodox form of Vedic Brahmanism, so Sufism was regarded with suspicion or even disdain by many orthodox Muslims. Vedic Hinduism is a community-centered, socially structured religion with a rigid sense of cosmic order and a requirement for adherence to the rules and outer forms of the faith. Tantra represents an individualistic alternative. Moreover, it is an alternative that emphasizes personal enlightenment and the acquisition of mystical powers, neither of which is normative to Vedic teaching. Sufism also emphasizes personal—one may say private—spiritual experience in the greater context of Islam which, like Vedic Brahmanism, requires adherence to the rules and the outer form of the religion.

Islam first arrived in Java around the 13th century, and was largely confined to the coastal communities where trading was done. The first Islamic sultanate in what is now Indonesia was located in North Maluku, an island far to the northeast of Java that was a center of the spice trade, particularly in cloves. The Sultanate of Ternate (as it was known) was established in the year 1257 and, remarkably, is extant still as an important cultural influence, although without any political power. Closer to home, we find the Sultanate of Demak on the north coast of Java (c. 1475–1548); the Sultanate of Banten on the northwest coast of Java, where it was a center for the trade in pepper (1526–1813); the Sultanate of Aceh, established in 1496 at the far western end of Sumatra, which lasted until the early years of the 20th century; and, finally, the great Mataram Sultanate that was founded at about the same time and that prospered until the coming of the European powers in the 18th century.

It is easy to see that the arrival of Islam in Indonesia was assisted by the trade in spices and gold. Ships arrived from India and the Middle East, through the Straits of Melaka and the Sunda Strait (between Java and Sumatra), seeking goods at ports mostly along the western and northern coasts of Java, which were also centers of first Hindu and Buddhist, and then Islamic learning. While the sultanates did not appear until the mid-13th century at the earliest, Islam was already in evidence in a casual way at least 100 years earlier. It was only the strength of the Majapahit empire that kept Islam from dominating the entire region until the early 16th century.

The Colonialists

In the 16th century, the mighty naval forces of Spain and Portugal began to extend their reach into the New World and Asia. Spain established colonies in Florida, the Caribbean, Mexico, and Central America, while Portugal took possession of Brazil. At the same time, these two countries fought for dominance in Southeast Asia. When the dust had settled, Spain had control over the Philippines, while Portugal held important ports in what is now Malaysia and Indonesia.

The Sultanate of Melaka (Malacca) was first on the list. Melaka is a city in what is now Malaysia, on the west coast of the peninsula and across the Straits of Melaka from the Indonesian island of Sumatra. Melaka was largely inhabited by Malays and Chinese (the so-called Straits Chinese). Around 1400 CE, it became a sultanate that lasted until the Portuguese came and invaded the territory in 1512. The Portuguese remained a force in the area until the mid-19th century, with an Asian empire that included Taiwan (Formosa) and the Chinese port city of Macau (which only recently was returned to Chinese sovereignty).

It was the Dutch who had the greatest impact on Java, however, starting with the arrival of the Dutch East India Company (the VOC) in 1602. It might be said that the presence of the Dutch in Indonesia had a similar influence on the native population as that of the British in India, but that is mistaken in some very important ways. The Dutch attempted to rule through artifice and cunning, pitting one sultan against another, dividing and conquering where possible, and using armed force when that failed. The interest of the Dutch in Indonesia was simple: plunder. It was a colony that existed only for the purpose of trade, particularly in spices. Until the late 16th century, the Netherlands had been under Spanish control. When the Dutch got their independence from Spain, they began to send their own ships to the East Indies and mounted a series of expeditions, many of which ended in only partial success at first. European conflicts between Spain, Portugal, England, and the Netherlands were being played out in Asia, as these economic and naval superpowers vied for control over the best trade routes and the most profitable commodities. At the same time, Indonesia received some high-profile visitors like Sir Francis Drake, Sir Thomas Cavendish, and St. Francis Xavier, while Queen Elizabeth I of England established an East India Company in the year 1600.

Except for very brief periods, the Dutch remained in control of Indonesia (and particularly of Java) for more than 400 years, until the Japanese invasions of the 1940s and subsequent Indonesian independence after the World War II. Contrary to British practice in India, however, the Dutch did not impose their language on the Indonesians and largely kept to the coastal cities where they plied their trade. While Indonesia was definitely a colony of the Dutch—with all the inequality, racism, and arrogance that implies—the lasting impact of Dutch culture and values on the native population was not as great as it could have been under Spanish or English masters. The Dutch played one sultan against another, one territory against another, as long as the result was the same: increased trade and increased security for shipping. On their side, the sultans did their best to follow the same practice of divide and conquer, working with the British to drive out the Dutch, or asking the Dutch for assistance in conflicts with other sultans. This was the period of the great Mataram Sultanate, with its charismatic leader, Sultan Agung. At one point, the Mataram Sultanate ruled nearly all of Java.

In terms of religious conflict, the Dutch were Protestant and the Spanish were Catholic at a time when religious wars were still being fought in Europe. These conflicts were imported into Indonesia and the rest of the zone of influence as well. However, the primary interest of the Dutch was trade and not religion. While the spread of Catholicism in Asia was resisted as much as possible by the Dutch, it was not the main focus of their activities. The 17th century was a period of tremendous military conflict in Java and throughout Indonesia, with sultans battling each other and foreign powers interfering when and where it suited them. Sultan Agung himself established relations with the Dutch East Indies Company in a bid for survival, as he witnessed the military and political strength of what originally was supposed to be a trading mission. In the mid-17th century, in fact, the VOC captured the port of Melaka, thus ending Portuguese hegemony in the region. In addition, the VOC captured ports in Ceylon (today's Sri Lanka) as well as on Taiwan. Any shipping of goods in the entire region under VOC control that was not authorized by the VOC was considered smuggling, and the perpetrators were imprisoned or worse.

The situation between the Dutch and the Indonesians deteriorated considerably during the 18th century, with sultans being forced to sign treaties and give away huge amounts of territory to the VOC, or risk wholesale slaughter. Rebellions broke out all over Java, and resistance to both the Dutch and their Javanese collaborators was fierce. In addition, the Dutch feared the presence of a large Chinese population on the island and conspired to get rid of them. Called "superfluous Chinese," they were assigned to ships to take them away from Indonesia to other areas under their control, but the Chinese feared they would be murdered at sea and began to stockpile weapons. In the resulting battle in the city of Batavia (now Jakarta), roughly 10,000 Chinese were massacred at the hands of the Dutch troops.

Wars and rumors of war dominated this period, but it also saw the establishment of the Sultanate of Yogyakarta and the building of its famous palace, the Kraton, in 1755. The first sultan of the present lineage, Hamengkubuwono I, moved into the Kraton the following year. However, the district of Yogyakarta borders on the Sultanate of Surakarta and, in 1790, the Sultan of Yogyakarta, along with VOC forces, attacked Surakarta because of intelligence received that the sultan there was planning to take over Yogyakarta and murder all the Dutch in Java. Eventually, the VOC took over Surakarta for a while and looted its treasury.

To make matters worse, war broke out with England in 1780. The Netherlands formally surrendered to the British forces and the Prince of Orange (of the Netherlands) proclaimed that all Dutch colonies would revert to the British Crown. Many of the VOC outposts refused to surrender, so the English-Dutch war continued in Java long after the end of hostilities in Europe.

However, by 1800, the Dutch East India Company had ceased to exist. Plagued by corruption, war, and the growing insecurity of maritime trade, the famous VOC went bankrupt. The Dutch government took over the company's assets and plotted ways to get the colonies back from British control. The Napoleonic wars had broken out in Europe, and the Netherlands was now under French control, which only confused matters even more. Not surprisingly, perhaps, an edict went out from the Napoleonic administration that the French Revolutionary ideals of *liberté, egalité, fraternité* would not apply in Indonesia.

By 1811, the British were, for a time, firmly in control of Java. The famous Sir Thomas Stamford Raffles (1781–1826), who is credited with the discovery of the enormous shrine at Borobudur, was appointed Lieutenant Governor of Java that year. Among his other accomplishments is the founding of the city of Singapore; the famous Raffles Hotel there bears his name, of course. While in Java, Raffles wrote a lengthy report of the area (*The History of Java,* 1817) that is still in print today and consulted by historians and anthropologists as a curiosity and a starting point for research into the region. However, he was not well-liked at the Javanese courts, where he was considered rude and impolite, an impression probably exacerbated by the fact that the British began an attack on Yogyakarta within six months of Raffles' visit to the Kraton. During that attack, they looted the Kraton and sent the sultan into exile, replacing him with a sultan of their own choice.

By 1814, there was yet another sultan on the throne in Yogyakarta—Hamengkubuwono IV, a thirteen-year-old who replaced the British-selected Hamengkubuwono III. That same year, the British sent a report back to England on the discovery of both the Borobudur and Prambanan temples.

The British viewed themselves as saviors rescuing the Javanese from the oppression of their Dutch masters. In the end, however, it is difficult to say with any conviction which of the two European powers had the most benign affect on the people. Both countries burned villages, razed cities, massacred civilians, looted antiquities and treasuries, acted in bad faith with the sultans, and conspired against them all in the name of profit and glory. The native peoples of Indonesia were objects—at best, things to be traded; at worst, obstacles in the way of (European) progress. Raffles believed himself to be in Java on a mission to rescue the Javanese from the Dutch; in the end, it was difficult to tell them apart. Anyway, it is a moot point, for by 1825, the Dutch were again in control. They restored Sultan Hamengkubuwono II, who had been sent into exile by the British, and the Java War began—a conflict that lasted for five more years.

As 1830 dawned, the Dutch were once again in nominal control of Java. By this time, realization had set in that the Government of the Netherlands was largely being financed by Dutch holdings in the East Indies, to the tune of 30 percent or more of the annual budget. A more aggressive and militant program was created to ensure that the Javanese remained docile and firmly under Dutch control. A Dutch East Indies Army was created, and formal programs were announced to force Javanese farmers to raise cash crops for export—like coffee, instead of rice. This eventually led to a famine in 1845. This, and other excesses and poorly designed programs, led to the Dutch East Indies costing more for the Netherlands to maintain than they were taking in. By the early days of the 20th century, Indonesian nationalism had found its stride and resistance against the Dutch was growing in intensity.

Strangely, one of the forces that contributed to this sense of nationalism was the Theosophical Society.

The Theosophical Society in Java

Although much of the Theosophical Society's work in India is a matter of public record, particularly the role Annie Besant played in the Indian Independence movement, not much is known about the role of the Society in Indonesia. In its heyday in the pre-revolutionary period, the Theosophical Society had dozens of lodges in Yogyakarta alone, not to mention the rest of Java. For instance, as a high school student, future Indonesian president Sukarno studied at a Theosophical Society library in Surabaya in the 1920s.[32] Members of the Society assisted in the restoration of the Buddhist shrine at Borobudur and it was the first organization to celebrate Wesak Day (the Buddhist holiday commemorating the birth, death, and attainment of enlightenment of the Buddha) at the shrine in 1932.[33]

Some claim that Madame Blavatsky, the founder of the Society, personally visited Java three times—in 1853, 1858, and 1883.[34] Indeed, some say that the

32 Martin Ramstedt, "Introduction,"in Martin Ramstedt, ed., *Hinduism in Modern Indonesia: a minority religion between local, national and global interests* (London: Routledge Curzon, 2005), p. 13.

33 Iem Brown, "The Revival of Buddhism in Modern Indonesia," in Ramstedt, *Hinduism in Modern Indonesia,* p. 47.

34 Ramstedt, *Hinduism in Modern Indonesia.* The first two dates are before the creation of the Theosophical Society in New York in 1875. According to a history of the Society by C. J. Ryan (1937), she visited Java from India in 1857. There she "met two other chelas [disciples of her Master]" and thereby

Society was largely responsible for the rebirth of Buddhism in that country. Of course, many members of the Society were Dutch and other foreigners, including Chinese, lured by the Society's mysticism concerning the mysterious East and its proselytizing of Hindu and Buddhist teachings. But there were a substantial number of Javanese intellectuals who were drawn to the movement as it seemed to offer validation for Asian spirituality as opposed to faiths imported by gunboat. The emphasis on Buddhism was also a reminder of the glory days of Indonesian history, when the great empires that dominated Southeast Asia were Hindu and Buddhist.

The importance of Java to the Theosophical Society may be seen in a review of the contemporary literature on the subject. In 1917, an issue of *The Theosophical Path Magazine* printed an article on Borobudur by C. J. Ryan, a frequent contributor to the publication and a staunch Theosophist all his life.[35] Ryan wrote on astronomy, archaeology, and related subjects, and eventually produced a book-length appreciation of the Society. His article on Borobudur contains some speculation as to the purpose of the shrine and its possible association with Central American architectural styles. In the issue of February 1924, Ryan writes on "Scenes in Java," with a photo of the Dieng Plateau north of Yogyakarta and the observation that the temples in Java resemble those of Central America:

> Relics of a great city, far greater than any now existing in Java, are found on the plateau. Its walls are twelve feet high and six feet in thickness. Nothing whatever is known of its history, its builders, or its date. The hundreds of temples on the plateau are another enigma of archaeology; though many conjectures have been made nothing has been finally established. The only definite statement that can be made is that the Dieng temples closely resemble in general form and ornamentation the pyramid-temples of Yucatan and other states of Central America; and yet how can we

missed the famous Sepoy Rebellion in India that year. The identity of the two "other chelas" of the Master is not revealed, but the idea that there would be two of them in Java, who were also disciples of the Master who was guiding Blavatsky, is compelling. Were they Dutch? Or local Javanese? From there, Ryan suggests she went directly to South America where "she gained archaeological information" before returning to Europe by 1860 (Ryan, 1937, p. 22). Blavatsky biographer Marion Meade, however, suggests that the entire episode was a complete fantasy (1980), while Geoffrey A. Barborka (1986) repeats it without comment except to say that she went to Java "on orders," presumably from her anonymous Master (Meade, 1980, p. 69; Barborka, 1986, p. 26).

35 C. J. Ryan, "Boro-Budur: The Great Pyramid of Java," *The Theosophical Path*, Vol. XIII, No. 5, November 1917, pp. 482–486.

> suppose that there was any communication between these far distant places in comparatively recent times! It is not improbable that the key to some revealing historical mystery lies in this resemblance, and it is not impossible that Theosophy may find the way to turn it.[36]

Ryan revisits this theory the following month, in an article entitled "Great Temples in Java," where he focuses on the Borobudur complex that includes Candi Mendut and Candi Pawon. He then makes mention of Candi Sewu, near Prambanan, as well as Candi Sukuh, of which he writes:

> ... writers speak of them as being probably the shrines of a faith earlier and simpler than any of which we have record. Nothing is really known about them. They are severe in form, and massive, and have caused much speculation on account of their resemblance to Central American or Egyptian monuments.[37]

This is the type of fascination and wonder that accompanied early European interest in the ancient temples of Java. Whereas no one denied that the temples betrayed their Indian influences, there was still speculation that there was some kind of communication or contact between Java and the civilizations of Central America. This type of speculation only increased with the decades, fueled in part by the *Chariots of the Gods* type of literature of Erich von Daenniken and his imitators.

This was not the extent of Theosophical Society interest in Java, however. As the Dutch researcher Herman A. O. de Tollenaere has pointed out in a series of papers given in the Netherlands in the 1990s and in his book *The Politics of Divine Wisdom: Theosophy and labour, national, and women's movements in Indonesia and South Asia 1875–1947*, the Theosophical Society was very involved in the independence movement, although its views on such things as conscription in the Dutch forces during World War I were at odds with Indonesian revolutionaries, as the Theosophists tended to come down on the side of an authoritarian interpretation of government.[38] Even though they seemed to favor self-rule—as,

---

36 C. J. Ryan, "Scenes in Java," *The Theosophical Path*, Volume XXVI No. 2, February 1924, pp. 120–128.

37 C. J. Ryan, "Great Temples in Java," *The Theosophical Path*, Volume XXVI No. 3, March 1924, p. 225–236.

38 H.A.O. de Tollenaere, *The Politics of Divine Wisdom: Theosophy and labour, national, and women's movements in Indonesia and South Asia 1875-1947* (Leiden: Uitgeverij Katholieke Universiteit Nijmegen, Nijmegen, 1996.

for instance, in India—the ideal of the Society seemed to favor a ruling class, the nobility, over a purely democratic form of governance.

Thus, "among the Dutch in the East Indies colony, the TS had the largest proportion of members anywhere in the world. It also had quite some support among the Javanese nobility (*priyayi*)." The author also points out that the influence of the Society was so strong in Java that there was a Blavatsky Park in Jakarta, as well as an Olcott Park in Bandung and an Annie Besant Square in Semarang.[39] This is a remarkable, if little-known, aspect of the Theosophical Society in Southeast Asian politics and philosophy.

It did not end there, however.

One of the Society's more colorful characters in a crowd of colorful characters was Charles Leadbeater (1854–1934), who worked closely with Annie Besant and who discovered the spiritual teacher Krishnamurti. Leadbeater also wrote on Java from a Theosophical angle, even to the extent of collecting some of his essays on the subject in a slight volume entitled *The Occult History of Java*, which contains an essay on the type of fairies you may encounter there.[40] When it seemed that Krishnamurti was no longer interested in being an occult leader of the Society, Leadbeater cast around for a substitute and came up with the idea of the "Seven Virgins of Java."

These were seven young Dutch women, taken from Java and brought to India to become a kind of mystic society. Leadbeater dressed them in blue robes and taught them the fundamentals of Co-Masonry, into which he had been initiated. It was all very bizarre.

Suffice it to say that Java was on the radar of the Theosophical Society for quite some time. Their relationship with the Dutch authorities is interesting, considering the Society's avowed preference for home rule and a general abhorrence of violence. It was perhaps this disinclination to support a violent rebellion that led the Society to tread carefully in Indonesia, as they had in India. Perhaps they were waiting for an Indonesian Gandhi, but in any event that did not take place and future revolutionaries like Sukarno drank at the well of Theosophical thought as they developed their ideas of liberation. The full story of the Society's influence in the Indonesian independence movement as well as the Buddhist revival in Southeast Asia has yet to be written.

---

39 H.A.O. de Tollenaere, "The Theosophical Society and Labour and National Movements in Indonesia, 1913-1918," Paper for the first European Social Sciences History Conference, Noordwijkerhout, The Netherlands, 9-11 May 1996.

40 C. W. Leadbeater, *The Occult History of Java* (Adyar: Theosophical Press, 1951).

With the Japanese invasion of 1942, the internal political situation in Indonesia grew even more grave. Various independence factions fought with each other or with the Dutch, only to find themselves having to side with either the Japanese against the Dutch, or with their despised Dutch rulers. The Dutch promised to hold discussions after the war on Indonesian independence, but that was seen as a pragmatic move to insure that the Indonesians remained on their side in the war. Nazi Germany had already invaded the Netherlands, so the Dutch who were left in Indonesia were fighting a war without any European support. Sukarno, who by this time had become an important nationalist leader, found himself imprisoned by the Dutch and then escaped, only to find himself in discussions with the Japanese who wanted to support his nationalist struggle, if only to give further problems to the Allied forces still fighting in the region. Sukarno could then accept the position of head of the Indonesian government, as long as he also accepted Japanese military control.

The Japanese proved as bad as the European powers when it came to brutalizing the local population, even going so far as to press Indonesian women into service as "comfort women"—i.e., prostitutes for Japanese soldiers. They also imposed forced labor, and maintained horrendous conditions in prisoner camps. Although the Japanese had promised Indonesian independence—as had the Dutch—it became clear that Indonesians were going to have to win their freedom on their own.

Once the war was won and the Japanese retreated from Indonesia, the Dutch, aided by the British, returned with a vengeance to try to retake their former colony. Resistance was immediate and severe. Independence riots broke out all over Indonesia, and remnants of Japanese forces on some of the islands were still fighting Dutch and British troops as late as December of 1945, long after the formal surrender. Guerrilla warfare continued until the end of 1950, when Sultan Hamengkubuwono IX of Yogyakarta supervised the transfer of political power from the Dutch to the new Indonesian government headed by Sukarno, which was formalized at The Hague and became official on December 27, 1949. Less than ten years later, Sukarno was calling on the spiritual forces exemplified by the sultan and the Serpent Queen to save his country. And, after Sukarno, his successor Suharto was also known to engage in occult activity.[41]

The importance of Yogyakarta to Javanese history—and to Indonesian history in general—cannot be overstated. Yogyakarta's commitment to the new Republic

41 See the chapter on Nyai Lara Kidul for a description of these events. Many books have been published in Indonesia dealing with this subject, for instance: Ki Ageng Pamungkas, *Rahasia Supranatural Soeharto* [Suharto's Supernatural Secrets] (Yogyakarta: Penerbit NARASI, 2007).

and support for Sukarno was such that it earned the right to be called a "special district," answerable directly to the capital in Jakarta. It was the only such district in the country and one of the last remaining sultanates. It is to Yogyakarta and its suburbs that we will go in order to understand the influence of Tantric thought and ritual in Java, for the city is surrounded with ancient temples, even in the midst of Dutch colonial architecture and modern Western hotels, restaurants, and advertising.

The Dutch were as brutal and aggressive as their English counterparts, but originally they were not in the missionary business or in the business of cultural domination. That had changed by the end of the 18th century, however, when the Dutch Missionary Society was formed and undertook an aggressive program of conversion to Christianity. The Dutch legal system was imported to Indonesia and became the basis for modern Indonesian jurisprudence—as the English system did in India—and a smattering of Dutch loan-words survive in Indonesian. By and large, however, their influence on the people, culture, religion, and customs of the people was scant, especially when compared to other colonial situations. When the Dutch finally left after the revolutionary movement kicked them out at the end of the World War II, there was little left of Dutch culture in the country. Today, the relationship between the two countries is a cordial one, with an ongoing exchange of students from Indonesian and Dutch universities.

Chapter 2

Introduction to Javanese Mysticism

Magic is a continuation of politics by other means.[42]

The foregoing brief summary of Indonesian history was important to emphasize two points: the importance of Hindu and Buddhist religion in the political and cultural development of Java and the fact that the European powers and cultures had much less influence and were perhaps seen as spiritual as well as political adversaries. When we discuss Javanese mysticism, we will find a great deal of evidence of Indian religions—in particular, Tantra—as well as Sufi influences, but rarely will we find Christian elements, even after 400 years of European Christian domination in the region. This is partly due to the parallel development of Islam alongside foreign influence in Java during roughly the same time frame. As the Mataram Sultanate was reaching its greatest power, so was the Dutch East India Company. In a way, it may be claimed that the Mataram Sultanate protected the indigenous population from European religious and cultural influence at a time when the danger was greatest.

The old royal esoteric beliefs survived alongside normative religious practices during the era of the Mataram Sultanate and contributed to a sense of national identity on a plane not always visible to the foreign interlopers, who saw only gold and spices. The sultans still respected the Hindu and Buddhist ceremonies of their ancestors and proudly proclaimed lineages tracing back to the older dynasties of Srivijaya, with their Tantric rites and observances. While idolatry is forbidden in Islam—as it is in the Jewish and Christian faiths—the gods of the Hindus and Buddhists, as well as of the indigenous peoples, were not abandoned but preserved, relegated to "spirit" status. In many cases, the Indian deities were identified with ancient Javanese gods. The Indian epic poems of the *Mahabharata* and the *Ramayana* were revered, in a sense, as historical documents, and the exploits of Rama, Sita, Hanuman, and Lakshamana were preserved in the famous shadow plays, the wayang, which—like the early days of theater in the West—had spiritual and political as well as entertainment value. While not abandoning Islam, many Javanese still respect and revere these ancient personalities and the supernatural powers they represent. They are able to do this because they have realized that

42 Nils Bubandt, "Sorcery, corruption and the dangers of democracy in Indonesia," *Journal of the Royal Anthropological Institute (N.S.)*, 2006, 12, p. 413.

there is a hidden, or esoteric, aspect of Islam, just as there is of the Indian faiths. This is what the Muslims call *batin*.

Thus, the relationship between the indigenous belief systems and Islam may be considered an esoteric one. The ancient gods have found a place within the Javanese Muslim worldview—not as gods, perhaps, but as spiritual forces. Just as the *jinn* in Arab lore are believed to be living creatures, some of whom have converted to Islam, just so the Javanese spiritual forces may be understood as living beings, creatures of God like the jinn in the Middle East. This, at any rate, became a means of accommodating or rationalizing Javanese belief systems within an Islamic context.

The form of religion that existed in Java before the arrival of Hinduism is a matter of conjecture, since contemporary written records of the pre-Indian period in Java do not exist. What we have, however, is a living tradition of what anthropologists have called "animism," and this needs some clarification.

Animism comes from the Latin term *anima*, which means "spirit" or "soul." It is a belief system that sees objects in nature as imbued with spiritual life and force. In Java, the environment provides many opportunities for this type of perception. There are active volcanoes like Mount Merapi near Yogyakarta, whose eruption in October 2010 is continuing as I write, with much loss of life and property, including that of the shaman who died on the mountain rather than escape its wrath. There is a pitiless sea to the south of Yogyakarta that is known as the abode of a serpent queen who must be propitiated by the sultan every year. It is believed that the end of the world will come when lava from Merapi meets the ocean, for the flow would have to cross the city of Yogyakarta and the Kraton itself to do that. As I write, the Code River that runs through the city is already reaching the high-water mark, filled with debris from the ongoing eruption, and hundreds of thousands of Javanese have fled their villages and fields to seek refuge in the public buildings in Yogyakarta. Many Javanese perceive this as a spiritual event as well as a purely physical disaster, and see no particular difference between the two. That there is a continuum—if not a strict identity—between the physical world and the realm of the spirit is a Tantric worldview that lies deep within the Javanese psyche.[43]

Recently, anthropologists and archaeologists have suggested that neither a pure form of Vedic Brahmanism nor Buddhism really took hold in Java. While the

43 This is not to say that the eruption was "punishment" for an imagined series of sins or religious infractions, as infamously was suggested by the Indonesian Communications and Information Technology Minister in a way that was reminiscent of the remarks by Evangelical minister Pat Robertson concerning the sins of the victims of America's Hurricane Katrina in New Orleans (Al Makin, "Mythical perceptions of nature and survival," *The Jakarta Post*, 8 November 2010).

sojourn of Atisha in Indonesia is well-attested, it is undeniable that the religion that took hold in Tibet after Atisha's travel there was a Tantric form of Buddhism, what is called Vajrayana Buddhism. In Java itself, there is now a tendency to speak of a Shiva-Buddha syncretism: a wholly unique amalgam of the two main forms of Indian religion. This syncretic form is Tantric and may even contain elements of some of the more extreme forms of Tantra—like, for instance, the Kapalika sect that focused entirely on rituals in cemeteries, death ceremonies, skull cups, and bone trumpets, and even, it is alleged, human sacrifice.[44] It is possible that these extreme forms of Tantra found fertile ground within the indigenous belief systems and that elements of them were absorbed and have survived today as elements of Javanese mysticism. That some form of human sacrifice was practiced in Java at the time of the building of the Prambanan temple complex already has been asserted by some modern anthropologists, as we saw in the last chapter. I focus on this, not to accentuate the more lurid possibilities of this subject, but in order to show that the form of religious and mystical practice that was imported into Java was a serious version of Tantra. As we continue our excursion into the remote temples and shrines outside modern Yogyakarta, we will encounter a wide variety of spiritual expression along the way, and many of these examples will be virtually indistinguishable from Tantric practices. First, however, we will look at those elements of Javanese mysticism that seem to be purely indigenous.

For the sake of convenience, we will organize the discussion into separate categories: sacred space, sacred time, sacred personalities, and occult techniques.

Sacred Space

Java is a land that is characterized more than most by its ecology. Prone to volcanic eruptions, earthquakes, tsunamis, and monsoons, the emotional and psychological impact of the land itself is profound and contributes to the type of thinking that sees hidden forces at work in the world. This is because there is no clear cause-and-effect relationship between the work of humans and the dramatic response of the ecology. A volcano will erupt when it wishes to; an earthquake occurs according to its own timetable. It is a very human response to seek meaning in events over which we have no control, whether it is sudden illness, tragic death, or an environmental disaster. On a general level, science can answer the "how" of an event, but not the "why"—the "why" in the question "why me?" That

44 See for instance, R. Jordaan and R. Wessing, "Human Sacrifice at Prambanan," *Bijdragen tot de Taal-, Land- en Volkenkunde* 152 (1996), no: 1, Leiden, 45–73.

is when human beings turn to divination, religion, or occultism for explanations, and for reassurance that even events as enormous in their effects as an epidemic or an earthquake reveal a purpose, a meaning, or the hand of God in a way that is relevant to an individual's life.

The loci that contribute to this sense of cosmic order behind the disorder are mountains—which, in Java, may frequently be volcanoes—and the ocean, as well as cemeteries, shrines, and certain areas of the forest. If prehistoric humans were so impressed by thunder and lightning that they deified them as gods, how much more dramatic are the rumblings, exaggerated plumes, and eventual eruptions of a volcano?

Outside the ancient city of Yogyakarta, Mount Merapi dominates the horizon. The word *Merapi* means "fire mountain," which is as apt a description as anyone needs. Yet, Merapi—like many mountains in Java—has also been associated with Mount Meru, the legendary center of the world in Hindu and Buddhist religion. Indeed, the word for mountain in Javanese is *meru.* In the 15th-century Javanese epic poem, *Tantu Pagelaran,* part of the original Mount Meru was transported to Java by the Trimurti: Brahma, Shiva, and Vishnu. Pieces of it fell off here and there, and these pieces created the volcanoes of today. So, in this sense, every volcano is a relic of the original Mount Meru and as such is sacred.

These stand-ins for Mount Meru are liminal spaces—places where the earth meets the sky and where humans meet the gods. The summits of these mountains are for communing with the ancient gods. Further down the mountains, in the dry ground above the rice fields and swamps, are other places of mysterious powers and spiritual forces. These sacred precincts are often under the control of human agents, usually men, called *juru kunci* or "keepers of the key." These individuals occupy the tangential place between this world and the other, invisible world. They are the conduits through which the cosmic force, *shakti,* flows. They are sometimes called shamans, because their role is parallel, to a certain extent, to that of the Siberian religious specialists who gave us that term. They commune with spiritual forces and report back; they also bring messages from the human world to the spirit world. In some locations—those with a specific story or legend associated with them—the juru kunci can assist with special prayers and offerings to the local spirits for such worldly concerns as health, wealth, and love.

A site can also be considered powerful due to an historical event—the death of a king in that spot, for instance—or to something more clearly spiritual, like a vision or perhaps a haunting. Ghosts are as prevalent in Java as they are anywhere else, and ghosts are believed to congregate in places like abandoned buildings, lonely sections of forest, or, of course, cemeteries.

Cemeteries can be a tremendous source of shakti, depending on who is buried there. Those that are believed to be the resting places of famous Islamic saints, for instance, are especially powerful. Pilgrimages are often made to these places, particularly during important Islamic holidays (like the Prophet's birthday) and on days considered most powerful according to the Javanese calendar. In Java, however, sacred spaces are not only sources of power; they are also places where people go to give power to the site.[45] Sacred spaces are thus seen as having a reciprocal relationship with the people. Pilgrims give power to the sacred space to keep it vibrant and valuable to the community in much the same way that sacrifices are made in temples in order to give power to the gods. However, some places have more power than others. The grave of an important person—political, spiritual, or artistic—has power. Sacred objects also have power, whether they are buildings or statues imbued with spiritual force or implements used by a person of power. In a way, the Javanese belief in this type of power is analogous to the scientific attitude toward energy: it is neither created nor destroyed, but it may be transformed from potential to kinetic. Although a royal personage may have been dead for centuries, the power represented by that monarch is still strong and can be accessed at the gravesite.

The mountain is a sacred space by its very existence. So are graves. They are boundaries between this world and the next, and for that reason are powerful. In the previous chapter, we saw how charnel grounds in India are similar in nature: places inhabited by the souls of the departed, tangential places between the two worlds.

It is not only the revered dead—kings and saints—whose spirits possess power; those of people who died a violent death may do so as well. This type of spirit, called *siluman*, manifests as a water spirit or sometimes as a snake. They dwell in swamps and caves, not on mountains or dry land, and their peculiar specialty is giving advice and protection, and even winning lottery numbers.[46] This idea that the spirits of the violently dead have power that can be used for positive purposes is also found among the Tantrikas of India, where the skull of someone who was executed or murdered is considered especially efficacious as a *kapala*, or skull cup used in Tantric rituals.

Another snake spirit found in the wet lowlands is the *ipri* or *iprit*. These may appear as beautiful women. In West Java, there is a tradition that one can marry such a spirit provided the way is paved by the juru kunci, the gatekeeper of the

45 Robert Wessing, "Spirits of the Earth and Spirits of the Water: Chthonic Forces in the Mountains of West Java," *Asian Folklore Studies*, Vol. 47, 1988: 43–61.

46 Wessing, "Spirits of the Earth and Spirits of the Water," p. 52.

area where the snake spirit dwells.[47] An iprit will be a source of great wealth for the man who marries her.

The most extreme form of this concept is found, not in the wetlands, but even farther afield, in the oceans themselves, another sacred space. The oceans, seas, and lakes are also liminal places, because they represent a state of being inaccessible to those who cannot breathe underwater. Whereas the mountains reach toward the heavens, however, the watery places—swamps, wetlands, and the ocean itself—draw the unsuspecting or the careless to the Underworld. These are places of chthonic forces, of darker powers. Their most important manifestation is in the story of Nyai Lara Kidul—the Queen of the Southern Ocean—and her marriage to the sultans of Yogyakarta and Solo,which forms the substance of a separate chapter to follow.

Sacred Time

In the West, it is taken for granted that a week has seven days, that there are roughly four weeks to a month and twelve months to a year. It is also understood that this is not a perfect calculation of time, since every four years an extra day must be added to keep the calendar in line with the orbit of the earth around the sun; otherwise, after a century, the calendar would be almost a full month behind.

In Java, a number of different calendars are in use simultaneously (similar to the types of calendars we find in ancient Central America, for instance). In addition to the Gregorian calendar used in the West—which is a solar calendar—there is also the Islamic calendar, which is lunar-based. These two calendars are consulted side by side. Indeed, some Javanese calendars give both the Gregorian (solar) and the Islamic (lunar) dates for each day. But that is the same throughout the Islamic world.

The Javanese, however, have another calendar that is usually added to these two—a "market calendar" or *pasaran.* This is composed of a five-day week, for a total of thirty-five days per Javanese "month"—i.e., the time it takes for the five days of the Javanese calendar to align with the seven days of the Gregorian calendar (5 x 7 = 35).[48] When computing the right days to begin a project or go on a pilgrimage, this calendar is consulted with regularity. Certain days are, of course,

47 Wessing, "Spirits of the Earth and Spirits of the Water," p. 54–55.

48 These five days are known as *Legi*, *Pahing*, *Pon*, *Wagé*, and *Kliwon* in the informal *ngoko* style of Javanese. In the more formal *krama* style, these five days are known as *Manis*, *Pait*, *Petak*, *Cemeng*, and *Asih*, respectively. They have no direct counterparts in Western calendars.

Table 1. Advice for Determining the Best Days for Marriage

Month	Good Day
Sura / Muharram	Wednesday or Thursday
Sapar / Syafar	Wednesday or Thursday
Mulud / Rabiulawal	Friday
Bakdamulud / Rabiulakhir	Friday
Jumadilawal	Friday
Jumadilakhir	Saturday or Sunday
Rejeb / Rajab	Saturday or Sunday
Ruwah / Sya'ban	Saturday or Sunday
Pasa / Ramadhan	Monday or Tuesday
Sawal / Syawal	Monday or Tuesday
Dulkaedah / Zulkaedah	Monday or Tuesday
Besar / Zulhijjah	Wednesday or Thursday

more powerful than others, and certain days may be contra-indicated for certain actions,like betting on the lottery or getting married. Astrology is also very much part of this system and a type of literature called *primbon* has grown up around these calendars with their auspicious and inauspicious dates.

A primbon is a kind of almanac or diviner's manual that is sold everywhere in Java: in bookstores, in sidewalk stalls along Yogyakarta's busy main street, Malioboro Road, and in stationery shops. Its origins are pre-Islamic and they reflect Javanese cosmologies in their interpretation of life events like marriage, birth, and sickness. Originally written in the Old Javanese script (*Kawi*), they are usually published in Bahasa Indonesia for the use of the average person. In the Kraton at Yogyakarta, there are several original versions that are considered quite sacred and that only a chosen few may read.

Like diviners' almanacs worldwide, the primbon is concerned with the right day, the right hour, and the right cardinal direction for the successful accomplishment of certain tasks. While terminology and concepts from Indian religions predominate, there are also Islamic influences. The great anthropologist Clifford

Table 2. Advicc for Determining the Best Month for Marriage

Month	Advice
Sura	Not advised, otherwise there will be trouble and constant fighting.
Sapar	Possible, though there will be loss and debt.
Rabiulawal	Not advised, for either one will die.
Rabiulakir	Possible, though there will be much gossip and verbal abuse.
Jumadilawal	Possible, but there will be deceit, loss, and many enemies.
Jumadilakir	Rich treasure.
Rejeb	Peace and many children.
Ruwah	Happiness and peace always.
Puasa	Not advised. There will be a big misfortune.
Sawal	Possible, but there will be frequent loss and much debt.
Dulkaidah	Not recommended. There will be frequent illness and fighting with friends.
Besar	Wealth and happiness.

Geertz characterized the Javanese religious system as "syncretism": a blend of various religious traditions that results in a new or unique form of religious expression. While his claim has been much debated, there is no escaping the fact that a study of Javanese religion and spirituality will introduce one to Hindu, Buddhist, Islamic, and indigenous Javanese terms, concepts, and even practices.

Therefore, in any given primbon, we will encounter all of these influences, sometimes even on the same page. This amalgamation of so many different cultural approaches to spirituality can have a stimulating effect, rather like a dream that juggles a dozen different, seemingly unrelated, images until one significant point is made. In the case of the primbon, the main focus is the division of time into discrete elements and the meaning associated with each of these.

This relief gives some idea of the mythology connected to the pasaran week of five days

In addition to the pasaran calendar mentioned above, there is the *pawukon* calendar, which, although common to Bali, is also in use among Javanese diviners. This is a 210-day lunar calendar composed of thirty weeks of seven days each. It uses a total of ten separate weeks of ten different lengths (from a one-day "week" to a ten-day "week") that run concurrently. In other words, this is a very complex system that usually can only be understood truly by a priest trained in its structure. Its purpose is strictly ceremonial.

When the pasaran calendar is combined with the seven-day-week Islamic lunar calendar, the result is the *wetonan* calendar, which gives the thirty-five-day month previously mentioned. Moreover, calculations of even greater complexity can be done by combining all of the above calendars to track dates that are especially auspicious or particularly inauspicious.

As if that were not complex enough, the Javanese also use a cycle of eight lunar years called a *windu*. Each year has its own name within the windu, and there are four windu in all, for a total of about thirty-one years in a complete windu cycle. However, the total number of days per year as computed using this system comes to about 354 or 355 days, which means that a single windu consists of about seven years and nine months, rather than a full eight years. Thus, each windu consists of eighty-one wetonan cycles of thirty-five days each, or 2835 days.[49]

49 That this is a lunar-based system may be obvious to a Kabbalist from the fact that the *windu* cycle consists of 81 *wetonan*, 81 being the number of squares in the *kame'a* of the moon, which is 9 x 9 = 81.

Let us look at a few examples, to get a flavor of the advice offered.

One primbon gives a table for determining the best days of each lunar month for marriage (see Table 1, page 60). The months begin with the name of the month in Java, followed by the Arabic form of the month, according to the Islamic lunar calendar. Thus, the first month, Muharram (Old Javanese, Sura), begins on November 26, 2011; in succeeding years, it falls back at the rate of eleven days per year.[50]

Another primbon, one of the most revered, gives advice for marriage in the twelve Islamic lunar months (see Table 2, page 61).[51]

In addition to the above, there is the following note:

> The months Jumadilakir, Rejeb, Ruwah and Besar are recommended for marriage if it can be held on a Kliwon Tuesday, and especially good on Kliwon Friday. If there is no Kliwon Tuesday available, then these months are considered inauspicious. In that case, one can consider the months Sapar, Rabiulawal, Jumadilawal or Sawal, provided that the month contains a Kliwon Tuesday and Kliwon Friday.

Note that the spelling changes between one primbon and the next. This is to be expected, especially when one is transliterating Arabic words into Indonesian. *Kliwon* is one of the days of the five-day pasaran week, which means that, if a Tuesday or a Friday falls on a Kliwon, then the day is auspicious for marriage.

This is just the beginning of what become rather laborious calculations, reminiscent of Indian Jyotish (Vedic) astrology with its many cycles of *dashas*, *antardashas*, etc. It is also similar in some ways to Chinese horoscope methods and the Chinese counterpart to the primbon, the *Tung Shu*. The relief on the previous page gives some idea of the mythology connected to the pasaran week of five days.[52]

So far, we have no information as to the meaning of the names of the days of the week, nor of the images themselves. It may be that the five figures at the top of the chart represent gods or spiritual forces "in charge" of each specific day, and that

---

A 9 x 9 square is also the basis for *Vastuvidya*-style temple architecture in India.

50 Ki Sura, ed. *Buku Primbon Jawa: Lengkap* (Javanese Primbon, Complete) (Solo: Ud. Mayasari, 1995), p. 5. Unless otherwise noted, all translations are by the author.

51 *Kitab Primbon Betaljemur Adammakna*, attributed to His Highness Prince Harya Cakraningrat of the Yogyakarta Kraton (Yogyakarta: Penerbit CV Buana Raya, 1994), p. 21.

52 This comes from John Crawfurd, *History of the Indonesian Archipelago*, vol. 2 (Edinburgh: Archibald Constable & Co. 1820). In 1811, Crawfurd was resident at Yogyakarta as part of a British mission there.

the five figures on the lower half of the chart are scenes appropriate to each of the spirits/days. Thus for Manis, we have an agricultural motif; for Pahing, we have either a domesticated animal or livestock. Kliwon (here spelled Kaliwon) seems to be martial in nature, while Wagé (here spelled Wagi) indicates the giving of food. Pon seems to indicate a servant and master.

A person born on one of the five pasaran days is believed to have certain characteristics and possible futures. When the pasaran day is matched with one of the days in the seven-day week, another set of characteristics is developed. Then there is the lunar month, the solar month, and the year cycle, plus the hours of the day—all of which must be taken into account.

In addition to the division of time, there is also a division of space based on the five-day pasaran cycle, with four of the five days representing cardinal directions and the fifth representing the center. In one primbon, this is shown as Pon in the North, Legi in the South, Wagé in the East, and Paling in the West, with Kliwon in the center.[53] Thus, time and space become enmeshed in this system, just as they do in Western esoteric systems. In yet another primbon, the twenty letters of the Javanese alphabet are arrayed around the four cardinal points as well, with five letters to each quarter, thus offering the possibility of creating mantras—words of power—based on divisions and articulations of time, space, and sound.[54]

This is not as odd as it may seem. There is a lot of mystification in Java concerning the supernatural elements of the twenty letters of the Javanese alphabet. In a book entitled *Horoskop Jawa* (Java Horoscope), there is a chapter entitled "Human Nature Based on Java Script."[55] This chapter offers a detailed analysis of each letter, something that will be familiar to any student of *gematria*, *notarikon,* or *temurah,* the methods used by Jewish Kabbalists to analyze textual material in the Torah. The cosmological system of the Javanese, therefore, has a great deal in common with Western esoteric cosmologies and systems of correspondences, at least where their general approach is concerned. The importance given to cardinal directions, the complicated calendar systems, and their association with letters of the alphabet are all elements they hold in common.

---

53 *Kitab Primbon Betaljemur Adammakna*, p. 215.

54 R. Tanojo, ed., *Primbon Sabdo Pandito* (Surabaya: Penerbit Karya Utama, n.d.), pp. 44, 104.

55 Purwadi, Dr., *Horoskop Jawa* (Yogyakarta: Penerbit Media Abadi, 2007), pp. 58–97.

Sacred Personalities

To the Javanese, shakti is everywhere, in everything. The universe hums with its force, and even the most untrained, unschooled person may be able to turn contact with that power to his or her own advantage. However, it is always better to consult an expert—someone who has devoted his or her life to maintaining contact with supernatural forces. Some of these experts—like the juru kunci or "key keeper"—may ensure that the supplicant performs the right ceremony at the right time for the right purpose. Others take on total responsibility for ritual and its effects. These latter are known by different names in different parts of the archipelago and are even categorized according to their specialty.

The term *dukun* is used for a wide variety of ritual specialists, from healers to mediums and workers in the darker arts. They cast spells, commune with spirits, and exorcise demons. Some specialize in love, others in health, or money, or other normal human concerns. One does not normally go to a dukun in search of enlightenment. A dukun is not a guru, *per se.* They are specialists in their field and offer a service.

Rituals performed by the dukun generally contain Islamic references to God or quotations from the Quran, mixed at times with Sanskrit mantras and more clearly Javanese elements like the names of local spirits. Often, newspaper accounts feature lurid tales concerning specific dukun who are believed to have caused death with their spells. This type of magic—called *ilmu hitam* (the black knowledge or the black art)—is universally feared and its practitioners are called "sorcerers" (*dukun sihir*).[56]

Dukun are not to be confused with juru kunci. Juru kunci are located in a specific sacred space and control access to the space and to the powers represented by that space. A dukun may be self-selected due to some perceived spiritual power, or because of special training and knowledge, or even because he is in possession of some object believed to have superior supernatural force. The role of the juru kunci remains consistent with the spirit of the place he tends; a dukun, like a *santero* in Afro-Caribbean religion, may offer a wider variety of services, calling on a number of spirits or spiritual forces.

Some of these types of spirits have already been mentioned. These include the ipri and the siluman, a human spirit who takes on the form of an animal, often a snake. The spirits of the dead are often evoked, particularly the spirits of those

56 Ronny Nitibaskara, "Observations on the Practice of Sorcery in Java," in C. W. Watson and Roy Ellen, eds., *Understanding Witchcraft and Sorcery in Southeast Asia* (Honolulu: University of Hawaii Press, 1993), pp. 123–133.

who died violently or who were very powerful in life, as well as those deemed to have been saintly while alive or who were powerful dukun themselves. People go to dukun for all the usual reasons—to find love, to keep a recalcitrant lover or wandering spouse, to win at the lottery, to heal sickness, or even to curse a rival or an enemy.

There are mantras specific to many of these desires, as well as appropriate herbs and other substances that must be offered or sacrificed in special ways. These prayers may include Islamic references mixed in with traditional Javanese elements. This short but poignant love spell is found in a locally available pamphlet, *Mantra Orang Jawa* (Javanese Mantras):

Aji Pangasihan Semar Mesem

bismillahirahmanirahim
Srikandi sayang, sang Arjunalah suamimu
aku berdiri bagai Togog,
duduk bagai Semar
kau belas kau kasih menyaksikan sosokku
wahai, Nengina, kasihilah aku,
kasihilah demi kasih Allah[57]

This translates as:

The Smile of Semar Love Spell

Bismillah i-rahman i-rahim
Dear Srikandi, your husband Arjuna
I stood like Togog
Sat like Semar
You pity, you love watching me
Oh, Nengina, love me,
Love me for the love of Allah.

As you can see, there are several religious influences brought to bear in these seven lines. In the first place, the love spell is called "Semar's Smile." Semar is an important figure in Javanese mythology and in the wayang—the shadow plays famous throughout the archipelago that carry important cultural and spiritual informa-

57 Sapardi Djoko Damono, *Mantra Orang Jawa* (Magelang: IndonesiaTera, n.d.), p. 75.

tion. The first line of the mantra or prayer is familiar to every Muslim, for it is the opening line of all but one chapter of the Quran: "In the name of God, the Compassionate, the Merciful." This simple phrase is said to encapsulate the entire meaning and core of Islam.

The next line invokes Srikandi and Arjuna, warriors famous from the *Mahabharata,* of course, but also from the wayang, where Srikandi is interpreted a little differently.[58] Togog is another character from the wayang, as well as Semar in the following line. The spell ends with a plea to Allah.[59] Thus, in this short prayer, we have ample evidence of syncretism at work. Islamic, Hindu, and purely Javanese themes and influences are blended together in one spell, a spell to capture love. In a way, this invocation represents the entire psychology at work behind Javanese mysticism and gives us an insight into Javanese culture, since these references would be familiar to every Javanese.

Javanese culture includes not only human agents of occult forces—the dukun and the juru kunci—but also spiritual ones. These are unique to Indonesia and particularly to Java, and they will appear again and again in our examination of the temples, so we shall look at a few of them now.

Semar

Semar, mentioned in the love spell above, is perhaps the most beloved of all the Javanese gods and is most likely a genuine indigenous personality—a being worshipped in Java before the coming of Indian religions and thus at least a millennium before Islam came to the island. Accounts of Semar's personality, origins, and function depend on some very scarce documents and especially on the wayang performances, which retain much of what we know about this mysterious being. Indeed, even his name is believed to be related to the Old Javanese word *samar,* which means "not clear," or "obscure."[60]

58 Srikandi, in the *Mahabharata,* was born a woman but transformed into a man who fought at Arjuna's side. She transformed back into a woman toward the end of her life. In the Javanese wayang, however, she remains a woman throughout her life.

59 I have not been able to identify "Nengina" from Javanese sources, although in some parts of Java the word *neng* is used as a polite form of address to a younger woman. It may also be a reference to the wayang character *Dewi Nagagini*—alternate spelling, *Dewi Ngagini*—who married Bhima in one version of the tale. *Nagini* is a female form of *Naga,* the serpent spirits of Java, the most famous of which is Nyai Lara Kidul.

60 For this and alternate meanings of *samar,* see S. A. Mangunsuwito, *Kamus Lengkap Bahasa Jawa* [Complete Dictionary of the Javanese Language] (Bandung: Yrama Widya, 2006), p. 505.

According to old Javanese hand Niels Mulder, Semar is "the God of Java, progenitor of the Javanese race." Even today, he claims, "messianic hopes seem to be pinned on Semar, the guardian spirit of Java who, as retainer of the Pendawa, represents the common folks, and their suffering."[61]

This is an important aspect of Semar for, even though he is of divine origin and identified as the elder brother of Shiva, his place is with the common people of Java and not with the hierarchy.[62] His appearance is crude. He is overweight and sloppy, with enormous belly and buttocks, sometimes with a limp, and he is even considered to be, in a sense, hermaphroditic. He sits attentively at the feet of earthly masters, even though he is far more powerful, far more ancient, and actually divine. He is a savior dressed as a kind of clown or country bumpkin, with a voice at times high-pitched and keening and at others grumbling and rude. He is wise, while appearing stupid or dense. In a way, he is reminiscent of the Sufi hero Nasruddin, whose gnomic utterances and bizarre behavior always reveal a profound meaning.

It is impossible to exaggerate the importance of Semar to the Javanese people and culture. He is their identity, their divine representative. He survived into the Indian period under Hindu influences; even after Islamization, Semar survived within the new cosmology. His is an incredible personality, a god who spent thousands of years alone in Java until people began to arrive and he found himself protecting them, acting as intermediary between the people and the kings.[63]

The Pendawa, mentioned above, are a group of five personalities that appear frequently in wayang performances. They have their origin in the *Mahabharata* as the Pandava. Among them are Arjuna, the Indian king and warlord who is mentioned in the love spell, and Bhima, another famous warrior whose cult spread to Java from India along with that of Shiva. Semar's role in Java is to intercede with these royal and divine figures on behalf of the native Javanese.

Both Semar and Bhima figure prominently in some of the temple architecture that follows in the next section. Curious carved reliefs on temple walls depict some of the stories told about these two beings that were preserved in various wayang traditions. For this reason, it is necessary to devote a little space to a discussion of the enigmatic Bhima.

---

61 Niels Mulder, *Mysticism in Java: Ideology in Indonesia* (Amsterdam: The Pepin Press, 1998), pp. 93, 31.

62 Mulder, *Mysticism in Java,* p. 93. We should also note that Shiva in the Javanese version (especially in wayang performances) becomes Batara Guru, a local name for this imported deity. Shiva's wife, Durga, then becomes Batari Durga.

63 According to the *Babad Tanah Jawi,* a history of Java written during the Islamic period.

Bhima (also spelled Bima)

Bhima's birth was miraculous. A caul was left in a forest on Java, guarded by Semar and Arjuna. It remained there for years, until a series of cosmic events signaled to Shiva that the caul was responsible. Shiva (or Batara Guru, depending on whether you are following the Javanese or the Indian version of the names of the characters in the wayang) then tells his son, Gajah Sena ("Elephant" Sena), to crack open the caul and kill whoever or whatever is inside. After many trials, Gajah Sena finally manages to break open the caul. A by-now-teenage boy emerges and "combines" with Gajah Sena to become one entity—Bhima.

Bhima, the son of King Pandu, joins with Arjuna and three others to form the Pandava or Pendawa. He is known by several characteristics, most notable among them two long and sharp fingernails, one on each hand, that are formidable weapons. His face is black, possibly as the result of incubating in an impenetrable black caul until his release by Gajah Sena. He is known for his honesty and humility, as well as for his enormous strength and loyalty. Curiously, his name has another association in Javanese—as the Milky Way (translated as *bimasakti*, literally "Bima Power"). As far as I know, scholars have not yet established this as an astronomical metaphor, but a story from Australia calls our attention to the fact that the Yumu people of the Northern Territory conceive of the Milky Way as two beings—a woman and a young boy, in this case—stuck together in coitus.[64] They are considered kangaroo ancestors. Since Bhima is the result of Gajah Sena (an elephant god) and the boy-in-the-caul "sticking together," it may be that this tale resonates with an ancient mythologem concerning this astronomical phenomenon, with a possible sexual connotation as well.

Bhima's wife, Nagagini, was the daughter of the king of the Underworld. As such, Bhima has associations with death and destruction. His nails are said to have cut down trees and slit the throats of fierce demons. He is also depicted as being so hungry that all the food in the world would not satisfy him, so he is shown with a flat stomach (indicating his half-starved state).

While Bhima is well-known from the *Mahabharata*, the Javanese wayang versions change the story, the personalities, and the names of central characters over time. The addition of Semar is one indication that the tales have been "Javanized," since Semar does not appear in an Indian context. We will find this happening in the story of Togog, the personality mentioned in the love spell, as well.

---

64 Found in Allen W. Johnson and Douglass Richard-Price Williams, *Oedipus Ubiquitous: the family complex in world literature* (Stanford: Stanford University Press, 1996), p. 236.

Togog and Batara Guru are the two brothers of Semar. Batara Guru is usually associated with Shiva. Togog, on the other hand (also known as Tejomantri), was a bad seed. He usually cooperated with unsavory types like giants and evil knights. In a way, he is the evil twin of Semar. According to the story as told in the wayang, the father of the three brothers threw an egg onto the ground. The shell became Togog, the yolk became Semar, and the white became Batara Guru. The spiritual development of a human being may be seen as analogous, going from the ridiculous (Togog) to the sublime (Guru). Semar represents the middle way. Sarcastic, crude, and sometimes obnoxious, his character is nonetheless pure. He partakes of the crassness of Togog without betraying his inner self. Batara Guru, however, represents the full realization of the human spirit and its complete identification with shakti.

Uma

Also known as Parvati and in various other manifestations (including Shakti, Durga, etc.), Uma is generally understood to be the wife of Shiva who, in Java, is also known as Batara Guru. Uma is responsible for the creation of the human race (while Semar is the creator of the Javanese race in particular). She does this through a kind of stratagem. Since Shiva chooses to ignore her advances as he maintains his meditative solitude, Uma must seduce him in order for creation to take place. Strangely, however, this approach works, but in a bizarre way. Shiva does not impregnate Uma in the usual way, through penetration; instead, he ejaculates into her hand (in some other versions of the story, into her mouth). The seed spills onto the ground and becomes the origin of humanity.

This is clearly similar to other creation myths. The Egyptian God Atum is said to have created the world in the same way, through an act of masturbation that resulted in the appearance of the gods Shu and Tefnut. He is sometimes shown standing and holding an erect phallus.[65] Since Shu is connected with the air and sky, and Tefnut with moisture and water, there is also an analogue to another Javanese myth concerning the embrace of Shiva and Uma, who produced a rainbow and a water buffalo from their union, symbols of sky and water, or more accurately of the upper world and the Underworld.[66] Indeed, it seems logical that a self-created god or a god who preceded creation would perform the act of creation solo,

65 Donald B. Redford, ed., *The Ancient Gods Speak: A Guide to Egyptian Religion* (Oxford: Oxford University Press, 2002.), p. 25.

66 Jacoba Hooykaas, "The rainbow in ancient Indonesian religion," *Bijdragen tot de Taal-, Land- en Volkenkunde* 112: 291–322.

and the best way to represent that concept to a somewhat literal-minded people would be to depict him in the act of masturbation.

However, in the creation story of Shiva and Uma, Shiva obviously already has a wife and, moreover, one who has instigated the act of creation. There should be no "requirement" for the type of sexual act that Shiva commits. Yet, it is an important element of the Javanese myth cycle.

In another version of the tale—the one that appears in a wayang performance known as the *Murwa Kala,* which is often performed as an exorcism or purification ritual—the goddess Uma rejects Shiva's sexual advances, which results in Shiva's seed spilling on the ground and creating a monster, Kala. For her perfidy in rejecting Shiva, Uma is transformed into the demon goddess Durga.[67]

Yet, it is not only monsters like Kala who are created from the spilled seed:

> For the Javanese, creation involves not a sowing, but a spilling of seed ... The falling seed becomes stone, the building blocks of the cosmos....[68]

As if to reinforce our own thesis, it happens that the Kalachakra mantra is used in one version of the Murwa Kala, thus bridging a gap between Javanese mysticism (and traditional wayang performance as purification ritual) and core Tantric sources.[69] It is also important to note that the Murwa Kala is still performed today, including at the Kraton in Yogyakarta, when there is a perceived need for purification even at the state level.[70]

The character of Uma is as malleable as the other sacred personalities in Javanese religion. She can become Durga, or Parvati, or a number of other Mother Goddesses, depending on the context. As Uma, she is the Mother Goddess as creator of life. As Durga, she can be a fierce protector or an enraged demon. As Parvati, she is the loving wife and mother of Ganesha and Skanda. She also manifests as Kali, Chandi, and so many others.

In a Javanese context, she is often depicted as the wife of Shiva and is also considered to be one form of Dewi Sri, the rice goddess of Java. Dewi Sri is one of the most important figures in Javanese culture, for she ensures the fertility of the rice

67 For thoughtful examinations of the Murwa Kala and its importance to Javanese ideas about morality and creation, see Stephen C. Headley, *From Cosmogony to Exorcism in a Javanese Genesis: the Spilt Seed* (New York: Oxford University Press, 2000).

68 Headley, *From Cosmogony to Exorcism,* p. 152.

69 Headley, *From Cosmogony to Exorcism,* pp.118, 121, 143.

70 Headley, *From Cosmogony to Exorcism,* p. 24.

crop, which is a staple in that country. (Indonesia is the third-largest producer of rice in the world after China and India.) Rice is grown in Indonesia using the "wet rice" method, in which rice is grown in horizontal fields, the paddies (as opposed to the "dry rice" method that uses the sides of mountains). These paddies are the domain of snakes, as they must be kept constantly irrigated with a steady supply of water. Thus there is a continuum of ideas between rice, water, and snake spirits. This leads to some confusion (among outside observers, at any rate) when trying to distinguish between Dewi Sri, Uma, the iprit or serpent-women, and even Nyai Lara Kidul of the Southern Ocean. That female goddesses and spirits represent—or are represented by—moisture and water is perhaps to be expected because of associations with menstruation. These various forms of the Mother Goddess may be said to reflect more their function rather than their form—thus Dewi Sri is represented when rice and associations with rice are under consideration, but Uma is introduced when concerns about motherhood and creation are the subjects under discussion.

At heart, however, the mysticism associated with sexuality affects all of these individuals, both human and divine, both male and female.

> Javanists would agree that the mystery of life is contained in reproduction. Analogies of growth and transformation are usually taken from plant life (the tree contained in the seed, etc), but the deepest mystery, and the absorbing focus of symbolism, is sexual reproduction. Sex is not only an image of union, but of fertile union.[71]

And that is the key to understanding, not only Javanese mysticism, but Tantra itself. While neo-Tantra practitioners focus on the sexual aspect—promising better and longer orgasms, etc.—the "deepest mystery" is fertility. Our investigation of Javanese esoteric practices may very well help us achieve a greater understanding of Tantra.

Kebatinan and Kejawen: Occult Techniques

There are, in general, two different types of Javanese mysticism or occult practice. The first is called *kebatinan*, after *batin,* the Arabic word for "inner" or "hidden."

71 Andrew Beatty, *Varieties of Javanese Religion: An Anthropological Account* (Cambridge: Cambridge University Press, 1999), p. 167.

The other is called *kejawen,* which comes from the word for Java itself, *jawa.* In a way, these two words can be considered to represent an inner-directed, mystical spirituality (kebatinan) and an outer-directed esoteric practice (kejawen).

Kebatinan involves the cultivation of inner serenity and peace of mind, but can also result in the acquisition of supernatural powers. It is a return to a pre-Islamic mentality, an attempt to re-connect with the Java of the Hindu-Buddhist and pre-Hindu-Buddhist culture. It may also be a reinforcement of Javanese identity, interiorized.

Kejawen, on the other hand, manifests in rituals and practices that involve the community as opposed to the individual, like the *slematan,* or ritual feast. One of these rituals, performed for the good of the community or for individuals within the community, is the *Ruwatan* rite. As this ritual becomes important in our review of the temples, it is wise to summarize it here.

Ruwatan is a purification ritual in the Javanese style. It takes the form of a wayang, a cultural performance like the Murwa Kala mentioned above, or the Sudamala with which it is often identified. There is the re-enactment of a story that has its origins in Indian literature, but which—with the passage of time and the Javanization of its elements—may not be recognizable to Indians any longer. Some of its *dramatis personae* are already familiar to us: Semar, Bhima, Uma, and Shiva.

The structure of the Ruwatan ritual is similar to most typical wayang performances. There is a *dalang,* who is the main puppeteer and who speaks the lines of the play.[72] The role of the dalang can be as important as that of a dukun, or shaman, when it comes to wayang of ritual significance, for the performance *is* ritual and there are resulting effects that are expected by the observers and participants. The wayang is usually performed behind a screen, with the images of the puppets projected onto the back of the screen by the dalang, so that only their shadows are seen by the audience. This is interesting from a psychological point of view. Although the puppets themselves are intricately designed and often gorgeously painted, the audience sees only their shadows—that is, their influence or effect and not their essential spirit, as if the radiance of their souls is hidden from view. In a sense, this is similar to the way many religions understand God; we can perceive God's effects, but not actually see the face of God itself. Even Moses was never able to look God in the face, but was burned by God's radiance (Exodus 33: 20–23).

72 As in the West, the term "puppeteer" (in this case, *dalang*) also is used to refer to a mastermind or a manipulator of events and persons.

Another interesting point about the wayang is that it mimics modern film-projection technology, but in a pre-electric-power context. It is as if the people who developed wayang more than a millennium ago had seen a modern movie theater. There is the screen, and a lamp behind the screen that throws the shadows of the puppets onto the screen, where they are seen by the audience. The puppeteers are out of sight, and there is a constant voice and musical accompaniment.

Wayang kulit, or wayang using flat puppets cut from pieces of leather, is the most common form of wayang and the one with which most foreigners are familiar. There are other forms, some using wooden dolls more closely resembling Western-style puppets, but wayang kulit gives us the traditional form of Javanese theater.

The Sudamala (a term meaning "to lessen misfortune" or "to remove evil") and the Murwa Kala are used to purify a person (or an entire community) who has had a run of bad luck. It operates as an exorcism, or as a general purification rite. It tells a story, like all wayang, but is attended with a greater degree of solemnity appropriate to the situation. In brief, the story is about the relationship between Shiva and Uma, and how Uma was cursed for rejecting Shiva's advances. In another version, she is cursed because she was told to bring medicine for Shiva and she spilled it. In yet another version, she has an affair with another god, or is forced to have sex with a man who owns the medicine (in this case, the milk from a virgin black cow, an image that is itself fraught with Tantric significance). There is also a version in which she is responsible for spilling amrita over the earth or into the Underworld. In any event, she becomes Durga, the demon goddess of the Underworld, until she is rescued by the Pandava brothers and exorcised.

The main rescuers are Sadewa, or Sahadeva, and his twin brother, Nakula. What transpires is an explanation for the existence of evil in the world that is very similar to the Sumerian story of the Descent of Inanna.[73] We have a goddess who descends to the Underworld and is rescued by two beings who pour the Water of Life over her.

In the version of this story called the Murwa Kala, Uma's transgression—whatever it may be, depending on the version presented—results in the creation of an evil creature, Kala, who delights in human flesh. This demon must be controlled, and eventually Shiva accomplishes this feat by incarnating as a dalang himself and instructing Kala to repair to a specific place in the forest, away from

73 See, for instance, Samuel Noah Kramer, *The Sumerians: Their History, Culture, and Character* (Chicago: University of Chicago Press, 1971), pp. 153–155 for a description of this myth. Perhaps coincidentally, the Javanese name for Uma when she descends to the Underworld is *Ra-Nini,* which suggests "Inanna" phonetically.

human company. Kala does this, but asks for supplies to take with him. These supplies are the basic necessities for life, and they form part of the sacrifices that devotees make during the rite.

The Murwa Kala ritual requires that the persons afflicted (called *sukerta,* which refers to their congenital or accidental status as bearers of bad luck according to a complicated formula) be bathed in water and have their hair cut symbolically (a few strands), after which the wayang performance proceeds. There are also sacrificial offerings in the form of specific types of food. The dalang must be a spiritually advanced person, or at the very least respected as a spiritual leader. Many of the spoken elements of the Murwa Kala (and Sudamala-style wayang in general) are chanted; they are in the form of mantras, including a mantra from the Kalachakra Tantra, as well as diagrams called *rajah,* which are Javanese versions of yantras (in this case, Rajah Kalachakras).

In the Sudamala version that is depicted on the walls of Candi Sukuh, Uma becomes the demon Durga, who must be saved; she is also the mother of Kala, the flesh-devouring monster.[74] In both cases, water is an essential component of the story and of the ritual itself. As we will see in the photographs of Candi Sukuh, there is ample evidence that water was an essential part of the Tantric rituals performed there. This water may represent amrita, the water of life and immortality.

One of the offerings at these cleansing rituals is porridge, both white and red. The significance of these two colors has not escaped the attention of anthropologists, who see in it another Tantric survival, with the red representing the female aspect of nature—blood, especially menstrual blood—and white representing the male aspect, semen.[75] This idea of the red and white representing female and male principles is echoed in the texts and iconography of Western alchemical literature as well, as in the emblems of European and American secret societies, as we shall see. In Tantra, the two *kapalas,* or skull cups, used in rituals to propitiate the deities are also used in the same fashion, one being filled with red liquid (wine or blood) and the other with white (milk or seminal fluid).

A central feature of the wayang is a "puppet" that is not really a puppet, in the sense of an anthropomorphic character, but instead is a representation of Mount Meru, the axis mundi and center of the Javanese universe. It is called the *gunungan* (after the Javanese word for "mountain," *gunung*) or *kakayon* (after the Javanese word for "tree," *kayu*). It is a symmetrical figure, roughly pyramidal or cone-shaped, that stands in the center of the performance area behind the screen. As can be seen by the words used to describe it, it is understood as either the *mountain*

74 Headley, *From Cosmogony to Exorcism,* p. 28.

75 Beatty, *Varieties of Javanese Religion,* p. 167.

in the center of the world or as the *tree* in the center of the world. These are both memes that are understood in many cultures as representing the axis of the world. Both the tree and the mountain reach to the heavens, but have their foundation in the earth. Like Jacob's Ladder, they enable an ascent to celestial heights (Genesis 28:11-19).The fact that "tree" and "mountain" are used interchangeably as names for the same object in wayang suggests an ancient heritage—whether Hindu or indigenous Javanese—for this concept.

In Javanese culture, the *axis mundi* is also found in the Kraton—in the palace of the sultans, particularly in Yogyakarta and Surakarta (Solo). In Yogyakarta, the Kraton is located halfway between the active volcano Merapi to the north and the Indonesian Ocean to the south, thus reinforcing topographically the metaphysical concept. The sultan himself, therefore, is the earthly representative of Batara Guru (Shiva), united with his Shakti. That identity is reinforced when we speak of the relationship between the sultan and what anthropologist G. J. Resnik calls his "second divine spouse"—the Serpent Queen of the Southern Sea, Nyai Lara Kidul, who, as much as any other deity (Uma, Parvati, Kali, Durga), represents Shakti.[76]

There have been performances of Ruwatan at the Kratons both in Yogyakarta and in Surakarta even in recent memory. In 1998, the Murwa Kala was performed at the Surakarta Kraton on behalf of the Suhunan (equivalent to Sultan) of Surakarta, Pakubuwono XII, and his family.[77]

Another public ritual that is performed with regularity in Java is the *slematan*, or ritual feast. Since this ritual does not figure prominently in the Tantric temples, we will not devote a lot of space to it here. In brief, the *slematan* is a type of communal sacrifice that is offered to ask for favors or to give thanks. The word comes from *slemat*, a Javanese variant of the Arabic *selam* or *salaam,* meaning "peace." Its timing depends on the Javanese calendar, but it is usually held in the evening after the evening prayer. According to pioneer anthropologist Clifford Geertz and Niels Mulder, it is the central rite of Javanese who consider themselves perhaps nominal

76 G. J. Resnik, "Kanjeng Ratu Kidul: The Second Divine Spouse of the Sultans of Ngayogyakarta," *Asian Folklore Studies*, Volume 56, 1997, 313-316.

77 *Sunan* and *Suhunan* are titles given to the ruler of Surakarta (Solo). Suhunan is equivalent to saying "His Highness" and Sunan is the name given to the sages and holy men who brought Islam to Indonesia thus implying a sacred lineage for the ruler of Solo, similar to *sheikh* in Arab countries. Sunan may also simply be an abbreviation of Suhunan. Authorities are somewhat divided over this.

Muslims, but nonetheless true Javanese.[78] It is sometimes used to heal or cleanse a community by bringing everyone together at a shared meal.

One should not underestimate or ignore the role that community plays in Javanese society. A Javanese community—especially in the smaller towns and villages, the *kampung* or *desa*—is a kind of extended family guided by principles of status, of relations between neighbors and families, and of what is considered *halus,* or graceful, smooth, and polite behavior. Javanese village society has managed to withstand more than 1000 years of foreign influence—both benign and malignant—by reinforcing communal identity, often at the expense of individuality. That is not to say that Javanese are hostile to foreigners or foreign ideas; far from it. But they are understandably cautious, and manage to incorporate that which they believe is useful or helpful into their own context. In this, perhaps, they are not much different from any other culture.

The *slematan,* therefore, performs a function of bringing harmony back into a community that may have become unbalanced due to conflicts or environmental or other calamities, or to give thanks for the birth of a healthy child, or to ensure good luck for a long voyage. While we may not come across too many instances of the *slematan* in our investigation, it is worthwhile to carry with us its main message of the seriousness with which the Javanese take community and social harmony.

While wayang and slematan may typify the social culture of kejawen, the techniques of kebatinan are more private and are directed toward the spiritual cultivation of the individual—although not at the expense of the community, or else it would not have become such a common aspect of Javanese culture. Its value to the community rests in the taming of the passions and mundane concerns of an individual so that he or she can exert a gentle, nurturing, spiritual effect on the community. Meditation, fasting, and prayer are essential aspects of kebatinan, known under the general rubric of *latihan* or "exercises." This practice is directed toward the heart of those who follow it—to bring it closer to God. Those who practice *latihan kebatinan* regularly are said to have a calming influence on those around them.

These methods are learned at the feet of a *guru kebatinan,* a teacher of the art. What are known as *aliran kebatinan*—mystical groups—grow up around the more famous of the gurus. Some of the more famous and better-organized of these include Subud and Sapta Darma. Subud has been exported successfully to the West and Subud chapters can be found worldwide today. Sapta Darma is more

78 Clifford Geertz, *The Religion of Java* (Chicago: University of Chicago Press, 1960, 1976), pp. 38–85. Mulder, *Mysticism in Java,* p. 85.

locally Indonesian and specifically Javanese; their logo shows Semar in the center of a triangle with their slogan in Javanese script running around it. The goal of these groups is the training of something called the *rasa*, or the inner, intuitive self. This usually requires a period of asceticism (or *tapa*), during which this refinement of the *rasa* can take place. It was during just such a period of asceticism that Batara Guru, or Shiva, was disturbed by Uma in one version of the *Sudamala*. (We recall that this story involves the spilling of seed onto the earth: in some contexts, the word *rasa,* or intuitive self, may also mean "semen."[79])

The teaching of the cultivation of *rasa* may take place in the guru's home, but groups often meet at places considered particularly sacred or potent. These *kramatan,* as they are called, can be located in cemeteries—as is Tantric custom—or they may be shrines, old temples, or a place in the wild that is believed to possess its own particular shakti. Gunung Lawu, the mountain that is home to Candi Sukuh and Candi Ceto, is also home to a number of ascetics and hermits who draw strength and spiritual sustenance from the very ground itself. Many of the people who live nearby are known to practice a form of spirituality that has much more in common with Hindu and Buddhist ritual than orthodox Islamic ritual.

One form of latihan kebatinan is the *dhikr.* Familiar to those who study Islamic mysticism, dhikr is the constant repetition of the name of God in an effort to reach a deep trance state. Virtually identical to the Indian practice of mantra and the Eastern Orthodox "Jesus Prayer," this Sufi practice was embraced in Indonesia very early on. In fact, the Sufis had a profound impact on Indonesian Islam and on Javanese spiritual ideas and practices, as they were among the first groups to arrive on the islands before the more normative sects.

The combination of Sufism with Hindu and Buddhist Tantra is a heady mixture. While anthropologists like Geertz write of syncretism, it might be better to call the result a kind of synthesis of the best of all the techniques—a synthesis by informed and capable spiritual specialists who discerned the value in each of the methods to which they were introduced. Sufism is already a form of batin, of inner spiritual practice. Tantra, both Hindu and Buddhist, is another form. They differ in some outward appearances and in ritual—and certainly in the metaphysics and philosophy behind them. But in certain essential ways, they are similar technologies aiming at the same goal. They use the functions of the body, of the nervous system in particular, as tools to achieve direct awareness of the divine. The rajah of the Javanese and the yantras of the Indians—the dhikr of the Sufis and the mantras of the Hindus and Buddhists—are cultural refinements of an engineered approach to spirituality that eschews theological hair-splitting and dogmatic com-

79 Mulder, *Mysticism in Java,* p. 81.

bat in favor of actual experience. Like Cold War scientists on either side of the Iron Curtain, these Sufis, Hindus, Buddhists, and Javanese gurus spoke the same language and understood each other far better than their leaders. They were fascinated with each other's findings, the research taking place on the other side of the great divide of culture, religion, and politics. They did not care as much for ideology as they did for the practicality of what they were studying.

This aroused the ire of conservative religious groups, of course. As an example, what is known as kebatinan and kejawen is frowned upon by conservative Muslims in Java. Religio-political parties like Muhammadiyah would like these "nominal Muslims" (called *abangan,* to differentiate them from *santri,* or orthodox Muslims) to abandon their "animistic" beliefs and practices and become normative Muslims. But occultism has always had an allure that transcends theological differences.

Eventually, the fact that this "pure science" of esoteric practice could be put to use for political and military purposes inevitably occurred to the kings and princes and sultans who incorporated Tantra into their palace ceremonies and who, in some cases, came very close to identifying themselves with the Divine.

Section II

The Tantric Temples

And what is the secret of that quiet, subtle magic exercised by the builders of Java? Nothing but a matter of technical skill, of such a control over the practical details of their craft as, for instance, made them scorn metal bindings, while using mortar only to a very limited extent? Or was it their faith, leavening design and execution, attaching the master's seal to general plan and minutest ornamental scroll?[1]

1 J. F. Scheltema, *Monumental Java* (London: Macmillan, 1912), p. 3.

The tantric temple complex at Candi Ceto in 2008. (See page 137).

Chapter 3

Borobudur

Of all the religious buildings in Indonesia, Borobudur is the most famous. A United Nations World Heritage site, it is the largest Buddhist building in the world. Built in the late eighth century CE, it was covered by a mountain of Merapi's volcanic ash some centuries later and basically forgotten; whether this was due solely to the volcanic eruption or to a shift in political power is still debatable. Located less than an hour's drive northwest of Yogyakarta, it was not discovered again until the 19th century, when a team began to dig it out of the ash and soil that had covered it for centuries.

What they found was staggering—nothing less than a massive mandala carved in stone. Borodubur is not a temple *per se*—it has no interior cella, no altar, no hall for prayer or meditation or sacrifice. It is an open-air pyramid with virtually every inch of its surface intricately carved, mostly with stories from the life of Buddha. It rises majestically to be crowned by seventy-two "perforated" stupas, each of which

Borobudur Temple

Ground plan of Borobudur, from a 19th-century text.

once held a statue of a sitting Buddha. The last, commanding stupa at the very top was kept empty, signifying the Void.

Above is shown the ground plan of Borobudur. The concentric circles in the center show the locations of seventy-two stupas, each containing a Buddha statue. Yet for all of this, there is still some controversy over whether or not Borobudur was always a Buddhist edifice. Some scholars suggest that it began life as a Hindu monument, but gradually became a Buddhist one. Others go so far as to suggest the opposite. It is possible that the confusion comes from the fact that the type of religion that was practiced in Java at that time was a fusion or synthesis of Shiva Tantra and Buddhist Tantra, for the monument has been accepted by most scholars to be Tantric. Since we have such a difficult time identifying what is and is not Tantric, it is no wonder that this confusion has extended to architecture as well. Yet, the Dalai Lama came to Java in 1983 to consecrate Borobudur as a shrine of

Vajrayana Buddhism, which is, as we have discussed, Tantric. That indicates that Borobudur is not only the largest Buddhist monument in the world, but the largest Tantric Buddhist monument as well.

The dimensions of Borobudur are one indication of its grandeur. Its base measures 123 meters x 123 meters, or 403 feet x 403 feet. The total height from the base to the top of the stupa is 35 meters, or about 115 feet. It consists of six square platforms rising from the first platform at the base and ascending in successively smaller platforms, until it is topped by three circular levels with a large central stupa at the summit. There are 2672 reliefs comprised of 1460 narrative panels and 1212 decorative panels, for a total of 2500 square meters (or nearly 27,000 square feet) of decorated surface area. And that doesn't include the thirty-two lion guardians (eight on each side) and 100 rainwater spouts carved in the image of *makaras*—strange sea creatures associated with water, possibly crocodiles, but also similar to a type of fresh-water dolphin known to inhabit the Ganges River in India. The Hindi word *makar* refers to this creature as the vehicle of both the goddess Ganga (who incarnated as the Ganges River) and the god Varuna, who is a god of the ocean as well as of the Milky Way. Moreover, the term also refers to the astrological sign of Capricorn which, in the West, is a half-goat, half-fish creature, and in India is a fish creature with four legs and a long snout with sharp teeth.

On the following page is one example of a makara at Borobudur.

The first level of Borobudur is not visible, but remains buried. It is called the "hidden foot" and contains 160 panels depicting the world of human desires and the effects that they cause. No one is certain why the level is hidden. One theory is that this was due to a construction concern. After the base was carved and the succeeding layers placed on top of it, the base layer may have shifted or had its integrity somehow compromised, leading the engineers to pile earth around it in an effort to shore up the rest of the structure. Another theory is that the structure began as a Hindu shrine and was later transformed into a Buddhist one, so that the message of the first layer was superseded by the message of the top layers.

There is also some evidence that Borobudur was originally sited in the midst of an ancient lake and was therefore surrounded by water early in its existence. Even the name Borobudur is an enigma, for no one seems to know what it means. In fact, there are so many mysteries surrounding this incredible feat of art and construction that one author writes of the need to "decode" it.[2]

Years of analysis of the six levels of reliefs has yielded the conviction that some of the panels represent stories from the life of the Buddha before his incarnation as

2 John Miksic, Marcello Tranchini, Anita Tranchini, *Borobudur: Golden Tales of the Buddhas* (Jakarta: Periplus Editions Ltd., 1991, 2004), p. 45.

A makara at Borobudur.

Siddhartha, stories that come from Buddhist texts known as the *Jatakas*. In addition, texts from various other Buddhist scriptures are represented as well, sometimes mixed together in no discernible order. These texts include the *Gandavyuha* and the *Avadanas*.

The *Gandavyuha* is a kind of Buddhist "Pilgrim's Progress." The hero, Prince Sudhana, is sent on a quest to find wisdom by Manjusri, a bodhisattva who is very important to Tibetan Buddhism (particularly the Gelugpa or "Yellow Hat" sect represented by the Dalai Lama) and to esoteric forms of Buddhism in general. After many trials and encounters, including long periods in meditation along the way, Sudhana encounters Maitreya (the so-called "Buddha of the Future" who has not yet incarnated), then returns to Manjusri and visits other bodhisattvas, eventually achieving his goal of complete spiritual illumination.

The *Avadanas* are accounts of famous Buddhist stories and saints, including, in this case, the tale of Princess Manohara, who was saved by Prince Sudhanakumara. Manohara was a *kinnari*—a creature that is half-human (in this case female) and half-bird. These creatures may be seen in several reliefs at Borobudur and Prambanan, and at other temples, and their appearance is rather startling among all of

A kinnara-kinnari pair from Prambanan temple standing at either side of a Tree of Life, the Kalpataru.

the purely anthropomorphic deities ones come across. They are usually depicted in pairs—kinnara (male) and kinnari (female)—and they are said to mate for life.

The Tree of Life, or Kalpataru, was said to have appeared at the famous Churning of the Milk Ocean, and is regarded as a wish-fulfilling tree. Not much else is known about its origins, nor is it known if it refers to a real tree, although there has been some attempt to identify it with the banyan tree, of which there are many in Southeast Asia.

Aside from the more than 2000 reliefs at Borobudur, there are the three major levels that contain them. The first level—the "hidden foot"—is said to refer to the Sphere of Desires, the *Kamadhatu* (*Kama* means "desires"; *dhatu* means "world" or "realm"). This is the realm of animal instincts and the other more sophisticated desires that originate there: love of money, power, etc.

The five square levels are said to represent the Sphere of Forms, the *Rupadhatu*. Those who manage to conquer their desires reach this sphere, but they are still in darkness, for this is the sphere of names, forms, and illusions.

An example of the dhyana *mudra, the gesture of meditation.*

The three circular levels represent *Arupadhatu,* the Sphere of Formlessness, which is the goal of the devotee. The last level is that of the great stupa at the very top of Borobudur. This is the stupa that contains ... nothing. It represents absolute attainment in the Buddhist sense of *advaita*, non-dualism.

Thus the whole edifice is said to represent Mount Meru, the cosmic center of the universe, the *axis mundi*. It is to Java what the pyramids are to Egypt, and what the ziggurats were to Babylon and Sumer. In fact, Borobudur is almost perfectly aligned with the points of the compass, with only a slight deviation. The famous ziggurat at Ur is also aligned with the compass, except that it is the corners that are aligned, whereas it is the sides of Borobudur that face the four directions. Another difference is that Borobudur is so heavily decorated on its exterior walls that we are left with an incredible text in stone. Imagine if each immense block of the Great Pyramid at Gizeh bore an intricate carving of gods, goddesses, and stories from the Egyptian scriptures such that one could follow a narrative from the lowest level to the very top.

A better image of the dhyana *mudra.*

To reinforce the idea of Borobudur as Mount Meru and as a vast mandala in stone, the Buddha statues themselves reveal more mystery, more intricacies. Each of the Buddhas is carved with a specific gesture, or mudra. The mudra shown above and on the previous page is called the *dhyana* mudra, the gesture of meditation. This is associated with Amitabha Buddha, and the cardinal direction of the west.

The photo on the following page depicts the *bhumisparsa* mudra, associated with the Buddha Aksobhya of the eastern quadrant. The word *bhumi* means earth, and it refers to the moment when Buddha attained enlightenment and called the earth as a witness. It also refers to the subjugation of the demons under their king, Mara, when Mara attempted to seduce the Buddha away from his meditations with a string of beautiful women. The photo shows the length of the eastern wall of Borobudur, with an array of Buddha statues in various states of disrepair, but all showing the same *bhumisparsa* mudra. There are twenty Buddha statues visible in this photograph and, although many of them show serious damage, it is still possible to get an idea of the grandeur of this edifice.

The eastern wall of Borobudur. The twenty Buddhas display the bhumisparsa *mudra associated with the Buddha Aksobhya of the eastern quadrant.*

The next image shows the *vara* mudra, the gesture of charity, which is associated with the Tantric deity Ratnasambhava and the south. Note in the photograph that there are creatures at either side of the Buddha—what appear to be little imps holding up the wall. These are called *ganas.* They are servitors of the Hindu god Shiva that predate the arrival of Buddhism by perhaps 1000 years. In fact, the name of the elephant-headed god Ganesha comes from the Sanskrit root *gana,* which means a group or a tribe, or some type of assembly. In Hinduism, ganas reside mainly in charnel grounds and cemeteries, which again reinforces some opinions that Borobudur reflects a Tantric viewpoint rather than a purely Mahayana perspective.

In the Borobudur reliefs, it is common to find these ganas sitting atop pillars. These pillars are "reversible," in that their structure is the same whether we look at them from the top down, or the bottom up. Their perfect symmetry may be an

The vara *mudra is associated with the Tantric deity Ratnasambhava and the south. The creatures at either side of the Buddha are called* ganas.

allusion to the *vajra,* or thunderbolt device used by Tantrikas as a symbol of Shiva's power. It would be consistent with the association of the ganas as Shiva's assistants, who hold up the cosmos on the god's behalf (like Atlas in Greek mythology).

Due to the deterioration of most of the Buddha statues—missing arms and sometimes heads—we do not have a good example of the other two mudras to show *in situ.* However, we do have examples of mudras from other reliefs at Borobudur, like that on the following page, which shows the *abhaya* mudra, the gesture that protects from fear. It is associated with the north and with Buddha Amogasiddhi, an important Vajrayana deity whose consort is Tara.

The mudra that represents the center or the zenith is the *dharma chakra* mudra, which represents turning the Wheel of the Dharma, or Law. Associated with the

The abhaya *mudra that protects from fear is associated with the north and with Buddha Amogasiddhi, a Vajrayana deity whose consort is Tara.*

Buddha Vairochana, it consists of holding both hands at chest level with the fingers of the right and left hands touching to suggest the turning of the Wheel. Unfortunately, there are no good representations of a Buddha statue at Borobudur showing this mudra, since many of them have lost arms or hands, and those that haven't are only visible from about the waist up. We do, however, have the example shown on the next page from the dim interior of Chandi Mendut—a temple associated with the Borobudur complex—that shows Buddha in an unusual position: sitting upright, on a throne, as if to emphasize kingship.

These Buddha statues, with their associated mudras, are quite explicitly Tantric in that they represent the five *Dhyani* Buddhas or the Five Wisdom *Tathagatas.*

The dharma chakra *mudra represents the turning of the Wheel of the Dharma, or Law, and is associated with the Buddha Vairochana.*

They are always associated with the five directions (the four cardinal points plus the center) and they have their origin in Vajrayana (Tibetan Tantric) Buddhism. This is a strong argument in favor of the identification of Borobudur as a Tantric monument, but there are still scholars who debate this. A system of correspondences that equates a particular Buddha with a specific mudra, cardinal direction, and—in the classic Vajrayana system—other attributes like colors, psychological states, or philosophical concepts indicates an esoteric, magical structure that is somewhat at odds with pure Mahayana Buddhist thought and practice and seems more likely to represent some form of Tantra.

The so-called "perforated" stupas are themselves marvels of religious architecture. Arranged along the three circular platforms of the Arupadhatu (the Formless

World) with a total of thirty-two on the first level, twenty-four on the second, and sixteen on the top level (below the main stupa), they number seventy-two in all. It is important to note that these numbers are all divisible by eight, which is a sacred number in Buddhism that refers to the Eight-fold Noble Path, an eight-step way to end suffering (Right Mindfulness, Right Concentration, Right Effort, Right Livelihood, Right Action, Right Speech, Right Intentions, Right View). Seventy-two also has resonance with Jewish mysticism and the *Shem-ha-Mephorash*, the Divine Name of seventy-two letters.

Each perforated stupa once contained a sitting Buddha showing the same gesture: the dharma chakra mudra. There were more than 500 Buddhas of various types at Borobudur and, of these, more than 340 are either missing or damaged, leaving at most 160 intact. Some of the damage was doubtless due to environmental factors, for Borobudur was buried under volcanic ash and soil for centuries. In other cases, it is entirely possible that the heads of the statues were taken and sold to museums and private collectors in the lucrative underground antiquities market.

Stupas were generally built as shrines for relics of the dead, particularly of saints. Thus, the seventy-two perforated stupas on the three levels of the Arupadhatu may signify seventy-two Buddhist saints, although as mentioned, each of them contained a Buddha performing the dharma chakra mudra. It is possible that the main stupa in the very center of Borobudur once housed a relic of Gautama Buddha himself, but this has not been proven nor is there any textual evidence to support the idea.

What was the purpose or function behind the construction of Borobudur?

Several theories have been proposed, but strongest among them is that Borobudur may have started as a temple or as a shrine for a particularly sacred relic, but that, as time went on, the monument took on a purpose of its own. The structure is part of an axis comprised of three temples or *chandi*: Borobudur, Mendut, and Pawon. These three buildings lie in a straight line, with Mendut and Pawon leading the way to Borobudur, which lies at the end of a ceremonial road. That Borobudur may have served as an initiatory device is a definite possibility. Visitors are told that one would walk up each level and around it entirely, bearing left and keeping the reliefs always on their right, taking note of the reliefs and the stories concerning the Buddha and the quest for spiritual illumination before ascending to the next level. The entire process eventually leads to the Formless Realm where there are no reliefs, only the stupas with the sitting Buddhas. Finally, at the very end of the path, lies the main—empty—stupa as a symbol of ultimate enlightenment, of *samadhi*.

ABOVE: *A group of "perforated" stupas with the main stupa rising in the background.*

BELOW: *Another group of stupas at Borobudur.*

In Javanese spirituality, the center, or zenith, of the palace or kraton is also the center of the kingdom and the axis mundi. It is a place occupied by both the sultan or king and his consort, his shakti. In Babylonian spirituality, the top of the ziggurat served the same purpose. Once a year, the king ascended to the top of the pyramid, where an empty room—and the presence of the goddess—awaited him. Some argue that the Holy of Holies in the Temple of Solomon at Jerusalem served the same purpose and, indeed, this has been claimed in the Gnostic texts.[3] If, as some insist, Borobudur is a Tantric edifice, is it possible that some sort of *hieros gamos* or sacred wedding once took place in the main, central stupa? Since this type of mystical union at the palace level did take place in Java—and continues to take place to this day—there is some degree of internal consistency to the idea.

What argues against the idea of Borobudur as a typical Tantric temple is the existence of the reliefs, which represent scenes from Buddhist scriptures, as we have seen. Yet, there is something a little odd about this fact, for there are no Buddhist structures anywhere in India that are designed the same way. There is no temple or shrine in which more than 1000 scenes are depicted in so much detail. In this respect, Borobudur is an instruction manual, and a scripture in stone. But what is being taught?

As mentioned above, the reliefs on the five visible rectangular levels depict scenes from the Jataka, Avadana, and Gandavyuha Sutras. The Jataka Sutra contains stories relating to the birth of Buddha; these are probably included due to their popularity as a kind of "humanizing" of the Buddha. The Avadana Sutra deals with various stories relating to Buddhist personalities ("saints") and their quest for enlightenment. The Gandavyuha Sutra tells us of the quest of Sudhana and is especially important to Vajrayana Buddhism; it is the last chapter of the much longer Avatamsaka Sutra and is usually studied as a separate document in its own right.

The specific themes of the Avadana Sutra that are represented at Borobudur are quite similar to the scenes of the Gandavyuha Sutra. In the former, we have Prince Sudhanakumara and his rescue of Princess Manohara, the kinnari. In the latter, we have Prince Sudhana and his quest for enlightenment. These personalities—Sudhana and Sudhanakumara—are actually one and the same. The suffix *kumara* means "prince" or "young, unmarried male." Thus, what we may have in the scenes of the Avadana and Gandavyuha Sutras depicted at Borobudur are the exploits of Sudhana *before* he begins his quest for enlightenment (Avadana) and *during* his quest (Gandavyuha).

3 See, for instance, the Gospel of Philip (II, 3) from the Nag Hammadi scrolls.

Another Borobudur stupa.

Sudhana's marriage to a kinnari may indicate a deeper Tantric message. The idea of a prince whose princess disappears and must be found is a familiar one in Indian literature. The most famous example, of course, is the *Ramayana,* in which Sita, Lord Rama's beautiful bride, is seized by the demon Ravana and must be rescued. In the Avadana story at Borobudur, Princess Manohara—the half-woman, half-bird creature—is forced to flee Sudhana's kingdom while the latter is away at war. She returns to her native land, and Sudhana is forced to find her there and win her back after an archery contest.

Thus, in the Avadana tale, Sudhana goes on a quest to find and bring back his bride. The bride's kingdom is none other than Kailash, the famous sacred mountain of Tibetan Buddhism and Tantric Hinduism. To the Hindus, Mount Kailash is the abode of Shiva and Parvati, the archetypal Tantric couple.

In the Gandavyuha tale, Sudhana is again on a sacred mission, only this time, it is for his own personal illumination. During the course of this quest, he visits a total of fifty-two sages and mystics, gathering important information from each one, until he finally realizes that the secret to enlightenment was within him all along.

We may suggest that these two stories have a lot in common, and that they were selected deliberately because they are related on a deeper level than is obvious at first glance. The Avadana story of Sudhana and Manohara can be interpreted as a dualist approach to spiritual integration, while the Gandavyuha tale is a non-dualist version. In the first, we have a man and wife who are separated and then re-united. The wife is a spiritual creature, a hybrid being who lives in an enchanted kingdom and thus may be construed as a source of spiritual power, of shakti. The union of the earth and the heavens, the mundane and the divine, is represented by Sudhana and Manohara.

In the second tale, Sudhana goes on his spiritual quest alone. It is strictly a boy's club at this point: fifty-two male sages, including two of the most famous in Buddhist (and especially Tantric Buddhist) lore: Manjusri and Maitreya.

Sudhana, therefore, becomes the stand-in for humanity in general, a means of identifying with both the austere spiritual quest of the Buddha and with the Tantric practice concerned with balancing male and female aspects of consciousness. There are many Jatakas, many Avadanas, and of course many sutras generally. The selection process that resulted in the emphasis on Sudhana and his various quests in the reliefs at Borobudur thus appears deliberate and meaningful.

In a paper written by the independent Java expert J. L. Moens, an attempt is made to underscore Borobudur's importance as both an initiatory center and a mechanism for consecrating the dynasty of the rulers that had created it: the

Sailendras.[4] According to Moens, many scholars ignore the most obvious fact about the shrine—the four stairways that descend from the main stupa down the four sides of the edifice. To Moens, this indicates that Borobudur was a device for incarnating the divine light, a *devavatara* or "descent from the sky" stupa that combined with the pedagogical nature of the entire building (its *dharma chakra pravartana,* or the "turning of the Wheel of the Law") to produce a kind of two-way traffic (like Jacob's Ladder). As the Buddha incarnates and spreads the light of his illumination downward, so the rest of humanity—by following the instructions and the inspiration revealed in the three levels of the temple—can ascend the staircases and attain unity. This had special implications for the rulers who built Borobudur, for they considered themselves *chakravartins*: those who turn the Wheel. To quote Moens:

> For the devavatara type of stupa implies the noble birth of the king ... whereas the dharmachakra-pravartana type emphasizes the fact that the king based his chakravartinship on his Buddha status ... [H]is dynasty ...was supernaturally endowed for the exercise of its worldly power. Consequently the massive edifice of Barabudur [sic] not only was the spiritual center of the realm, but also the political center of the kingdom.[5]

Mark Long, a translator of Moens who has written extensively on Borobudur, has discovered evidence to prove that Borobudur was a supreme example of sacred architecture, what is known as *Vaastu*: the Vedic equivalent of the Chinese system of *Feng Shui*.[6] Further, the Tantric element found at Borobudur—and at the accompanying chandi of Mendut and Pawon—is inescapable. The arrangement of their specific Buddhas and their mudras is completely consistent with Vajrayana Buddhism and, in particular, the cult of Vairochana, who symbolizes Emptiness, or *shunyata,* and at the same time is shown using the dharma chakra mudra.

This identification of political rulers with spiritual enlightenment is most pronounced, of course, in Tibetan history. The Dalai Lama is at once the head of the

4 J. L. Moens, "Barabadur, Mendut en Pawon en hun onderlinge samenhang," *Tijdschrift voor Indische Taal-, Land-, en Volkenkunde uitgegeven door het Bataviasch Genootschap van Kunsten en Wetenschappen,* LXXXVI, 1951. In English translation as "Borobudur, Mendut, and Pawon and their mutual relationship," translated by Mark Long, 2007 at *www.borobudur.tv* accessed 18 November 2010.

5 Mark Long, "Borobudur, Mendut, and Pawon," p. 63.

6 Mark Long and Cesar Voute, *Borobudur: Pyramid of the Cosmic Buddha* (New Delhi: DK Print World, 2008).

Tibetan government-in-exile and its most famous religious leader. Tibet was a theocracy until the Chinese invasions, and the Sailendras of Java were no different. Thus it should come as no surprise that the Dalai Lama himself came to consecrate Borobudur as a Vajrayana shrine.

In ancient times, there was no "separation of church and state." The secular rulers of Java were also its spiritual leaders, especially in the esoteric sense that they embodied the shakti of the land, of the kingdom. The correct performance of rituals not only ensured the success and prosperity of their kingdoms, it also helped to reinforce the idea in the minds of the people that the kings had a "divine right" to rule. While we may regard this cynically, it is entirely possible that this was a mutually dependent relationship. The rituals performed at Borobudur may very well have created the atmosphere necessary for the peaceful pursuit of secular goals. When things did not go their way, the failure of the kings could be perceived as a sign from the gods of divine displeasure, thus giving the people the moral right to choose other leaders.

This mythologem of sex, power, spirituality, and politics is one that we will encounter again and again, making Java an excellent example of what the medieval European monk and magician Giordano Bruno called "the link."[7]

7 Giordano Bruno, *De vinculis in genere,* (A general account of bonding), in Richard J. Blackwell and Robert de Lucca, *Giordano Bruno: Cause, Principle and Unity, and Essays on Magic* (Cambridge: Cambridge University Press, 1998), pp. 143–176.

Chapter 4

Prambanan and Sewu

While Borobudur's identity and purpose may be controversial, we have no such problems with Prambanan. Located to the east of Yogyakarta, Prambanan is a clear example of Hindu architecture and iconography. Dedicated to the *Trimurti* (Trinity) of the three most important gods of Indian religion—Brahma, Shiva, and Vishnu—Prambanan contains all the elements we expect to find in any Hindu temple complex. There are lingga and yoni, statues of the gods, and accommodations for the Homa, or fire ritual. Scenes from the *Ramayana* abound, as well as depictions of sages and gurus.

Prambanan (also a UNESCO World Heritage site) was built about the same time as Borobudur. While the latter is considered Buddhist in nature, Prambanan

Prambanan Temple.

Some of the 224 ancillary temples at Prambanan.

is Hindu. The reasons for building two such different temples at the same time, at opposite sides of what would become Yogyakarta, are still open to conjecture. While both sites may be considered Tantric, their approach is decidedly different.

There are three main temples at Prambanan, with that of Shiva, located in the center of the complex, being the largest. Those for Brahma and Vishnu are shorter and are located at either side of Shiva. In addition, there are smaller temples for Nandi, the mount of Shiva (usually portrayed as a white ox or bull) and for Hamsa, the Swan of Brahma, and a temple for Garuda, the mount of Vishnu. These six temples—plus two small "flanking temples" (*candi apit*) whose function is unknown at this time—are in the center of what is actually a huge complex comprising more than 200 separate temples and shrines. Most of these are in terrible states of disrepair and amount to little more than piles of stones whose original purposes can only be imagined. This was the state of the complex when it was "discovered" by men working for Sir Thomas Raffles in the 19th century. While some restoration work was begun and the center complex restored to its former glory, a series of earthquakes and volcanic eruptions has since threatened the site

The central Shiva temple at Prambanan.

again. When the author first visited Prambanan in 2007, access was drastically limited due to the 2006 earthquake that had devastated much of the region to the east of Yogyakarta. It was in better condition in 2010, but the complex close to Prambanan, Candi Sewu, was still in the process of being rebuilt after the tremors knocked down huge stones from the many temple buildings there.

The photograph on page 102 shows some of the 224 ancillary temples at Prambanan that are still in a state of ruin. The number and arrangement of these temples—called *Perwaras,* or "bridesmaids"—has led some observers to suggest that there was an astronomical purpose behind the design.[8] There are fifty-six ancillary temples per quadrant—which is interesting from a Western esoteric perspective, for it is the number of cards in the so-called Minor Arcana of the traditional tarot deck. The Minor Arcana have astronomical associations, according to complex calculations put forward by the founders of the British esoteric group The Golden Dawn.[9] In the case of Prambanan, these perwaras are believed to be connected to the position of the sun at its highest point, or zenith, 112 days after or before (112 x 2 = 224) the June solstice at the time Prambanan was being built, around the ninth century CE.

The central Shiva temple, on page 103, is the tallest of the complex, measuring 47 meters (154 feet) in height. The main, eastern chamber of the temple houses a large statue of the god, and chambers on either side house Durga (north chamber) and Ganesha (west chamber), with a statue of Shiva Mahaguru (Great Teacher) in the southern chamber. Durga, of course, is one manifestation of Shiva's shakti, his consort, called variously Uma, Parvati, and even Kali. In this instance, Durga is depicted as the Goddess of Death; her ornaments are mostly weapons. Ganesha, the elephant-headed god, is one of their two sons. Thus, we have the equivalent of a "divine family" at this temple.

While Durga is represented here at Prambanan, in later temples, as we shall see, Shiva is accompanied, not by Durga, but by Uma or Parvati, representing gentler manifestations of his shakti. While Durga is associated with warfare and death, Uma is associated with the creation of the world. Durga, however, is a very familiar goddess to the Tantrikas, for she is often worshipped in charnel grounds and cemeteries.

The statue of Shiva sits atop a lingga-yoni pedestal, as do the other primary statues in the other temples. What cannot be seen, however, is the existence of a deep well beneath the statue that extends below ground. At the bottom of this

8 See the series of articles on Prambanan found at *www.borobudur.tv* accessed on 17 August 2010.

9 See Israel Regardie, *The Golden Dawn* (St. Paul: Llewellyn Publications, 1971, 1986), pp. 540–621 for a description of this system and its relationship to the tarot, astronomy, astrology, etc.

well were found offerings that were made at the time the construction began. This was—and in some cases still is—a common practice in the building of temples and other public buildings in Asia. The type of offerings change depending on the purpose of the building and other factors. It is interesting that this idea of putting a lingga-yoni over a well containing offerings is mirrored in the Western practice—in Roman Catholic and Eastern Orthodox churches—of situating the main altar over a relic of one of the saints. The following photos of the Brahma and Vishnu statues—the Shiva statue was off-limits at the time I was photographing Prambanan due to post-earthquake restoration work—gives an idea of how these statues and pedestals are designed.

Brahma at left and Vishnu at right stand upon lingga-yoni pedestals.

The entrance to the Brahma temple with makaras in either side of the doorway.

Lingga-yoni pedestal at the Hindu temple of Sri Mariamman in Singapore.

As one can see, the Brahma statue is standing on a pedestal placed directly atop a yoni, thus implying that Brahma is the lingga of this yoni. Water or other liquid offerings were made and the excess flowed down the narrow channel on the left of the statue (to the right in the photograph), where it could be collected as "holy water." Vishnu is shown in a position identical to that of the Brahma statue, but viewed from the side.

The photo on the opposite page shows the entrance to the Brahma temple. Note the guardians and the makaras to either side of the entrance, and the one gana on the left.

The picture above, taken at the Sri Mariamman temple in Singapore, a shrine to a South Indian mother goddess, shows how the lingga-yoni pedestal normally appears in a Hindu temple. Here we can see the lingga in its usual form as an erect penis, with flower offerings. The yoni has a rather large channel—seen to the left—for the collection of oil or other liquid that is poured over the lingga. What is unusual about this configuration is the placement of a rectangular slab next to the lingga, whose purpose is a mystery to me.

Thus, at Prambanan, in place of a simple lingga, the entire statue of a god is placed atop the yoni, which clarifies or identifies the type of power that is being invoked. The function of the yoni—as a symbol of the feminine—is to manifest the transcendent power of the universe. Until shakti is involved, power remains in its potential state—like Shiva meditating alone in the forest. It requires the activity of shakti to transform the potential energy into kinetic energy—that is, to create worlds.

Lingga are almost always seen as symbols of Shiva, so much so that they are usually referred to as "Shiva lingga." For Brahma and Vishnu to take the place of lingga implies a refinement of the Shiva message, or the Shiva power. But at Prambanan, it is still Shiva who takes center stage.

The Ramayana

Around the Shiva temple, there are numerous reliefs showing scenes from the *Ramayana*: the famous Indian epic of the relationship between Rama and Sita. Rama is usually considered to be an incarnation of Vishnu, not Shiva. However, Shiva plays an important role in the story, for it is Shiva's bow that Rama uses to win Sita as his bride. Further, it is said that the *Ramayana* itself was told by Shiva to his wife, Uma, to keep her entertained. Other sects believe that the Monkey King Hanuman is an incarnation—or "avatar"—of Shiva, and Hanuman's role in the *Ramayana* is a critical one. According to a verse in the Shiva Purana (3:20:3–7), Hanuman was born from the seed of Shiva that had been spilled when Shiva lusted after Mohini (a female incarnation or avatar of Vishnu). Thus, there is a strong tradition linking both Hanuman and Shiva to the *Ramayana*. The question, of course, is one of emphasis and, in Java, the strongest form of "Hinduism" was the Shiva sect that was also the most Tantric.

The following relief from the Shiva temple at Prambanan shows a decisive scene from the *Ramayana* as Rama attacks the demon king Ravana with his bow.

In the very center of the photograph, one can see the face of Hanuman the Monkey King and, indeed, Ravana—at the far right—is being attacked by a horde of monkeys. At the far left of the picture is a bearded image holding a trident. This is the sage Agastya, one of the legendary Seven Sages of Vedic India who once swallowed the cosmic ocean in order to trap some asuras (demons) who were hiding in its depths. He is related to the cosmic ocean, and his name means literally "mountain thrower," so there seems to be a connection between Agastya and both the ocean and the mountain, which are symbols of the Samudra Manthan. Agastya is

A relief at the Shiva temple at Prambanan with a scene from the Ramayana.

credited with having created many of the mantras of the *Rig Veda*, and he is also the sage visited by Rama and Sita during their fourteen-year sojourn in the forest.

The trident that Agastya is holding is a symbol of Shiva, representing three ways in which the cosmos is manifested (as creation, destruction, and preservation). It is not unusual to see three horizontal lines marked on a Shiva lingga, or the same three horizontal lines painted on the foreheads of Shiva devotees.

Other reliefs from Prambanan afford us an opportunity to see various mudras, incarnations of gods, and scenes of an idealized domesticity. The story of Rama and Sita is a love story, and begins as such. As those who are familiar with the *Ramayana* know, however, the story ends in tragedy. It may be the original Romeo and Juliet tale, except that in the *Ramayana,* it is only Juliet who dies!

Rama, desiring to marry Sita, approaches her father, a king. The king has determined that whoever is able to bend Shiva's bow will be Sita's husband. Rama attempts to string the bow and, in doing so, manages to break it. Such power indicates to the king that Rama is the natural choice and he permits the marriage to take place.

Rama and Sita repair to his palace, where his father is dying. Rama is to be king, but the crown was promised earlier to his brother. In order to avoid political difficulties Rama and Sita—and their loyal friend, Lakshamana—go in exile to a forest far from the castle walls. There, they have many adventures, but the one critical to our story is the scene in which Sita sees a beautiful golden deer and asks Rama to shoot it with his bow and bring it back to her. Rama goes off into the forest chasing the deer, but it was a ruse. Sita is captured and taken to the distant land of Lanka, where she is held hostage by the evil Demon King, Ravana, who wants Sita for his own wife. A stand-off ensues, during which Rama enlists the aid of his friends—prominent among them Hanuman—to rescue his wife.

After Sita is rescued from the clutches of the demon Ravana—who lives on an island that most scholars agree is today's Sri Lanka—Rama is worried that she has succumbed to the advances of Ravana, either through desire or force. Sita, of course, is blameless; but, in order to prove her faithfulness to her husband, she jumps into a burning pyre to immolate herself. As it happens, the flames do not burn her and she walks out of the fire unscathed. In fact, in some versions, she walks on live coals as she leaves the fire. Fire-walking is still an Indian ritual indicating spiritual purity.

In some recitations of this tale, we are left with this somewhat upbeat ending. The performance of the Ramayana ballet that takes place at Prambanan throughout the year uses it. "And they lived happily ever after," we can almost hear them say. This is because the Javanese version of the tale, the *Kakawin Ramayana,* has a vastly different second act that includes the appearance of the indigenous Javanese deity, Semar, and all sorts of other variations. This is the version found in the shadow puppet theater, the wayang kulit, all over Java. The original ending, however, is somewhat more troubling.

The original tale tells how Rama and Sita return to their kingdom to live a peaceful life, but rumors soon begin to spread. They say that Rama is a fool to take back a woman who lived with another man. Gossip turns ugly, and Rama feels forced to send Sita away to live alone in the forest. What he does not know is that Sita is pregnant with his twin sons.

Sita lives long enough to see her sons grow up and become acquainted with their father, but her heart is broken and the gods hear her weeping. The earth opens, and Sita is carried away into another world, where she will be happy and at peace at last.

It is possible to see this story as a kind of condemnation of Rama, even though this is not countenanced in India, where Rama is worshipped as a god and as an example of the Perfect Man. After all, he waged a long and terrible war in order to get Sita back from the demon king. He lost friends in battle, and relied heavily on Hanuman when things looked impossibly bleak. He finally overcomes all obstacles and rescues his wife—only to question her chastity! She proves herself faithful, literally undergoing a baptism by fire, only later to succumb to evil gossip and rumors of impropriety, and to be banished from the kingdom to bear and raise her children alone—the archetypal single mother.

Perhaps what is troubling to a Western reader of the *Ramayana*, taking the story as literally as possible, is the apparent lack of cause and effect when it comes to blaming Sita for the bitter gossip of the chambermaids who condemn her. In a world where it is common to believe that one is innocent until proven guilty, this treatment of Sita seems outrageous and cruel. It is possible that there is another level of interpretation to the story, however, one in which Sita somehow shares the blame for her misfortune. This may be the aspect of the tale that resonates with Indian audiences, to such an extent that they believe the mere recitation of parts of the *Ramayana* is enough to cure them of disease or to banish evil spirits. There is, in other words, something else going on here. It may be simply that Rama and Sita both understand that the peace of the kingdom is more important than their own wedded bliss—something like the end of the film *Casablanca,* where Rick banishes Ilsa to the United States while he stays behind to fight the Nazis.

Sita's origins are a mystery. The name Sita is mentioned briefly in the *Rig Veda* as an earth mother figure, but does not appear again until the *Ramayana* was composed, about the fourth century BCE. In that epic, she is discovered as an infant lying in a plowed field; this may be an allusion to the earlier Sita as earth mother. In the *Ramayana,* she is considered to be the daughter of Bhumi Devi, the Goddess of the Earth, to whom she returns at the end of the tale. Therefore, it is entirely possible that this story is a much later version of an earlier agricultural myth regarding an Earth Mother, fertility, plowing, planting, and reaping. This would have made Sita attractive to the Javanese, who already had an agricultural goddess in their pantheon—the Goddess of the Rice Field, Sri Dewi.

That is not the only metaphor involved, however. As we have seen in the previous chapter on the reliefs at Borobudur, one of the Avadanas concerns Prince Sudhana, who loses his wife, the kinnari, and must win an archery contest to get her back from her father. Rama wins Sita from her father by bending (and ultimately breaking) the bow of Shiva. In the Arthurian legend of the West, the young Arthur becomes recognized as king when he pulls the sword Excalibur from a stone—a feat of superhuman strength or perhaps paranormal ability. The same achievement is Rama's, for the Bow of Shiva was so strong it was impossible for any mortal man to bend. Rama, who simply wishes to string the bow, breaks it as if it were made of bamboo, thus revealing his superhuman status. The relationship between archery and the winning of a bride from her father is perhaps a compelling one for future research and investigation, but the association of weapons with divine as well as temporal power is something we will encounter again in a more blatant form in the chapter on the temples of Gunung Lawu, where, as in the Arthurian legends of England, we find miraculous swords, sacred sexuality, and an *elixir vitae* (an Indian "holy grail") literally written in stone.

The Cosmic Ocean

Several scholars have noted that the *Kakawin Ramayana* describes Prambanan, and specifically the Shiva temple, as representing Mount Meru, especially in the context of the story of the Churning of the Cosmic Ocean, one of the set-pieces of both the *Mahabharata* and the Vishnu Purana, as well as of the *Ramayana.* In Sanskrit rendering, it is known as *Samudra Manthan,* with *samudra* meaning "ocean" and *manthan* meaning "to churn." As this story is central to the idea of amrita—the elixir of life and immortality that has many analogues to alchemical processes as well as to Tantra itself, and that is virtually an obsession with the temples under review in this study—it is worthwhile to summarize it here. The story takes place at the beginning of the Golden Age according to the Vedic calendar. The gods and demons—*devas* and *asuras*—cooperate to churn the cosmic ocean to produce amrita, the elixir of immortality. In order to do this, they need a churn, which they fashion out of the sacred mountain at the north pole, the axis of the world. They remove the mountain from the pole and take it to the cosmic ocean, where they rest it on the back of a turtle. The mountain is then churned by means of the king of the Nagas, the serpents. The devas and asuras each take one end of the huge serpent, which is wound around the mountain, and the churning begins. Eventually, they produce a vessel full of amrita.

According to the *Kakawin Ramayana*, the Shiva temple at Prambanan is an earthly representative of the cosmic mountain, the churn that produces amrita. The implication is that the Shiva temple might have been used for that purpose in some esoteric sense. It is a kind of counterbalance to Borobudur, which may have been intended as an initiatory device, as well as a means of legitimizing the political power structure through association with divinity. At Prambanan, the emphasis is on occult power and physical immortality rather than pure spiritual illumination—if the two can be separated so arbitrarily.

Both Borobudur and Prambanan are believed to have been surrounded by water, probably through the construction of artificial lakes. This would satisfy the image of Mount Meru rising from the midst of the cosmic ocean. The similarities end there, however. Borobudur is composed of concentric squares and circles that taper upward to form a pyramid, with the main stupa at the very top. At Prambanan, there is a central square with three main temples—for Brahma, Shiva, and Vishnu—with three smaller temples for their mounts, plus two "flanking" temples whose purpose has not yet been discovered. There are also another eight smaller constructions at the quarter and cross-quarter points, for a total of sixteen temples in the central square. Outside of that square are more than 200 smaller temples, most of which are in complete ruin. Yet, both Borobudur and the Shiva temple are believed to represent Mount Meru, the axis mundi and the Asian version of Jacob's Ladder. That they were also built by kings of temporal kingdoms—perhaps to emphasize their spiritual authority—is not in doubt.

In the three main temples, the statues of Brahma, Shiva, and Vishnu are standing on yonis. Understanding how lingga-yonis were (and are) used in the Indian world, we know that oil, water, or some other liquid is poured over the lingga and drains off in the channel at the side of the yoni, where the excess liquid is collected as sacred or charged with supernatural power. In the case of the statues at Prambanan, it may be that they were similarly anointed and the resulting liquid preserved for its perceived occult properties.

In many Indian temples, a *kalash* (a water pot) is suspended over the lingga so that the water can drip onto it in a constant manner. This is said to "cool down" Shiva so that he does not incinerate those who come to pray to him, as he is notoriously ill-tempered and does not like to be disturbed during his aeons-long meditations. (In some Ayurvedic medicine practices, a kalash is suspended over a patient and special oils or other substances are allowed to drip onto an affected part of the body, often the forehead.) This would seem impractical in the case of the rather large statues at Prambanan if, indeed, they functioned as lingga to their respective yoni.

The number of reliefs at Prambanan that allude to the Samudra Manthan seems to indicate that these temples were used for such a purpose, however, even though the manner of the rituals employed is still a mystery. That human sacrifice also took place at the site—probably at the time of its construction—further reinforces the idea that the function of Prambanan was Tantric in nature.

The Rishis

As we discussed in the first chapter, Tantra employs various methods for the attainment of spiritual power. These include mantra, mudra, yantra, meditation, and yoga (in most cases, Kundalini yoga) in place of, or in addition to, the pancatattva ritual of the five Ms, which adds additional levels of sensory awareness. At Borobudur, we saw the Buddha statues in various mudras.

At Prambanan, we have examples of the *rishis*. In India, the term refers to those who originally received the *Rig Veda*. They may be considered sages, except that, in the case of the rishis, the word should not be used in its purely intellectual sense of "wise," but also has connotations of "seer" or "ecstatic"—that is, someone with direct experience of the divine.

In Vedic astronomy, the constellation Ursa Major is referred to as the Seven Rishis. As this constellation has special importance in connection with the axis mundi and Mount Meru,[10] the presence of the rishis in reliefs on the Brahma temple at Prambanan may point to an astronomical interpretation of the site, as some authors have suggested.[11] The Prambanan rishis are all depicted seated in *ardha padmasana*—a half-lotus pose. This is a relaxed asana for meditation that places the right foot on the left thigh. In a full-lotus, or padmasana, the right foot is placed on the left thigh and the left foot on the right thigh.

There seem to be only four mudras depicted in these reliefs: the dhyani mudra for meditation; a mala mudra (a method of holding the mala, or rosary beads, in the right hand for counting off the mantras); a mudra that uses the left hand instead of the right to hold a mala that has been draped around the neck; and a mudra that cannot be identified due to the extensive erosion that has taken place. There is also another rishi who is holding what may be a vase of amrita in his left hand, at chest level.

One of the rishis from the Brahma temple (shown on the next page) holds a mala. The trident on his right and the fly whisk on his left shoulder are prominent and are actually present in almost all of the rishi reliefs at Prambanan. The trident,

10 See Peter Levenda, *Stairway to Heaven* (New York: Continuum, 2008), pp. 110–119.

11 See, for instance, the series of articles on *www.borobudur.tv* concerning the proposed astronomical significance of the design and construction of Prambanan.

BRAHMA TEMPLE RISHI 1: *Holding mala.*

while normally an emblem of Shiva as well as of Durga, may also represent the three *gunas*—the basic operating principles of the universe: creation (*rajas* guna), preservation (*sattva* guna), and destruction (*tamas* guna). These three concepts are also represented by the Trimurti as Creation (Brahma), Preservation (Vishnu), and Destruction (Shiva), except that, to a Shiva worshipper, Shiva himself represents all three principles—hence his symbol of the Trident.

The fly whisk is another common symbol in Hindu religion (shown above resting on central figure's left shoulder). It represents both an instrument to scatter evil influences—represented by flies in much the same way that the Semitic demon-god Beelzebub was the "Lord of the Flies"—but is also a symbol of royalty.

On the following pages are a selection of rishis from the temples of Brahma and Vishnu

BRAHMA TEMPLE RISHI 2: *With mala and trident.*

BRAHMA TEMPLE RISHI 3: *With fly whisk, trident, and mala, in varada mudra.*

BRAHMA TEMPLE RISHI 4: *The trident is partly eroded and the fly whisk only barely discernible.*

BRAHMA TEMPLE RISHI 5: *With trident. The mudra is, unfortunately, impossible to identify due to the erosion.*

BRAHMA TEMPLE RISHI 6: *In pose of dhyani or meditation, with fly whisk and trident.*

BRAHMA TEMPLE RISHI 7: *With fly whisk, trident and mala.*

BRAHMA TEMPLE RISHI 8: *With fly whisk and trident, badly eroded. This one is unusual due to the elevation of the left hand to the level of the chest: it does not seem to be making a particular mudra, but rather is holding onto a mala necklace.*

BRAHMA TEMPLE RISHI 9: *The trident and fly whisk are evident, as is the mala. Hanging off the trident is what appears to be a kalash, either a water-pot or perhaps the vase of amrita also known as Amrita Kumbha.*

BRAHMA TEMPLE RISHI 10: *Varada mudra. This time the fly whisk is obvious, but there does not seem to be a trident in evidence.*

BRAHMA TEMPLE RISHI 11: *With trident and fly whisk, holding mala.*

BRAHMA TEMPLE RISHI 12: *The trident and fly whisk are there, but in this case the mudra is done with the left hand, which appears to be holding a container. If so, then it may represent the vase of amrita.*

Vishnu Temple Figures

VISHNU TEMPLE FIGURE 1: *Unidentified male figure flanked by two female figures. He is holding a lotus plant, which is a symbol of Vishnu. It is difficult to know if the mudra is the varada mudra or the bhumisparsa mudra, but considering that this is a Hindu temple and not a Buddhist one, we may consider that the varada mudra is intended.*

VISHNU TEMPLE FIGURE 2: *Another unidentified male figure flanked by two female figures and holding a lotus flower.*

VISHNU TEMPLE FIGURE 3: *A figure believed to be Rama, flanked by two female figures (the one on the right clearly holding a lotus flower) and brandishing a bow. As Rama is an avatar of Vishnu, this is consistent with the overall theme of the temple.*

VISHNU TEMPLE FIGURE 4: *Another unidentified figure from the Vishnu temple, holding a lotus flower and flanked by female figures. There is some controversy over this relief, since it appears to represent a human ruler with noticeable facial features and expression and a more prominent stomach (see text below).*

Regarding the image shown above as Vishnu Temple Figure 4, it was the practice in Java at the time to carve statues of the gods that resembled human monarchs as a way of saying that they were the earthly form and representatives of those gods. Imagine, for a moment, if this practice had become common in the West, with images of the saints, the Virgin Mother, or even of Jesus or Moses patterned on human kings and queens. In a pre-literate society, or one in which literacy was within the reach of only a chosen few, the impact of these images would have been profound and the message inescapable—disobeying the monarch is tantamount to refusing a god.

It is the genius of the Javanese, however, that they found ways around this problem, for if the monarch was seen to be ineffectual, it was assumed that the spiritual powers had left him and that he was no longer worthy of support.[12] Like Arthur in Camelot, once the Grail disappeared and the kingdom was in ruin, it was a clear sign that shakti had left the monarch and had to be regained.

It will be noted that none of these figures are shown sitting on a lotus pedestal, unlike the Buddha statues at Borobudur, which are all on lotuses. This may refer to the human—i.e., non-divine—nature of the Prambanan figures, since the statues of the gods themselves are shown standing on lotus pedestals on top of yonis. It is difficult in Hindu religion to make a sharp distinction between human and divine figures, since quite often there is some cross-over between the two, hinting at an intermediary stage. The rishis, for instance, may refer to individuals who were once human, but who since have attained divine or quasi-divine status, like that of saints in the West. In Java, the kings were just such liminal figures. They straddled the worlds of human and divine, not unlike the juru kunci, who mediate between the human world and the supernatural realm.

That there is much we do not know about Prambanan is revealed in the course of any serious study of the subject. Scholars debate even points that were once considered beyond question—like whether or not Prambanan is truly a Hindu structure or if it underwent a kind of Buddhist "conversion" at some point; or whether Prambanan's environs were once flooded to simulate the Milk Ocean. Even the identities of many of the reliefs are still being debated.

The Guardians

Some visitors find the guardian reliefs and statues at Prambanan to be the most compelling of the figures because of their obvious fierceness and hostility. There is an immediacy about the guardians that provokes an almost visceral reaction. Their intense expressions leave no doubt as to their intentions, yet they face in only one direction—away from the temples. Once intrepid visitors have passed the demon gates, they need fear the guardians no longer.

---

12 The story of Adiwijaya, the Sultan of Pajang, is a case in point. Having lost a battle against his enemies that was accompanied by an eruption of Mount Merapi, he went to the mausoleum at Tembayat in Central Java where it is believed one of the nine saints of Java is buried. When the gate refused to open, he was told by the juru kunci that "the light of royalty" had passed from him to the new Mataram dynasty. See Claude Guillot, "The Tembayat hill: clergy and royal power in Central Java from the 15th to the 17th century," in Henri Chambert-Loir and Anthony Reid, eds., *The Potent Dead: Ancestors, Saints and Heroes in Contemporary Indonesia* (Honolulu: University of Hawai'i Press, 2002), p. 148.

A makara with a serpentine body ending in a ferocious mouth.

These makaras are present in Borobudur as well as at Prambanan, as we have seen in the previous chapter. What is not so well known by visitors is that the makaras also represent sexual desire. As water symbols—and as half-goat, half-fish composites—they clearly have resonance with the satyrs of European mythology and pre-Christian religion. As one of the symbols of the God of Love and Desire, Kamadeva, the makaras carry a charge of sexuality in a spiritual or sacred context. As guardians, they may indicate the raw power of shakti in a natural state, but under the conscious control of the initiate or god. The image above shows a typical makara with a serpentine body ending in a ferocious mouth. These were used—as at Borobudur—for water drainage, but it is also possible that this seemingly mundane function had an esoteric analogue as well.

In addition to the makaras, there are also many instances of dvarapala—door or gate guardians that are a typical feature of Indian Buddhist and Hindu temples, as well as those found on Java and on Bali. In some cases (as at Prambanan), only their heads are shown (see page 124). This is usually an allusion to the demon Rahu who swallowed some of the amrita before being decapitated by Vishnu. Thus his head became immortal, while the rest of him died. In Indian astrology, it

Two dvarapalas or door guardians at the Prambanan Temple

Here we see a typical arrangement of door guardians surrounding the entrance to the Shiva temple. These dvarapala are shown with bulging eyes, wide grins, and sometimes talons. They are the enemies of evil spirits and protect the gods from harm.

Another configuration of guardians

is Rahu who devours the moon, thus causing a lunar eclipse. (In Western astrology, he is known as the Moon's North Node.).

The photo above shows yet another configuration of guardians. In addition to the monster at the very top of the door, there are smaller ones at the foot, surmounted by Shiva's assistants, the ganas. On top of the ganas, you can see makaras at either side of the door and, at the sides of the staircase, more demonic beings.

On the opposite page is an almost comical dvarapala with an unhappy-looking gana on top. Above the gana, you can see another makara.

The next four photos show some badly eroded examples that nonetheless retain their explicit personalities.

An almost comical dvarapala with an unhappy-looking gana on top.

The two photos at left show some badly eroded examples that nonetheless retain their explicit personalities.

The two dvarapalas above are also badly eroded but retain their personalities. For comparison, the photo at left is of an identical creature atop the entrance to a Hindu temple in Bali

The dvarapala shown above from the entrance to a Hindu temple in Bali has exaggerated eyes and ears that may imply a kind of omniscience on the part of this entity—the ability to see and hear evil, to detect it, not only in the form of malevolent spirits, but also in the fissures of our own hearts and consciences. The gaping mouth with the hideous fangs clearly represents the devouring function of the guardian.

When Rahu is intended, the allusion is specifically to the quest for amrita, the elixir of immortality that is a focus of the Tantric sects. The profusion of Rahus (monsters without bodies) and makaras at Prambanan may indicate the special purpose of the temple complex, which revolved around amrita and the Churning of the Milk Ocean. One could say that the bodiless immortal Rahu represents the purely intellectual approach to the subject—an approach by someone who has done the studying, but has not made the actual sacrifices required. As in our discussion of the Homa ritual in chapter 1, it is clear from any unbiased reading of the Tantras that actual, not virtual, sacrifices are intended. The language is explicit, and the practice should be as well. Thus the body must be as engaged in the pursuit of Tantric illumination as the mind. It is amusing (and perhaps too unkind) to imagine the scholars of Tantra as so many Rahus who, having tasted of the divine wisdom, warn the rest of us to keep away from the inner chamber of the temple, a chamber they have never seen.

Candi Sewu

Not far from Prambanan and sometimes considered part of the same complex is Candi Sewu, a name that means "1000 temples." At the time the author was there, the site was in the midst of restoration after the damage caused by the earthquake of 2006. While there is a lot of construction and reconstruction taking place there, it is still possible to get a glimpse of some of the original art and architecture.

Although the site is named 1000 Temples, there are actually only about 257 in evidence today. They are all part of what had been a huge mandala. Candi Sewu is believed to be a Buddhist site, and the pattern of the temples and arrangement of the statues and reliefs is thought to represent a vajradhatu mandala, the mandala most associated with the Kalachakra Tantra.[13]

Rather than belabor this study with more discussion of the individual reliefs—those that are in a state to be identified—it is perhaps more interesting to focus on the Rahus of Candi Sewu, which are more elaborate in some cases. The tradition that the mouth of the Rahu drips with jewels is perhaps linked to the story of a monster who steals the amrita and takes a drink of it before being beheaded. The jewels may be the crystallized essence of the amrita he drank. The reliefs at Candi Sewu give us some excellent examples of this idea. This Rahu, found over the entrance to the main temple, is resplendent with ornamentation. Like many Rahu in the Indian tradition, this one lacks a lower jaw. Also note the makara on either side of the entrance.

The photograph on page 132 shows an image of a boddhisattva with a similar Rahu overhead.

---

13 See Jacques Dumarçay, *Candi Sewu and the Buddhist Architecture of Central Java* (Jakarta: Kepustakaan Populer Gramedia, 2007) for a thorough study of the architecture of this site, along with a discussion of how the Candi Sewu "cubit" (0.34 meters) was calculated.

Rahu relief at Candi Sewu over the entrance to the main temple.

In addition to the elaborate Rahus, visitors to Candi Sewu are greeted by some of the largest dvarapala ever seen. These guardians are truly enormous, and worthy of reproduction here (see page 133). They are depicted draped in serpents and carrying a club, with a knife or short sword tucked into their belts. Their function is protective, yet they are not shown standing, but in a half-sitting, half-kneeling position that probably fits their role as spiritual guardians of the second-largest Buddhist shrine in Indonesia, after Borobudur.

Candi Sewu is believed to be related to the famous Javanese story of the *Loro Jonggrang*, or "Slender Virgin." In this story, two Javanese kingdoms are at war. A cruel giant, ruler of one kingdom, is at war with a wise prince with supernatural powers, ruler of the other. The giant, however, has a beautiful daughter—the *Loro Jonggrang*.

An image of a boddhisattva with a Rahu overhead.

Gigantic dvarapalas at Candi Sewu.

The giant is defeated, and the armies of the wise prince invade his palace. The prince sees the giant's beautiful daughter and at once proposes marriage. She refuses at first, but after much urging agrees to the union on two conditions: the prince must build a well and he must build 1000 temples in only one night.

The prince agrees and builds a very deep well using his supernatural abilities. The giant's daughter, however, piles rocks into the well to trap the prince—to no avail, for the prince manages to escape.

The next night, the prince enters into meditation and summons all of his supernatural forces, including spirits and genii. They begin building the 1000 temples. When the 999th temple is complete, the giant's daughter becomes alarmed and begins pounding rice (an activity that normally takes place in the morning). The prince's spirits and genii, fearing the sun is about to come up, abandon the task. Only 999 temples are built, and the prince has lost.

Except ... the prince realizes he has been tricked and, in a fit, curses the giant's daughter, causing her to turn to stone. It is this stone statue that he uses to adorn the 1000th temple, where she will remain forever.

In Java, there are several statues that are believed to be the Loro Jonggrang. One of them is found at Candi Sewu, and another at Prambanan. These are probably statues of the Indian goddess Durga, but Javanese culture has appropriated her as one of its own or, conversely, has recognized that Durga is the Indian avatar of the Slender Virgin of Javanese folklore.

Magic, Politics, Religion, Sexuality

What the summary of the temples of Borobudur, Prambanan, and Sewu have given us is a basis for understanding the temples that appear in the following chapters, as well as some practices that are still being observed in Java—practices that have Tantric significance. Borobudur and Prambanan both provide evidence of the way in which the Hindu-Buddhist culture of pre-Islamic Java managed to equate secular rulership with spiritual attainment, and political power with spiritual power. While the contemporary Western world understands and respects a legal division between Church and State, older civilizations (both European and Asian) did not see rulership that way. Power is shakti—at its base, a psycho-spiritual form of consciousness whose essential motivating factor is all but obscured by dogma, culture, and social expectations. It is the locus where matter and energy are one—a state of potentiality, a coiled serpent at the base of the unconscious spine, at once a promise and a threat.

Chapter 5

The Temples of Mount Lawu and the Production of Amrita

Of all the temples found in Java, there are perhaps no more blatant examples of Tantric iconography than those found on the slopes of Mount Lawu.

This mountain—actually a quiescent volcano—is on the border between Central Java and East Java, not far from the city of Surakarta (Solo) and easily accessible from Yogyakarta (Jogja). As one climbs into the foothills, the temperature becomes cooler and there is extensive agriculture in the form of terraced fields of tea and other commodities. A curving road hugging the side of the mountain takes the visitor past simple houses, an occasional ox, and scenery of incredible beauty. For centuries, Mount Lawu (or *Gunung Lawu,* in Javanese) has been a spiritual center, a kind of Indonesian Mount Shasta.

The people who live on the western slope of Mount Lawu practice Hinduism and have a local priest who officiates at Hindu rituals. The shrines and statues at the two temples under discussion—Candi Ceto and Candi Sukuh—are well-tended. There are flowers left in front of statues, incense burning near trees or before stone phalluses, all left by unseen hands. Mount Lawu is a mystical site, and the temples of Ceto and Sukuh are especially potent. The temples are places of pilgrimage for traditional kejawen-type gurus and their students. Yet, for all their local popularity, they are rarely visited by foreign tourists.

The temples on Mount Lawu are believed to have been built during the 15th century CE, meaning that they were already in use when Columbus landed in North America. They represent a form of Tantra that had been fused with indigenous Javanese practices and reflect the tensions building in Java with the ascendancy of Islam during the same period.

To understand the cultural and religious environment that gave rise to these temples, it is necessary to know a little about the history of Java in the13th century, immediately before construction began at Candi Ceto and Candi Sukuh.

One of the most famous Tantric Javanese kings was Kertanegara, the last of the Singhasari dynasty. An initiate of Hevajra Tantra (which became one of the central Tibetan teachings), Kertanegara represented a fusion of Hinduism and Buddhism within a purely Tantric context. Indeed, he believed himself to be the avatar of both Shiva and Buddha. He was also one of the most notorious of all the Southeast Asian rulers of the period, for he openly opposed none other than the great Mongol emperor Kublai Khan.

School children know of the Great Khan from their study of the voyages of Marco Polo, who visited Kublai Khan's court. A grandson of Genghis Khan, Kublai sought to extend his empire throughout Asia and eventually turned his attention to the Javanese kingdoms to the south. He sent envoys to demand tribute from the court of Kertanegara, who promptly had the men arrested, cut off their ears, and sent them back to China, where the Khan reacted with predictable anger.

At the same time, Kertanegara had sent an army to Sumatra to subdue the Islamic kingdom of Jambi. Since Jambi had already formed an alliance with the Khan, Kertanegara assumed that it would align itself militarily with him as well. When the Khan's forces finally did arrive in Java around the year 1290, they found the Singhasari dynasty in disarray. A revolt had taken place against Kertanegara while his troops were off fighting the Jambi kingdom in Sumatra. Kertanegara was himself slain during a Tantric ritual at which large quantities of wine had been consumed, rendering him and his retinue intoxicated and defenseless.

The rebellious commander was eventually slain by Kertanegara's son-in-law, the *Raden* (Prince) Wijaya, who not only defeated the rebel armies, but also managed to rout the Mongol forces sent by the Khan. It was through Raden Wijaya's line that the last non-Islamic dynasty of Java, the Majapahit, was founded in 1293. This dynasty lasted for over 200 years, during which time most of present-day Indonesia as well as present-day Malaysia were incorporated within the Majapahit empire. It was in the later period of this dynasty that the famous and mysterious Tantric temples of Candi Ceto and Candi Sukuh were built and consecrated, probably during the reign of King Brawijaya V, the last monarch of the Majapahit and thus the last non-Islamic monarch in Java. As enemy forces began squeezing the armies of the Majapahit, many fled to neighboring Bali, where the Hindu way of life and religion was preserved. Others wound up scattered throughout Java, hiding in the mountains and building their temples and shrines to the Javanese-Hindu-Buddhist religion they practiced so faithfully.

Candi Ceto and Candi Sukuh are two of these temples. They remained largely forgotten and in ruin until the 19th and 20th centuries, when foreign officials took note of the sites and began excavation and restoration. The sites were still revered by the people who lived on Mount Lawu, who regarded them as sources of spiritual power.

We will look at Candi Ceto and Candi Sukuh in turn.

Candi Ceto

The photo below shows the entrance to the temple—a lintel-less gate that is typical of Javanese religious architecture. The stone figure at the entrance, called Nyai Gemang Arum, does not appear to be a guardian, but a devotee.

Nyai is a term of respect for women, especially women of high social rank, although the statue in this case does not appear to be female. In Bali, the same term may be used to signify "you" or "thou," also terms that imply respect for someone of higher social status. Thus the confusion may rest there, as the Balinese were and are devout Hindus and Candi Ceto is a Hindu-Javanese shrine.

Entrance to the Candi Ceto temple.

Compare this statue to the two others on the facing page that flank the main entrance. They are called Nyai Agni, which may be a reference to the Sanskrit word for "fire" *(agni)* and which is also the name of the God of Fire in Hinduism, both of which are male. The Hindu deva Agni is usually shown with two heads or two faces. The fact that there are two Nyai Agni here may be a reference to this, but the religious symbolism of the temple has been so Javanized that any clear association between it and classical Indian religion is a bit problematic.

To add to the confusion, the restoration of the temple was conducted in a cavalier fashion. All of the wooden elements had, of course, deteriorated to the point that new wooden roofs, beams, and structural supports had to be made. Much of the stonework was in disarray as well, leaving some of the reconstruction design up to the imagination of the workers. However, enough elements of the original Candi Ceto (begun about 1451) remain to allow us to develop theories about the purpose for the entire site.

At the top of page 139 is one of the two Nyai Agni found at Candi Ceto. From the beard, we can assume that the figure is not female. However, the statue is back-to-back with a female figure, shown in the second image, that is not identified, thus adding a greater degree of confusion. Notice also the offering of rice and incense that has been made to the statue. What appear to be wristwatches on either arm of the figure have contributed to some hilarity among some visitors.

The second Nyai Agni at Candi Seto, shown opposite below, is in much disrepair, but also sports facial hair.

On page 82 we see the Candi Ceto temple complex as it appeared in 2008. All of the wooden structures are, of course, new and part of the restoration work that was begun in 1970.

On page 140 is another view of the complex that gives some idea of the layered effect of the fourteen terraces that made up the original design. Only thirteen of the terraces remain at the present time.

The complex contains two statues of historical figures, advisors to the last king of the Majapahit dynasty. They are shown on page 141. The first is Sabdapalon, a loyal subject of King Brawijaya V, and a priest as well as a spiritual and political advisor. According to the story, he cursed the king when the latter converted to Islam in the year 1478. He foretold that the Hindu-Javanese kingdom would return in 500 years, but not before widespread devastation on Java. The 1978 eruption of Mount Semeru—also known as Mahameru or Mount Sumeru, after the Indian original—was believed to be one sign that the prophecy was being fulfilled.

ABOVE LEFT AND RIGHT: *Nyai Agni statues flank the main entrance. The Hindu deva Agni is usually shown with two heads or two faces. However, the statue at Candi Seto is back-to-back with a female figure, shown above right.*

LEFT: *The second Nyai Agni at Candi Seto is in much disrepair, but also sports facial hair.*

The terraces of the Candi Seto Temple complex.

The second statue is of the advisor Naya Genggong, who is sometimes believed to be one and the same person as Sabdapalon.

Because of the prophecies made by Sabdapalon, recorded in an ancient document entitled *Ramalan Sabda Palon Naya Genggong* (The Prophecy of Sabda Palon Naya Genggong), and the latest eruption of Mount Merapi outside of Yogyakarta in November 2010, there has been a resurgence of interest in this narrative and, consequently, something of a mystical revival taking place at the temples on Mount Lawu. Sabdapalon himself is believed to have left Java for the island of Bali, where Hinduism still flourishes, but so many stories are told about him that he has acquired a mystical status in his own right.

One of the few surviving reliefs at Candi Ceto shows what may be a typical scene from the shadow puppet theater. In the center of this stone is what appears to be Mount Meru, the cosmic mountain of Indian religion, depicted in wayang fashion. At either side are archers. This may be a scene from the *Ramayana*, but the erosion that has taken place has made it difficult to make out much detail.

ABOVE LEFT: *Sabdapalon, a priest and spiritual advisor to King Brawijaya V.*

ABOVE RIGHT: *Naya Genggong, perhaps the same person as Sabdapalon.*

A relief at Candi Seto may be a scene from the shadow puppet theater.

Palang

One of the most shocking elements of Candi Ceto is the huge stone lingga and yoni on one of the terraces that marks the entrance to the main building. As you can see opposite, these lie flat on the ground rather than standing vertically, and their sheer size is arresting. The photo on page 144 shows a close-up of some curious ornamentation found on the lingga in the form of round balls or spheres at the head of the phallus, below the glans at either side and on top. This may reveal a cultural practice called *palang*.

Palang is a practice known in one form or another throughout Southeast Asia, but also mentioned in the Kama Sutra.[14] It is a practice that involves the insertion of a rod in the penis—laterally, perpendicular to the head of the penis and just below the glans—and the attachment of small balls or beads on either end of it. This is supposed to increase female enjoyment during the sex act. The method has undergone a renewal in the modern world, much like piercing the body in other areas, like the tongue, navel, and breasts. After the first incision, a small length of bamboo is inserted to keep the wound from closing. When the sex act is to be performed, the bamboo is removed and replaced with a metal rod and the two balls attached, one at each end.

Other methods involve the insertion of precious stones, pearls, or gold balls in the skin of the penis where they usually remain.[15] In some cases, small bells, ball

---

14 See Richard Burton's translation (1883), Chapter II: "The people of the southern countries think that true sexual pleasure cannot be obtained without perforating the lingam, and they therefore cause it to be pierced like the lobes of the ears of an infant pierced for earrings. Now, when a young man perforates his lingam he should pierce it with a sharp instrument, and then stand in water so long as the blood continues to flow. At night, he should engage in sexual intercourse, even with vigour, so as to clean the hole. After this he should continue to wash the hole with decoctions, and increase the size by putting into it small pieces of cane, and the wrightia antidysenterica, and thus gradually enlarging the orifice. It may also be washed with liquorice mixed with honey, and the size of the hole increased by the fruit stalks of the simapatra plant. The hole should also be anointed with a small quantity of oil. In the hole made in the lingam a man may put Apadravyas of various forms, such as the 'round', the 'round on one side,' the 'wooden mortar,' the 'flower,' the 'armlet,' the 'bone of the heron,' the 'goad of the elephant,' the 'collection of eight balls,' the 'lock of hair,' the 'place where four roads meet,' and other things named according to their forms and means of using them. All these Apadravyas should be rough on the outside according to their requirements."

15 There has been some recent research on this subject among modern Indonesians, Thais, Burmese, and Filipinos. See, for instance, Terence H. Hull, "Penis enhancements: popular with sailors and miners, but not necessarily with their women," *Inside Indonesia*, Vol. 68, Oct–Dec 2001; and Terence H. Hull and Meiwita Budiharsana, "Male Circumcision and Penis Enhancement in Southeast Asia: Matters of Pain and Pleasure," *Reproductive Health Matters*, Vol. 9, No. 18, Nov. 2010, pp. 60–67. Also Donald E. Brown, James W. Edwards, and Ruth P. Moore, "*The penis inserts of Southeast Asia: an annotated bibliography with an overview and comparative perspectives,*" occasional paper No.15, Centre for South and

Closeup of lingga with palang at Candi Seto.

bearings, and even silicon are inserted. The use of semi-precious stones, gold, and pearls is believed to provide the added benefit of increasing supernatural power, while also advertising the bearer's wealth and social status, thus increasing his desirability as a potential husband or mate.

Another supposed benefit of palang is the ability to remain in sexual intercourse for hours at a time.[16] That is one of the Tantric ideals, of course, just as prolonged periods of meditation are considered evidence of the supernatural power and sincerity of the practitioner.

Palang has profound implications for the way in which Tantra was understood in Java at that time. The method of palang does not provide much enjoyment to the male; its purpose is strictly to increase stimulation in the female partner. The

---

Southeast Asian Studies, University of California at Berkeley, 1988. This paper discusses the idea that palang indicates higher social status of women.

16 See Laurence Bergreen, *Over the Edge of the World: Magellan's Terrifying Circumnavigation of the Globe* (New York: HarperCollins, 2004), p. 266, pp. 372–373 for the account of a 16th-century explorer visiting Java less than 100 years after Candi Ceto was erected.

At left is a shrine at Candi Seto containing the stone phallus shown at right.

number of rods and balls can be considered signs of status—two, three, or more such rods could be inserted in the penis, with the respective number of balls; or a large number of balls or jewels could be directly and permanently inserted under the skin of the penis. This degree of attention to the female experience in the sex act indicates a focus on the female and her enjoyment that seems to be inconsistent with generally accepted ideas concerning patriarchal societies and their emphasis on the male orgasm. For instance, in cultures where "female circumcision" (clitoral mutilation) is practiced, something like palang would be inconceivable.

Why, then, would this practice attain the elevated status it enjoys in the stone sculptures of Candi Ceto? Is there another level of meaning that escapes the uninitiated observer? After all, these are not the usual phallic monuments we expect to see in Shiva temples. Lingga and yoni are prevalent throughout the Indian cultural sphere. Yet, it seems that we find lingga pierced in the style of palang only in Java (and Bali).

A possible answer will become clear as we move through the very detailed stonework of the temple, for Candi Ceto, like its sister Candi Sukuh, was designed for a very specific purpose—the collection of amrita.

The sculptures and iconography at Candi Ceto are very selective. All the symbols found there today can refer to one concept only—amrita—and the methods used to collect it. The juxtaposition of the lingga (with palang) and yoni, next to what appears to be a giant Garuda indicates that the entire complex was dedicated to this most Tantric of Tantric rituals. In order to decode it—and Candi Sukuh—we need to understand a bit more about the mysticism concerning biological fluids that was current in Indian Tantra and alchemy.

Precious Bodily Fluids

> **Group Capt. Lionel Mandrake:** Uh, Jack, Jack, listen, tell me, tell me, Jack. When did you first become . . . well, develop this theory?
>
> **General Jack D. Ripper:** Well . . . I first became aware of it, Mandrake, during the physical act of love.
>
> **Mandrake:** Hmm.
>
> **Ripper:** Yes, a profound sense of fatigue . . . a feeling of emptiness followed. Luckily I . . . I was able to interpret these feelings correctly. Loss of essence.
>
> **Mandrake:** Hmm.
>
> **Ripper:** I can assure you it has not recurred, Mandrake. Women uh . . . women sense my power and they seek the life essence. I, uh . . . I do not avoid women, Mandrake.
>
> **Mandrake:** No.
>
> **Ripper:** But I . . . I do deny them my essence.
>
> —*Dr. Strangelove, or How I Learned to Stop Worrying and Love the Bomb*

We can isolate two separate phenomena that take place in the context of Tantric worship and ritual, and specifically of the *pancatattva* or Five Elements ritual that incorporates sexual intercourse. One of these is the sex act itself, which may be considered from a psycho-biological viewpoint as the mating of two humans in an intense and focused ritual that may even take place before the gaze of onlookers (other members of the Tantric circle). Like the sex act between two people in love with each other, this act is both passionate and "animal," but also contains higher elements, like a desire for union that transcends the physical. In that sense, the Tantric ritual of Maithuna is a kind of re-enactment of the moment when two lovers first embrace, as opposed to a sex act that takes place, for instance, between a prostitute and her client, or between a rapist and his victim.

This is the element of the Tantric rite that is pure consciousness, a symbol of the creation of the world (and of the specific creation—i.e., the conception—of the two individuals performing the rite). The moment of orgasm is usually delayed for a long period of time so that the partners reach a plateau of experience—much like an intense state of meditation that can last for hours or even longer—during which both partners lose themselves completely in the act, to the extent that it is difficult to know where one body ends and the other begins. Orgasm, if and when it occurs, can be intense, breath-taking, and, in some cases, truly illuminating.

The second phenomenon derives from the first, and involves the use and even the consumption of the bodily fluids created by the sex act. This is the element of Tantra that is often overlooked or ignored—if it is even understood or recognized—by practitioners of New Age Tantra, who focus primarily on improving their sexual experience and their relationships with lovers. However, it is as important to the process as the sexual act itself, for, just as sex often leads to conception and procreation—that is, the materialization on the physical plane of what began as something ephemeral like desire, lust, or love—so the Tantric act must also lead to a kind of procreation or materialization. And just as the sex act within the Tantric circle mimics the Ur-intercourse of the gods that led to the creation of the cosmos, so are worlds created through the medium of the sexual fluids.

We cannot understand some of the Western alchemical writings unless we recognize the importance of physical substance and its potential for transformation. The same true in Tantra. The seminal fluid, mucoid excretions, and blood that may be the effluvia of the sex act are all preserved or, in many cases, consumed on the spot by the practitioners. There is, actually, no bodily excretion at all that is considered tabu in the Tantric context.

The exoteric explanation is usually the recognition that the initiated adept has gone beyond a dualistic view of creation, and sees bodily excretions as no different from a field of wildflowers or a lover's sigh. All is Maya; all is illusion—the manifestation of desire in the created, albeit illusory, world. All is one; there is no difference between you and me. Thus, there is no reason to feel disgust at the sight of fecal material, just as there is no reason to feel desire at the sight of a beautiful person. There is no beauty, no ugliness. This is the exalted state of advaita, or non-duality. To demonstrate that one has achieved this state, one can as easily consume menstrual blood as a glass of wine.

the female genital organ was the source of other "essences," depending on its time within the menstrual cycle. These essences were called *kalas*, a reference to the Sanskrit word for "time," as well as to "essence" and "unguent" (*kala).* It was believed there were sixteen of these kalas, based on the sixteen "digits" of the lunar cycle in Indian astrology and hence related to a similar division of a woman's menstrual cycle. Thus, at different times of her period, a woman "excretes" a different kala, a different essence. This, of course, would be of intense interest and subject to observation by Tantric practitioners, who would time rituals of collection of these essences for optimum results.

The importance that the Javanese Tantricists gave to this concept is evident in their obsession with the mythical hero Garuda and with the story of how Garuda seized the amrita—the elixir vitae—from the grasp of the Nagas, the serpent gods. Depictions of Garuda are found everywhere in Indonesia, of course; their national airline is named after him. In Java, however, Garuda appears in a somewhat different form from the way he is normally shown in India and even in Bali. In Java, Garuda is thin, tall, even gangly. He has the head and talons of a bird of prey, and the body of a man. He is almost always shown with his claws on the backs of serpents and with the vessel of the precious amrita within reach of his talons.

At Candi Sukuh—arguably one of the most blatantly Tantric of all Javanese temples—Garuda is present in various forms throughout the complex. In the photo on the facing page, the heart-shaped instrument at his waist is the vessel of amrita. Considering that Candi Sukuh is where we find shrines to the phallus and statues of men with prominent members, the Garuda statues, with their serpent bases and their vessels of amrita, can only have been understood in a purely Tantric sense—especially as the sacred vessel itself is shown tied to Garuda's belt and dangling in front of his groin, as if it were a heart-shaped fig leaf, as the photograph shows.

In this case, the statue has been beheaded—possibly by art thieves—but the rest of the image is clearly that of Garuda, from his wings to his talon-like feet and the amrita vessel at his waist.

There are, of course, at least two different approaches to the concept of amrita. Like the quotation from *Dr. Strangelove* above, there is one school that cautions practitioners to retain their "precious bodily fluids" rather than lose them in the sex act. In this case, the male either refrains from ejaculation altogether or draws the ejaculated seminal fluid from his partner's vagina back through his penis into his own body. The latter practice requires long training and is potentially quite dangerous, as it reverses the normal action of the genital organ, making it, in effect, a kind of vacuum cleaner. The safer approach is to refrain from ejaculation

A statue of Garuda at Candi Sukh.

and retain the seminal fluid, coaxing it (or, more correctly, its etheric counterpart) to enter into circulation in the body, raising it to the level of the pineal gland in the brain. This practice is well-known to practitioners of Hatha yoga and, in particular, Kundalini yoga.

Those who are familiar with Kundalini yoga remember that the goddess Kundalini is represented by a serpent. The serpent is made to rise through the seven levels of the human etheric body—the seven chakras—in order for initi-

The serpent king Ananta or Shesha at the Bangkok Suvarnabhumi International Airport in 2008.

ates to attain enlightenment. This association of a serpent with the vital force, or amrita, is found in the stone carvings at Candi Sukuh representing the mission of Garuda, who stole the elixir from the serpent gods, the Nagas. The iconography is remarkably consistent with what we know of the actual practice of Tantra.

To give an idea of the creation of amrita from the churning of the cosmic ocean, we have the following photographs, which were taken in Bangkok Suvarnabhumi International Airport in 2008 of a huge sculpture commemorating the event as it appears in the *Mahabharata*.[18] The first two show the serpent king—Ananta or Shesha—with many heads and his demonic devotees (the asuras) pulling him in a weird tug-of-war with the divine warriors (the devas). The third photo shows us a close-up of the churning Milk Ocean, in the midst of which we see a turtle, with the coils of the serpent on top. This particular juxtaposition of turtle, serpent, and elixir vitae (and Milk Ocean) is one we will come across again—particularly in the case of Candi Ijo and its mysterious shrine to creation itself.

18 The sculpture has since been moved.

ABOVE: *The asura pulling the serpent king.*
BELOW: *Churning Milk Ocean with a turtle in the midst and the coils of the serpent on top.*

Vishnu at the Bangkok Suvarnabhumi International Airport.

In the foreground of the churning Milk Ocean on page 153, you can see a conch on a pedestal. It is believed that the conch was the first created form to emerge from the ocean, followed by the goddess Lakshmi. The conch symbolizes life itself and is an important element in many Hindu rituals, or *puja*, where it is used either as a horn (much like the shofar is used in Jewish ceremonies) or as a vessel for holding sacred water. Vishnu is often shown holding a conch in his hand, as in the detail from the sculpture on the facing page.

Thus, as we have seen, there are two important narratives concerning amrita. The first is the Churning of the Milk Ocean, which produces amrita; the second is the theft of amrita from the Nagas by the mythical bird-man Garuda. In both of these narratives, serpents (Nagas) are essential elements. Turtles also appear, forcing us to ask the obvious question: What is the relationship between amphibious creatures and the production/procurement of amrita?

In the following photograph, we can see some detail of the "yoni" figure that accompanies the lingga-palang figure at Candi Ceto. In the center of the yoni triangle can be seen a crab (another amphibious creature) with what appear to be three frogs in the very center of the sculpture. At the ends of the triangle barely can be seen the figures of lizards.

Yoni figure at Candi Ceto.

The turtle figures in situ at an unnamed shrine at Candi Ceto.

We can conclude that it requires the assistance of amphibians to obtain the amrita, for it is hidden in the ocean. Both the turtle and the serpents are essential to the story of the Milk Ocean. The addition of crabs and lizards (and possibly frogs) to the large stone emblem at Candi Ceto seems to place emphasis on this aspect of the story. Our attention is being drawn to this part of the code in a very deliberate manner.

In the next two photographs of an unnamed shrine at Candi Ceto, we see the use of turtles once again. They seem to be functioning as steps, but I am not

Close-up of turtle figures at Candi Ceto.

comfortable with that description. They may serve a sacrificial purpose and, as can be seen, offerings of flowers and incense were made some time before my arrival.

In fact, the large sculpture of a Garuda that is flat on the ground next to the lingga-yoni bears yet another turtle on its back, as can be seen in the photo on the next page. The turtle's head can be seen rising from the circular form atop the large, winged sculpture lying flat to the rear of the yoni. Between the Garuda-cum-Turtle and the triangular yoni, there is a small circular sculpture representing a solar disc with seven rays. This was the symbol of the Majapahit dynasty.

The yoni in this sculpture is virtually crawling with amphibious creatures, and Garuda is himself carrying a huge turtle on his back. This is excessive, even

Garuda figure flat on the ground with a turtle on its back at Candi Ceto.

by Tantric standards, unless a point is being made. The ability to rise from the sea to dry land and to return indicates that amphibians are liminal creatures, like divine kings and juru kunci. They thus have a special affinity as shamanic totems. Birds can be seen as liminal in the sense that they fly, and this may be why both a bird—Garuda—and a turtle are involved in the amrita narratives. If present-day paleo-zoological theories are true, dinosaurs are the direct ancestors of birds, which indicates an even greater degree of liminality—a connection with an ancient time and with a world where humans did not yet exist.

This idea of liminality may be enough for a general appreciation of the iconography, but when it comes to Tantra, there are always deeper levels of meaning. Tantra is about action and action is the manifestation of process—and this specific process involves fluids of various kinds.

The human foetus begins its existence as an amphibian, living in the fluid-filled sac of its mother. Even earlier, it is created through the mingling of fluids from both parents. When the infant is born, there is an expulsion of more fluid from the mother, and the almost ritualistic bathing of the newborn. These associations were not lost on those who created the Tantric worldview. They understood that there was a power in these specific fluids that far exceeded their appearance as mere bodily excretions. Blood and semen became the Red and the White tinctures of alchemy, of course, but the esoteric philosophers and alchemists who began this investigation did not stop there. They extended their research to other bodily excretions as well, including urine and feces, but also vaginal secretions at various times during a woman's period. They attempted to understand precisely which organs and other elements of the human body owed their creation to the male contribution of fluid, and which to the female essence. Attempts were made to synchronize bodily rhythms to solar and lunar patterns, to create complex matrices that would enable practitioners to caress the entire web of existence and provoke one or another response based on their understanding of the process.

Once it was understood that such a matrix did exist, the realization set in that it existed in every aspect of human experience—biological, psychological, chemical, spiritual, physical, architectural, musical, even political. Hence the elaborate calculations and iconography at Chartres Cathedral in France, for instance, which contains much alchemical symbolism in the form of statues and other images, but which also was built as a kind of device for enhancing the spiritual experience according to the mysticism associated with its geometrical proportions—what in Asian religion is called mandala. The science behind the creation of these mandalas in stone is known as Vastu in India, and the mathematical and geometrical considerations that go into their design are specific to their purpose. Candi Ceto and Candi Sukuh—as well as Borobudur, Prambanan, and other monuments in Java—were designed with a goal similar, if not identical, to the Gothic cathedrals of France.

Candi Sukuh

> The temple keepers have erected wooden gates to prevent visitors from tripping on the genitalia.
>
> *Jakarta Post*, 26 October 2008

Less than a mile from Candi Ceto is Candi Sukuh. This temple is so notorious that one Indonesian academic felt compelled to write an article entitled "Candi Sukuh is not a Porno Temple."[19] To be sure, there are even more Tantric references

19 Prof. Dr. Bani Sudardi, "Candi Sukuh Bukan Candi Porno," on the website of the Fakultas Sastra dan Seni Rupa Universitas Sebelas Maret (Faculty of Literature and Fine Arts at the March 11 University in Surakarta, Indonesia) at *www.fs.uns.ac.id*.

Temple at Candi Sukuh.

at Candi Sukuh than at Candi Ceto. The photograph of a headless man clutching his em-palanged phallus opposite represents only one of them.

While Candi Ceto's main iconography was the lingga-yoni and Garuda sculptures flat on the ground, at Candi Sukuh we have an extensive inventory of reliefs in a typical Javanese (rather than Indian) style. As you can see in the image above, we also have some interesting architecture that many visitors have associated with a type of design more common in Mexico and Central America than in Southeast Asia, which has given rise to all sorts of von Daennikenesque speculation.

These reliefs are informative, for they emphasize once again the relation of these temples to the gathering of amrita. Considering the time at which they were built—toward the end of the last Hindu-Javanese dynasty—one could also claim that their builders' obsession with amrita and with associated ideas of immortality, health, power, and fertility seem nearly desperate. It may be this very desperation in the face of imminent collapse that led the builders to reveal more of the secrets than they might have otherwise.

The reliefs depict scenes from various stories familiar to audiences of the wayang kulit, the shadow theater. Prominent among them are Semar and other Java-

Closeup of headless man grasping em-palanged phallus (see page 195).

nese personalities, including several strange Garuda figures that actually may or may not represent Garuda, as well as ithyphallic reliefs of various types. Unfortunately, the same haphazard restoration work that plagued Candi Ceto is also evident at Candi Sukuh.

According to published reports, there were "scores" of yoni figures at Sukuh, but the workers who managed the restoration had no idea where to put them, so instead they stacked them in a warehouse. The yoni were made in the typical Indian style, "with a groove for water to flow through ... these were used to collect and make holy water ..."[20]

In the Indian religious context, "holy water" is, of course, amrita.

In addition, the main lingga—nearly six feet in height, and complete with palang balls—that stood at the entrance to Sukuh was removed and brought to the National Museum. Therefore, in order to understand the complete design, one has to visualize the replacement of these critical structures. What is presented, then, is a temple to the sacred sexuality of Java.

20 Godeliva D. Sari, "The sexual wisdom of the Sukuh temple," *The Jakarta Post*, 26 October 2008.

On the opposite page are three photographs that show the structure at Sukuh. The first shows one of the wooden gates erected by the temple custodians. Above the gate is the inevitable guardian, shown close-up in the second image. The style more closely resembles those of Bali than the previous examples at Borobudur and Prambanan. The third shows the other side of the shrine, with another set of wooden gates and the obligatory guardian at the top. At the left of the picture, you can see a figure with an exposed (and uncircumcised?) penis. The photo at the top left of page 164 gives us a closer look at this enigmatic creature.

On the other side of the gate there is another figure, shown top right on page 164, in a serpentine motif. These odd, almost surreal, images are believed to be chronograms, or *candrasangkala* in Javanese. They are a graphic method of stating the year in which the edifice was completed. It is a kind of Javanese Kabbalism, in which an image represents a word and that word represents a number. This one—which shows an elephant, a serpent, and other images—is understood as representing the year 1378 in the Saka (Hindu) calendar, or 1456 CE. While this interpretation is certainly accepted by most scholars, there are those who see in the use of these symbols something deeper than the calendar.[21] That may be because the range of numbers is limited to the digits 1 through 9, but the number of words that can be used to represent numbers varies widely and seems to be at the discretion of the person creating the chronogram.

Thus at Candi Sukuh, we find images—representing words, which themselves represent numbers—that seem to be consistent with the theme of the temple and that are not merely "dead" numbers. An elephant swallowing a snake is representative of the Tantric nature of the site, for both elephants and serpents are very much in evidence in the other reliefs and have decidedly Tantric associations. The type of word-play involved in developing these chronograms will be familiar to anyone who has studied Western alchemical literature, as well as to those familiar with the elaborate word games found in the Zohar. It's one example of the twilight language that we described earlier, which serves both to conceal and reveal the intentions of the creators.

In the photograph on page 165, we find what the wooden gates are protecting—a lingga-yoni figure on the floor of the shrine, at the entrance where visitors would have had to step over it in order to get into the inner areas. In this case, the lingga is clearly piercing the yoni. No ambiguity here. The yoni is roughly

21 See Ann R. Kinney, *Worshipping Siva and Buddha: The temple art of East Java* (Honolulu: University of Hawai'i Press, 2003, p. 266): "The demonic behavior of these figures may refer to sexual rituals and suggests the prevalence of Tantric practices during this period."

Candi Sukuh Temple:

TOP LEFT: *One of the wooden gates erected by the temple custodians.*

TOP RIGHT: *Above the gate is the guardian, shown here in close-up.*

BOTTOM LEFT: *The other side of the shrine, with another set of wooden gates and guardian at top.*

AT LEFT: *A figure with exposed penis.* AT RIGHT: *Another serpentine motif.*

heart-shaped, with what appear to be fingers at either side, and the whole image is surrounded by what may be a serpent or serpentine motif with eleven coils. The debris that can be seen in and around the figure are the remains of flower offerings.

Taken as a whole, the lingga-yoni depicted here resembles a chalice with the lingga as the stem and the yoni as the cup. Considering some of the speculation that has surrounded the identity of the Holy Grail in Western esoteric literature, this device may very well add another level of interpretation.

There are several narratives displayed on the reliefs at Candi Sukuh—several different myth cycles that reflect legends common to Javanese culture and to the wayang kulit performances. In fact, the figures at Candi Sukuh are almost certainly based on the designs of the leather puppets that are used throughout Java even today. Their departure from traditional Indian styles is obvious and dramatic, yet their themes remain remarkably consistent with Indian Tantra.

The story of Sudamala, the first of these narratives, bears some explanation. As usual, it centers around the relationship between Shiva and his consort, Uma.

Dramatic lingga-yoni on the floor of the inner shrine of the Candi Sukuh temple.

In this case, Shiva wanted to make love to Uma, but she refused him on the basis that the time was inappropriate. Angered, Shiva cursed Uma, turning her into the dreaded Bathari Durga. Durga, of course, is the demonic form of Uma. Desperate to have the curse removed, she turned to the five Pandawa brothers (heroes of the Indian epic *Mahabharata*). Impersonating their mother, she asked them to purify her. One of the brothers, known as Sadhewa, agreed and she was purified.

The transformations of gods and goddesses is well-known in world religions. The Greek gods frequently transform into animals or humans. Transformations

incredible physical strength. He is the son of the Lord of the Wind and Air, Vayu, and brother to Hanuman, the trickster and monkey god who is the loyal friend of Rama and Sita. (Vayu is also known as the first of the gods to taste the amrita when it was produced by the Churning of the Milk Ocean.) Esoterically, Bhima is associated with the "ether," the source of existence and "fulfiller of desires of all living or lifeless beings," according to the *Linga Purana*.[22] This is consistent with his lineage from Vayu, the Lord of the Wind and Air.

Bhima's attraction for the Majapahit rulers was probably his role as the fabled military commander in the *Mahabharata*. Some of the reliefs at Candi Sukuh show Bhima defeating his enemies. The panel on page 169 depicts Bhima in the center—recognizable by his curled hair—lifting an enemy into the air with one hand.[23] The enemy figure is usually described as the giant Kalantaka (a form of Yama, the God of Death) or his twin, Kalanjaya, both of whom have been cursed by Shiva to live in a cemetery as servants of Durga.[24] This may be part of the Sudamala story (see below), or it may represent the search of Bhima for amrita and his war against the God of Death, who must be defeated before the amrita is secured.,

Political legitimacy was as much a requirement for the Javanese rulers as military superiority, however, and legitimacy was bestowed by the identification of the political rulers with spiritual forces. Thus, Bhima had two functions for the state: military strength and invincibility, plus his role as the provider of amrita. The supply of this elixir vitae was seen as evidence of both the supernatural power of the rulers and the favor of the gods. It was also essential to the rites of purification that were undertaken by the Tantric ascetics at Sukuh. Purity was at the heart of the process of spiritual transformation, just as it is in chemical transformation. Impurities can hinder or even derail the process at the very outset, so steps must be taken to remove those impurities before the process begins and all during the course of the process itself.

Purity may be understood in two ways: as ritual purity, which comes from strict adherence to laws concerning mostly biological functions (eating, drinking, sex, menstruation), and as moral purity, which is more difficult to establish on an

22 Quoted in Alain Danielou, *The Gods of India: Hindu Polytheism* (New York: Inner Traditions, 1985), p. 205.

23 Some authors have identified this headdress with Arjuna rather than Bhima. See Kinney, *Worshipping Siva and Buddha,* p. 241.

24 Not to be confused with the same name as an epithet of Shiva in the sense of "Vanquisher of Death." In the *Mahabharata* (6.109.13), *Kalantaka* has even been used to describe Bhima.

Relief at Candi Sukuh shows Bhima lifting an enemy in the air with one hand.

individual basis. Often, moral purity was understood to be a reflection of ritual purity: if one followed all of the rituals laws, it was assumed one was in a pure state.

Ideas of purity and tabu preoccupied social anthropologist Mary Douglas, who saw in these rituals an attempt to impose order on chaos. She also understood that there are political implications where purity and tabu are concerned, and that "bodily orifices seem to represent points of entry or exit to social units, or bodily perfection can symbolize an ideal theocracy."[25]

Purity, especially of water, was an obsession among the ancient Jewish Qumran community as well. Discovered by accident in 1947, the Dead Sea Scrolls tell us of a group of men and women for whom purity was so important that

25 Mary Douglas, *Purity and Danger: An analysis of the concept of pollution and taboo* (New York: Routledge 1996, 2008), p. 4

was himself overthrown shortly thereafter. He fled to the mountains east of Yogyakarta and declared his independence sometime around 1437 CE, consecrating a royal lingga at Candi Sukuh in 1470 CE.

This political situation was interpreted in the context of Javanese religion. The Queen of Majapahit was identified with Durga, in this case a form of Durga that inhabits cemeteries. As we discussed above, this narrative belongs to the Sudamala story in which Uma is cursed by Shiva. The reason for the curse is interpreted variously, depending on the text involved (whether normative Hindu texts like the *Mahabharata*, or a Javanized form like the *Kakawin Ramayana*, or others). In one version, already mentioned, Shiva wanted to have sex with Uma at a time she deemed inappropriate; in another version, Uma had illicit intercourse with Brahma, which incurred Shiva's wrath. Regardless, the reason for the curse had to do with sex and, moreover, inappropriate or illicit sex.

Uma is cursed for a period of twelve years. She must spend the time as Durga, haunting a frightening graveyard, until her sentence is over or until she has been freed by Sadewa. Her companions are ghosts and other creatures of the night. The implication is that Queen Suhita is Durga, the evil goddess, who must be overthrown by the heroic Pandawa brothers. Bhima is one of those five brothers. In the relief shown opposite above at Candi Sukuh, he is shown with Semar, the quintessential Javanese god, banging a gong and preparing for war.

In the next photograph, opposite below, we see the story of the Evil Queen—in this case, Durga. She is in the cemetery of the gods, standing in the center of the relief and surrounded by ghostly emblems. In front of her, tied to a tree, is Sadewa, who alone has the power to free her from the cemetery. Durga is threatening to kill him with her sword unless he relents and releases the curse that Shiva has put upon her. In front of her is a bodiless head reminiscent of Rahu, but perhaps intended to be a ghostly figure. There are other weird creatures behind the tree to which Sadewa is tied.

Behind Durga are two of her female servants, one of whom possibly represents Kalika (her demonic servitor). The hanging, pendulous breasts are usually signs that the women being depicted are evil, sometimes witches. For comparison, see the example on page 175 from Prambanan, where an evil goddess or witch is suckling two imps on her rather tubular breasts.

The only way Sadewa can lift the curse from Durga is if his own mother, Kunti, asks him to do so. Kalika, the female servant of Durga, demonically possesses Kunti, who then demands that Sadewa lift the curse. Reluctantly, mother and son return to the cemetery, but Kalika leaves the body of Kunti too early and

ABOVE: *Bhima banging a gong, with Semar, preparing for war.*
BELOW: *Uma, as Durga, in the cemetary of the gods.*

the ruse is revealed. Mother and son then return home, but Kalika once again possesses Kunti.

To make a rather long and intricate story a bit shorter, Sadewa finally does lift the curse from Durga, who then turns back into the beautiful Uma. Shiva blesses Sadewa and gives him the name by which this story is known, Sudamala ("one who cures sickness"). Further along in the story, Sudamala cures a hermit sage of his blindness and is rewarded with a wife.

Many elements of this story could have been applied easily to the political situation at the time, even going so far as to legitimize the reign of Bhre Daha. Queen Suhita is, of course, Uma-become-Durga. Bhre Daha is himself Sudamala, or perhaps Bhima. The nobles who stayed with Queen Suhita can be portrayed as having been possessed by Kalika, and so on. In a sense, it is a blameless way of presenting political events: the Queen has been cursed; her supporters are possessed by demons; all will come right in the end if Bhre Daha remains steadfast and lifts the curse from the Queen so that she comes to her senses. Perhaps Queen Suhita was "cursed" for the same reason Uma was cursed by Shiva: for whoring after the foreign elements, the Chinese and the Muslims.

The warlike atmosphere represented by some of the reliefs at Candi Sukuh certainly seems to reflect a preoccupation with armed conflict. The relief on pages 176 and 177 is controversial, and scholars disagree on what exactly is being represented, since the figures seem anomalous for a temple. There is some agreement that there is a panel missing between the left panel and the center. Nevertheless, what we have is certainly suggestive for anyone who has studied the works of Eliade concerning alchemy.[30] The general impression is of an iron worker (left panel) who is engaged in making weapons of war, among them the famous *kris*—a weapon believed to have mystical properties. At the far right is a figure of a person working the bellows that keep the fire burning hot. What seems totally out of place is the rather strange dancing elephant and dog in the center panel.

A closer look allows us to see the weapons being made more clearly, just to the right of the iron worker's head. They are obviously swords and axes used in battle, minus their wooden hilts. Above the figures of the swords are enigmatic symbols that some observers claim are mystical signs associated with the creation of weapons.

Looking yet more closely, in the photo on page 177, we can see that those symbols are tridents (usually associated with Shiva), a sword shape, an hourglass-

30 Mircea Eliade, *The Forge and the Crucible* (Chicago: University of Chicago Press, 1962, 1978).

An evil goddess or witch is represented at Prambanan suckling two imps on her rather tubular breasts.

OPPOSITE ABOVE: *Relief at Candi Sukuh suggestive of the manufacture of weapons of war.*
OPPOSITE BELOW: *Detail showing swords and axes.*
ABOVE: *Close-up showing tridents associated with Shiva and other weapons.*

type figure, and several serpentine forms. The author has yet to see a convincing identification of these figures.

As reference to Eliade's work suggests, the presence of these reliefs at a Tantric temple may not be as out of place as it seems:

> In our view, one of the principle sources of alchemy is to be sought in those conceptions dealing with the Earth-Mother, with ores and metals, and, above all, with the experience of primitive man engaged in mining, fusion and smithcraft. ... Now these techniques were at the same time mysteries, for, on the one hand, they implied the sacredness of the cosmos and, on the other, were transmitted by initiation ... mining and metallurgy put primitive man into a universe steeped in sacredness.[31]

Eliade identifies alchemy and alchemical processes with ceremonial initiation, as well as with psycho-biological processes, and rightly understands that Indian alchemy and Tantra are linked.[32] By completing the circle with metallurgy and smithcraft, Eliade has given us a tool for understanding the role that this relief plays in such an erotically charged Tantric temple as Candi Sukuh. The German Tibetologist Siegbert Hummel goes even further when he demonstrates that the blacksmith represents fertility and shamanic initiation in Tibet, a country with close ties to Java, as we have seen.[33]

We can as easily identify the figure at the far right of the relief as operating a churn as a bellows, and it was the churning of the ocean that gave us the water of life, the sacred amrita. The iron worker on the left panel is transforming the raw material of the earth into items sacred to Shiva, a process analogous to human procreation. The kris—the long knife (or short sword) familiar to anyone who has spent time in the region—has long been understood to represent Shiva and the vital life force. The mysticism surrounding this iconic Indonesian and Malaysian weapon is profound and extensive. Even such a well-known personality as Gerald Gardner (1884–1964), founder of the modern Wicca or Witchcraft movement that bears his name, wrote a monograph on the kris during his sojourn in the archipelago that is still reprinted today in studies of this enigmatic device.[34]

---

31 Eliade, *The Forge and the Crucible,* p. 142–143.

32 Eliade, *The Forge and the Crucible,* p. 127–141.

33 Siegbert Hummel, "Der Goettliche Shmied in Tibet," *Folklore Studies* Vol. 19, (1960) pp. 251–272.

34 See G. B. Gardner, "Notes on Two Uncommon Varieties of the Malay Keris," in *The Keris and Other Malay Weapons* (Kuala Lumpur(?): MBRAS Reprint Number 16, n.d.), reprinted from *The Malaysian*

To Indonesians or Malaysians, the kris (sometimes spelled *keris* or *kriss*) is equivalent to the Arthurian Excalibur. The knife often (but not always) has a wavy, serpentine blade that is immediately recognizable. A kris must be made by a qualified craftsman who is also part shaman. It is a sacred duty, to be begun on propitious days and tied to the personality of its owner; the knife itself is believed to embody the maker's soul or spirit, his shakti. Like Excalibur, it is a personal weapon; not everyone can lift the sword from the stone. No one should touch or use another's kris, except under particular circumstances. They are worn by sultans and (male) members of noble households on ceremonial occasions. They can be very simple, or as ornate as possible, their scabbards studded with precious gems and cased in gold and silver.

That the kris has peculiar characteristics is something to which the author can readily attest. Once, in the city of Melaka in Malaysia, he was browsing through a small curio shop crowded with the usual odds and ends, souvenirs, and bric-a-brac. On one shelf, behind rows of tiny figurines and other precariously arranged merchandise, was a simple wooden kris. He noticed it, but did not retrieve it for a closer look (worried as he was that he would knock down an intervening row of delicate clay figurines in the process). Instead, as he made to leave the aisle, the kris "fell" off the shelf and landed on the floor directly in front of him.

The sheer impossibility of this was astonishing. None of the merchandise that blocked the knife had moved or been disturbed in any way. It was as if the kris had flown over them from the back of the shelf and through the very narrow space between the figurines and the next shelf above them. (For what it's worth, this took place on October 31. Halloween, however, is not a holiday celebrated in that predominantly Muslim country.) Of course, the author felt compelled to purchase the kris, which is shown in the photo on page 180.

The panel in the controversial relief shown above that contains the elephant and the dog has given rise to all sorts of speculation. The author believes it refers to one of the stories in the Jataka—the tales of the previous incarnations of the Buddha, some of which are depicted on the panels at Borobudur. In this case,

Branch of the Royal Asiatic Society (MBRAS), December 1933. Gardner spent eleven years in Ceylon (now Sri Lanka) and Borneo (Kalimantan) and then twenty-five years in what was then called Malaya, conducting numerous archaeological digs on his own, notably at Johore. He then returned to England, where he founded the Gardnerian witchcraft movement and wrote several books on witchcraft. He opened a witchcraft museum on the Isle of Man and was a colleague of Aleister Crowley, who initiated him to the VIIth degree of the OTO.

Magical kris purchased by author.

the Jataka in question is the *Abhinha Jataka,* which is quite short.[35] In the story, a dog befriends an elephant. The dog eats whatever falls from the elephant's mouth and grows fat in the process. Gradually, the elephant becomes aware of the dog and they develop a close friendship. It should be noted that this is no ordinary elephant, but the elephant of state—a member of the royal retinue.

One day, however, the mahout (the man in charge of the elephant) sells the dog. The elephant falls into a deep depression, and no one knows why. Finally, a wise man discovers the truth and asks the king to demand that the dog be returned, or else a penalty will be imposed on the owner. This is done, and the dog and the elephant live happily ever after.

According to this Jataka, the dog was a lay disciple of the Master (the Buddha). The elephant was an aged Elder, and the wise man was the Buddha himself.

35 A translation of this Jataka appears in Robert Chalmers, *The Jataka, Volume 1* (Oxford: n.p., 1895), p. 69–70.

This story was told as an illustration of reincarnation, for the frame of the tale concerns several monks remarking on how close a lay disciple and an Elder are and wondering at its meaning. The Buddha tells them that they knew each other in a previous life, as a dog and an elephant.

What relevance does this episode—from an anomalous Buddhist and not a Hindu or Javanese source—have for Candi Sukuh? Is it another allegory of the political situation? Since we seem to be missing at least one of the relevant panels, we may never get to the bottom of this mystery. Is it possible that the elephant represents the Majapahit kingdom, and the dog represents the kingdom's subjects, who have been "bought" by the evil Queen Suhita? Does the restoration of the dynasty by force—the iron worker making an arsenal of weapons—represent the king demanding the return of the dog, under dire penalty?

Realizing that Candi Sukuh is a temple, and a Tantric one at that, it is necessary to look a level or two deeper. We have seen that the panels showing the manufacture of weapons at an ironsmith's anvil is a metaphor for the alchemical—i.e., Tantric—process. The other erotically charged emblems at the site reinforce the idea that this was not the place to make a naked political statement, but a machine in stone for effecting cosmic change and transmutation. A necessary quality of the "twilight language" is that it can refer to multiple layers of meaning simultaneously. A political illustration is also an alchemical figure, is also a Tantric yantra or mandala, is also a spiritual truth.

The Bird-Men of Candi Sukuh

The stonework at Sukuh is awash in references to amrita, to the transformation of gods into demons and back again, and surprisingly to the practice of Kundalini yoga, the art of transforming physical energy into spiritual force. Let us look at some of these examples before we come to any conclusions.

First, let us examine the "bird-men," which some assume to represent Garuda. These figures—most of them missing their heads and thus causing more difficulty in identification—are usually associated with the gathering of amrita from the Nagas, or serpents. They seem strangely humanoid, unlike the usual depictions of Garuda. In some cases, they are shown standing on serpents, which is a direct reference to the story of Garuda and his seizure of the amrita from the Nagas. Some have talons; others, like the one on page 182, seem to have human feet and hands, although they all have wings.

A "bird-man" statue at Candi Sukuh.

A "bird-man" at Candi Sukuh, standing on serpents.

Garuda holding an elephant and turtle in his talons.

The relief opposite shows Garuda holding an elephant and a turtle in his talons, a reference to the tale of Garuda in the *Mahabharata* that occurs immediately before he is sent to retrieve the amrita from the Nagas, the serpent gods.

The photo opposite and the two photos below clearly show the Nagas at the base of one of the reliefs and one at the entrance to the complex, thus reinforcing the idea that at least some of these bird-men are Garuda and that the theme of the statuary is amrita.

Serpent gods or Nagas at the base of a Garuda relief.

Nagas at the entrance to the temple complex.

Massive turtles at Candi Sukuh above and opposite.

Now let us look at the massive stone turtles that are one of Sukuh's most impressive features. The next three images show stylized turtles at the base of the temple entrance. The last shows, in a close-up, sticks of incense inserted in the ground next to the turtle.

The turtle has a special significance, of course. It was on the back of the turtle that the Churning of the Milk Ocean took place, so their appearance at Sukuh only serves to reinforce the idea that the purpose of the temple was the collection of amrita. Many authorities believe that these statues served some function as offering tables or altars. Another scholar, however, has offered a different interpretation of the turtles at Sukuh and it is worth considering.

Victor M. Fic was a Czech student at the end of World War II who escaped to Canada at the time of the Communist takeover, after having been arrested and sent to prison. He became involved in Asian studies and, in the 1960s, was executive secretary of the Institute of Southeast Asia at the prestigious Nanyang University in Singapore. Fic has written extensively on Communism and Eastern European politics on the one hand, and on Asian religion, culture, and politics on

Note sticks of incense sticking in the ground.

the other. His special interest seems to be Indonesia, and he has published several books on that country. In one of these, he makes the startling claim that the turtles of Candi Sukuh represent nothing less than an esoteric maneuver from Tantra yoga known as the *vajroli* mudra.[36]

According to the *Shiva Samhita*—a core text of Hatha yoga that has influenced generations of scholars and practitioners alike—the vajroli mudra is "the secret of all secrets, the destroyer of the darkness of samsara."[37] The term *vajroli* comes from the word *vajra*, or "thunderbolt" (in Tibetan, *dorje*). In order to prevent the loss

---

36 Victor M. Fic, *The Tantra: Its Origins, Theories, Art and Diffusion From India to Nepal, Tibet, Mongolia, China, Japan and Indonesia* (New Delhi: Abhinav Publications, 2003), p. 68–69.

37 James Mallinson, trans., *The Shiva Samhita: A Critical Edition* (Woodstock, NY: YogaVidya.com, 2007), p. 95. *Samsara* in the above citation refers to the endless cycle of birth and rebirth, liberation from which practices like yoga, Tantra, etc. seek to accomplish.

of psycho-spiritual energy, yogins attempt to restrict the flow of semen during sex using various methods. Some of these permit orgasm but restrict ejaculation, instead diverting the ejaculate back into the body using one of two methods. The first, called *sahajoli* mudra, involves blocking the urethra in such a way that the seminal fluid flows into the bladder, from where the grosser physical elements are eventually expelled, but not the rarer, spiritualized elements. The second, known as *amaroli* mudra, uses the penis as a kind of vacuum cleaner to draw the ejaculated semen as well as any fluid discharge of the female partner—a mixture of male and female fluids known as the amrita—back into the male body. These methods are subsumed under the rubric of vajroli mudra, the "thunderbolt" mudra.

In both cases, yogins train by exercising various muscle groups, contracting the urethral muscles used to restrict the flow of urine (for example), or, in the case of yoginis (female practitioners of yoga), the vaginal muscles. The idea is to retain the energy that would otherwise be dissipated in the sexual act and redirect it upward along the nadis or etheric nerve channels in the body, activating the chakras along the way until the sacred marriage of Shakti (the energy) and Shiva (consciousness) takes place in the chakra in the brain, behind the eyes.

The relationship of the turtle to this process becomes clear if we think of how the turtle withdraws into its shell. This retraction mimics the retraction of the urethral or vaginal muscles during the vajroli mudra. Understanding that this mudra is the "secret of all secrets" and is at the very heart, not only of Hatha yoga, but of Kundalini yoga and Tantra, we can appreciate the importance of Candi Sukuh as a temple designed specifically to train its devotees in the most powerful of all Asian esoteric practices. This mudra is designed specifically to collect amrita—the commingled male and female essences that together guarantee immortality and liberation. It is represented in a temple complex surrounded by symbols of amrita and transformation. Should the temple ever be completely restored to its original design—complete with the many yonis and lingga—the overall effect would be deeply profound, for it would become obvious that Candi Sukuh was much more than a mysterious pile of rocks and stones, but was as important in its day as Chartres Cathedral was in France. They were both designed as a book of instruction, as well as engines of alchemical transformation. Although both monuments refer to the same process, they use different forms of the twilight language to do so. In the case of the Gothic cathedrals, the form the language takes is Biblical; in Candi Sukuh, the references are to Hindu-Javanese religion and scripture. The differences may reflect cultural distinctions and not a different process entirely.

At Sukuh, we find the fascinating relief on page 190, showing a personage holding two thunderbolts. Depictions of stylized thunderbolts, known as *vajra*

Figure holding two thunderbolts at Candi Sukuh.

or *dorje,* are rather rare in Javanese temples, so this one commands a great deal of interest, aside from its vaguely Central American appearance (another reason many visitors are reminded of Mayan temples when they see Candi Sukuh). Whether this figure is a king or a god is difficult to tell. He is standing on what seems to be a crescent moon, and is wearing a crown, reminding us of the famous Burney relief (shown on the opposite page), now at the British Museum, of a Mesopotamian goddess (Ishtar, or Ereshkigal?) or the demoness Lilittu (the original "Lilith").

In the Burney relief, the winged figure is depicted holding the "rod-and-ring" insignia in her two hands. This is believed to represent a measuring cord and rod, implements that the Sumerian goddess Inanna took with her during her descent into the Underworld. They were also given to the god Marduk—who defeated the dread monster Tiamat—as symbols of his authority and as weapons.

With her wings and taloned feet, the figure in the Burney relief easily could be the female version of the Garuda statues at Candi Sukuh. In fact, in one episode

The Burney relief with "rod-and-ring" insignia.

in the life of Garuda, he lifts an elephant and a turtle with his talons in order to devour them. As we have seen above, there is a relief at Sukuh that depicts this episode, and the iconography is reminiscent of the goddess in the Burney relief with her talons on the twin lions. There is even a similarity in the headdresses of the two.

The author is not suggesting there is a direct link between these two figures, but rather that the idea of half-human, half-birdlike creatures that descend into the Underworld to steal the secrets of immortality is a meme that deserves greater investigation than can be accomplished here. Either the two cultures—Mesopotamia and India—developed the same concept independently, or there was actual contact between the two at some remote period in history, either directly or through an intermediary culture. If the former, then the concept may reflect some common experience rooted in agricultural beliefs and practices of a chthonic (and perhaps lunar) nature.

Phallic image with palang insertions.

Ithyphallic image at Candi Sukuh.

Some of the other figures are more clearly phallic in nature, as the reliefs shown on pages 192 and 193 demonstrate. The photograph on page 192 shows a figure that is probably only partially restored. While the penis is not erect, it nevertheless shows the presence of the palang insertions discussed earlier. On page 193, we see a relief showing an ithyphallic creature holding two instruments. The one in his right hand seems to be a horn, but the one in his left hand is unidentified. The creature's open mouth may serve a functional purpose, for the dispensing of holy water or simply for drainage. Its posture calls to mind the ganas of Shiva that are found at Prambanan.

Then there is the famous statue of a headless man grasping his penis shown opposite. While the palang insertions can be seen just below the glans, what is not evident is any sign of other ornamentation or any means of identifying who this is supposed to be. The figure's stocky quality may lead us to believe that this is Bhima, and there is something on his right hand that adds some credence to this.

One of Bhima's characteristics is a long, curving thumbnail on his right hand. This is said to be his most important weapon, and it can be seen on a relief showing him lifting Kalantaka, one of the giants of the Underworld. There is some similarity between that depiction and this one, so it may be purely speculation at this point, but it is probably safe to say that this relatively unadorned statue represents Bhima. From the presence of incense sticks in front of the statue, we realize that the local Hindu population reverences this figure as much as any other in the Sukuh pantheon. Its placement is also significant—next to what appears to be a Bhima shrine, as shown in the photograph at the top of page 196. On either side of the shrine are figures in relief that appear to be standing on pedestals, with supplicants standing or kneeling before them. This is an image we will come across later.

Another side of the same shrine shows rows of figures, including some monstrous entities on the lower panel, one of whom displays a phallus with the palang inserts (see bottom photo on page 196).

Perhaps the simplest expression of the phallo-centric nature of Candi Sukuh, however, is the standing stone shown on page 197. It is possible that this stone predates the construction of Candi Sukuh, and that may be one of the reasons why Mount Lawu and this site in particular was chosen for the temple. Mount Lawu was said to be sacred before Sukuh was erected, and was a place where ascetics came to pray and meditate.

There is something carved at the top and side of the phallic stone, but the degree of weathering and erosion is so great that identification is difficult. One can hazard a guess, however, that it represents an animal of some sort, perhaps a serpent or something with a long hanging tail.

Headless figure at Candi Sukuh holding phallus with the palang.

ABOVE: *Bhima shrine at Candi Sukuh.*
BELOW: *Closeup of relief on the other side of shrine shown above.*

Ancient phallic stone at Candi Sukuh.

Phallic statues—although they are the features that usually dominate any discussion of Candi Sukuh—are only one aspect of the site, however. We have seen the multiple Garudas with their Nagas, and the giant turtle sculptures that may or may not represent the vajroli mudra; we have seen the forge where the ore from the earth is refined into sacred objects and the mysterious dancing elephant with his pet dog. We have also gazed at the reliefs that tell the Sudamala story, with their Durga and Bhima, their Semar and Kalantaka. But there is one final relief that demands our attention and it, too, is as mysterious as the rest of the complex. It is replete with symbolism and open to a variety of interpretations.

It is a large panel, shown opposite, ovoid in shape, suggesting the Greek letter *omega*. The shape is defined by the tails of two birds that meet at the top, where a wrathful Kala figure is seen as if it were guarding the entrance to a temple. Within the omega are two figures, standing on a serpent with two heads. One of the figures is on a pedestal, which implies divine status. The other figure is human and may represent Bhima. The divine figure is offering something to the human figure—and there has been some speculation that what is being offered is a flask containing the amrita whose collection is at the heart of the entire temple complex.

Once again, we are faced with an artistic expression that is unique in Java. This is not the standard Indian-inspired iconography of the other temples we have discussed so far. And, although the figures bear resemblance to the wayang-style designs of the Sudamala reliefs, the overall composition of the panel is quite strange. Due to the restoration work on the site that has been proceeding on and off for decades, we cannot say for certain that the panel is even in its original location. Its association with Bhima and the symbols of birds and serpents, however, seem to emphasize its relation to the amrita theme.

Another possibility is that the ovoid shape represents what, in the West, is called a *vesica piscis*. The association of this shape with female emblems and symbolism is well-known, and it may represent the vaginal opening. This would not be out of the question at a site that contains "scores" of yonis. If this analysis is correct, then the figures within the ovoid—a double-headed serpent, a god on pedestal, a human receiving amrita—are consistent and may illustrate the actual practice of mingling the male and female essences in the vagina of the yogini in order to extract the elixir vitae.

Scholars have noted the many ways in which Candi Sukuh does not fit the traditional criteria of Hindu-Javanese design. One theory is that the truncated pyramid style of Sukuh was intended to replace the traditional tri-partite Indian mandala model of Underworld/world/heaven with a simpler this-world/other-world design. The top of the truncated pyramid may be the "interstice" between

The ovoid shape of the large panel is formed by the tail of two birds.

the two worlds—the place where the king or high priest met with the gods.[38] Whereas Borobudur, for instance, is a model of Mount Meru, Candi Sukuh seems to represent a more functional architectural design that is concerned more with magic than religion—with the summoning of supernatural powers and attaining illuminated status in the here-and-now rather than in numberless incarnations. There is no sign of Buddhism at this site, other than the rather anomalous ele-

38 See for instance Timothy E. Behrend, "Kraton and Cosmos in Traditional Java," *Archipel.* Volume 37, 1989, pp. 173–187.

Side view of the pyramid.

phant-and-dog relief that seems to represent a story from the Jataka that may have become part of Javanese sacred literature purely on its own merits.

This is Javanese spirituality pared down to its bare essentials. It was clearly understood, at this late date in Hindu-Javanese culture and political hegemony, that amrita was the key to the mysteries, and that time had run out for the patient wooing of divine succor from above. Although many previous monarchs had been active in the practice of Tantra, as we have seen, at this late stage in the last Hindu-Javanese dynasty, the impulse was stripped of its "higher" spiritual accoutrements and reduced to pure alchemy.

> Even more interesting is the fact that in the ... Bhima relief from Candi Sukuh the existence of a sanctuary with purifying water is brought into prominence. The relation between Bhima and the elixir of life is evident from contemporary literature concerning Bhima ...[39]

39 Marijke Duijker, *The Worship of Bhima: the representations of Bhima on Java during the Majapahit Period* (Amsterdam: EON Pers Amstelveen, 2010), p. 192.

View from the top of the pyramid.

The image above and the one on page 200, give two different views of Candi Sukuh: the first is a side view of the "pyramid"; the second is a view from the top.

When viewing the site from the entrance, as in the photo on page 202, the anomalous design is plain to see, keeping in mind that the landscaping is new and not part of the original site. In this photograph, the terraces are easily discerned. The temple is on the western slope of Mount Lawu and thus this entrance faces east.

ABOVE: *Terraces at entrance of the temple on the western slope of Mount Lawu.*
OPPOSITE: *A close-up of the entrance showing the two guardians flanking the steps.*

The photograph on page 203 gives us a closer look at the narrow staircase and its two guardians.

Both Candi Ceto and Candi Sukuh were sanctuaries that had water purification and the elixir of life as their most salient characteristic. This process was not the simple "immersion" type of baptism known to generations of Christians, or even the *mikvah,* or ritual bath, of the Jewish religion. This process was buttressed by symbols implying a grand, sacred project of tremendous importance and energy. Guardian statues abound, as well as images of Garuda, the serpents, and the turtles. These were not temples devoted to ablutions as a preliminary rite, but sites sacred to the very idea of amrita as transformative. An inscription at Candi Ceto concerning purification reinforces this idea in a profound way:

> The first part of this inscription is similar to the Sukuh inscription, but has a few added words at the end, *hawaki ra ya hilangi,*

> which translates into "the disappearance of the body." This has no other meaning than the deliverance of the immaterial soul from the material body.[40]

The phrase "disappearance of the body," which is said to take place through the rituals of amrita at Candi Sukuh, has levels of meaning that may transcend the concept of the deliverance of the soul from the cycles of samsara. This "disappearance" is what takes place during the ritual of the *pancatattva,* or "five elements," which culminates in maithuna: the ritual sex act. For the rite to be successful, both partners must become gods. Their physical bodies are transcended in the act and their grosser elements disappear in the process of marrying Shakti to Shiva. Otherwise, why would a temple devoted to purification be surrounded by emblems of lingga and yoni? Traditional Western ideas of baptism by water are pale imitations of the type of purification that is required by the *acharyas* or priests of Sukuh.

What is also noteworthy about the system of symbolization at Candi Sukuh is that the male and female elements are always shown separated. There are massive phalluses and the many (missing) yonis, but aside from the single relief of the lingga-yoni at point of penetration at the very entrance to the complex, there is no overt depiction of the sex act. When we remember some of the more blatant imagery found in India, and particularly at the famous Khajuraho temple in Madhya Pradesh with its countless depictions of men and women cavorting in a variety of sexual positions, the system at Candi Sukuh seems to be purely utilitarian and functional. Sukuh is not a temple devoted to sexual pleasure and eroticism, but to the deliberate use of sexual functions for a different purpose and in a different context. The stress is entirely on the collection of amrita, which is also the central obsession of the Western alchemists, as well as of the Chinese Daoist alchemists. Immortality and transformation are the key elements here, in a remote temple that was designed as a very serious application of Tantra to spiritual growth and political stability, seen as different manifestations of the same process—and at a time of tremendous cultural and political tension.

40 Duijker, *The Worship of Bhima,* p. 189. See also the Śrīsrirāmakṛṣṇakathāmṛta, III, 141–142, as cited in Edward C. Dimock, Jr., *The Place of the Hidden Moon: Erotic Mysticism in the Vaisnava-Sahajiya Cult of Bengal* (Chicago: University of Chicago Press, 1989), p. 179 for the concept that the yogin is no longer conscious of his body in this state of samadhi brought about by the practice of Kundalini yoga.

Chapter 6

Candi Ijo and the Creation of the World

High on a hill overlooking Yogyakarta and the airport is a temple complex now largely in ruin. Built in the terraced style of Candi Ceto and Candi Sukuh, this was evidently once an important spiritual center. This complex dates to the end of the ninth century, however, and as such is actually contemporary with Borobudur and Prambanan and about 500 years older than Candi Ceto and Candi Sukuh. The highlight of the complex is the enormous lingga-yoni in the main building, with a few discrete bas-reliefs of Shiva and Uma depicting the moment of the creation of the world.

I visited the site on a rainy spring day, after a hazardous ride up the dirt road that clung, sometimes precariously, to the side of the mountain. The temple was

Main building in temple complex of Candi Ijo.

deserted and the rain had just stopped. The silence was impressive and a little unsettling. There was a sense of presence, something otherworldly, about the place. Why that should be was not immediately apparent, since, at first glance, Candi Ijo (the "Green" temple, named after its location on Green Hill) is similar to many other temples I had visited in Java over the past four years. Perhaps the utter lack of tourists or other visitors contributed to the solemn feeling that was generated by the rain-swept stones and the glaring Kalas over the temple entrances.

Then, as I prepared to take photographs of the site, there came the sound of a great buzzing of insects that suddenly rose up all around the silent shrines. This, combined with the gloom of the morning and the feeling of isolation from the rest of the world, almost made me forget my purpose in coming there.

In fact, according to legend, the site is inhabited by a Naga called Kyai Poleng, who manages a flock of doves that the villagers claim can sometimes be heard flying at night.[41]

As mentioned, the site dates to the late ninth century CE. It is not imposing in the sense of Borobudur or Prambanan, with their hundreds of detailed reliefs and enormous statues to the gods. Instead, this complex—which originally encompassed eleven terraces and is now reduced to only a few—is simple in design and construction. It, too, has suffered from tremendous deterioration and ruin over the centuries, and has tolerated a degree of restoration work in places. The four main structures have been wholly or almost wholly restored, and these comprise the main building and three ancillary buildings facing it.

The main sanctuary, which houses the lingga-yoni, is quite impressive in its simplicity. The lingga-yoni structure is about nine feet tall—the yoni about six feet high and the lingga another three feet on top of that. It towered over me, and I am almost six feet tall. The most interesting aspect of this structure, aside from its enormous size, is the carving of the snake and the turtle holding up the spout of the yoni. We shall return to this in a moment.

The three buildings that face the main structure are believed to have housed statues of the Trimurti—Brahma, Shiva, and Vishnu—but this really does not seem to be the case. Perhaps due to "creative" restoration, one of the buildings houses a Nandi bull—the vehicle of Shiva—next to a pedestal on which there is no statue at all.

In another of the three buildings, there is only what appears to be a fire pit, probably for the Homa sacrifice. And in the last of the three buildings, there is a

41 See Sasono, Elbaz, and Ardyanto, *Situs-Situs Marjinal* [Sites out of Sight] (Yogyakarta: PT Enrique Indonesia, 2002), p. 35.

The main structure in background with three smaller structures in foreground.

simple yoni, minus lingga or any other statue. If the three buildings represented the Trimurti at some point, those associations have since been lost.

In the photograph above, you see the main structure in the background and the three smaller structures in the foreground. There is a utility pole marring the view, whose purpose was not revealed to me during my visit.

Below is a closer view, with the main temple in the background and the smaller temple housing the Nandi and pedestal in the foreground. The wall that surrounds the four temples is easily visible, as well as another terrace a level down.

Closer view of the main temple in background and smaller temple in foreground.

Some detail of the wall and roof of the main temple contain motifs familiar from the shrines at Prambanan like the Kalas, the carved pillars on the reliefs, and some of the ornamentation. There are a few figures in asana barely visible in the niches on the roof of the structure, but the main niches in the walls are all empty.

The photos below show two empty niches in the wall of the main temple. The familiar Kala is there, as well as some carving above it of buildings that may represent Mount Meru, judging from the triangular shape of the relief, which suggests a hill or mountain. The niche at right shows most of the same features.

The entrance to the main temple housing the lingga-yoni is shown opposite. It has the dvarapala at the top and makaras at either side, as well as the pyramidal shape of the roof, which once again suggests Mount Meru.

The lingga-yoni in the main temple at Candi Ijo is shown on page 210. As we will see in a moment, there are two small reliefs on the wall behind the structure, one on the right showing Uma and one on the left showing Shiva.

To stand in this temple, in the presence of this device, is truly moving. There is a heaviness about the place and the same eerie sense of presence felt at the site is enhanced or magnified when standing inside this building. It is difficult to describe a sensation that is at once claustrophobic and somehow menacing. One

Two empty niches in the wall of the main temple with dvarapals and makaras.

Entrance to the main temple.

is reminded of the phrase *Terribilis est locus iste* that one finds in the chapel at Rennes-le-Chateau. The large Naga serpent holding up the yoni only contributes to the feeling that one is in the presence of forces ancient and potent, and largely incomprehensible to the intellectual faculties.

The photo on page 211 gives a closer look at the serpent and turtle holding up the yoni. What is remarkable about this arrangement is that it differs from other lingga-yoni designs in which the turtle is at the base supporting the serpent—which would be consistent with the Churning of the Milk Ocean, in which the turtle supports the entire operation. The author submits that this design is deliberate, and refers back to the significance of the turtle in Kundalini yoga and in

The lingga-yoni in the main temple of Candi Ijo.

Tantra, representing the vajroli mudra. This placement of the serpent—obviously a phallic reference—below the turtle may indicate just that practice.

The relief on the top of page 212 shows the goddess Uma, riding on a cloud and carrying objects in her hands that resemble *damaru*—the Tibetan drum made from two conjoined skulls. The reference is somewhat obscure, for the gods are rarely shown flying on clouds. The implication is that the events being related took place before the creation of the world, before there was dry land. The author was fortunate that is was raining when he took this photo, for the water dripping onto the relief made it more visible in the meager light available in the building.

He was not so fortunate in the relief shown at the bottom of page 212. Here Shiva is also on a cloud, and also holding similar objects in his hands. That these

Turtle supporting the yoni resting on the head of a serpent.

may be containers of amrita is a distinct possibility, for the creation of the world between Shiva and Uma required an act of sexual intercourse that is not exactly what may generally be understood as intercourse.

In virtually every episode in which Shiva and Uma "mingle essences," Shiva rarely penetrates Uma in the usual fashion. Instead, his seed falls either in her mouth or her hand.[42] Occasionally, it falls to the ground, where it creates monsters or, in one version, Skanda (also known as Kartikeya, one of Shiva's two sons, the

42 Wendy Doniger O'Flaherty, *Śiva: The Erotic Ascetic* (Oxford: Oxford University Press, 1973, 1981), p. 271: "Even when Pārvatī receives the seed, she receives it not in her womb but in her mouth or hand."

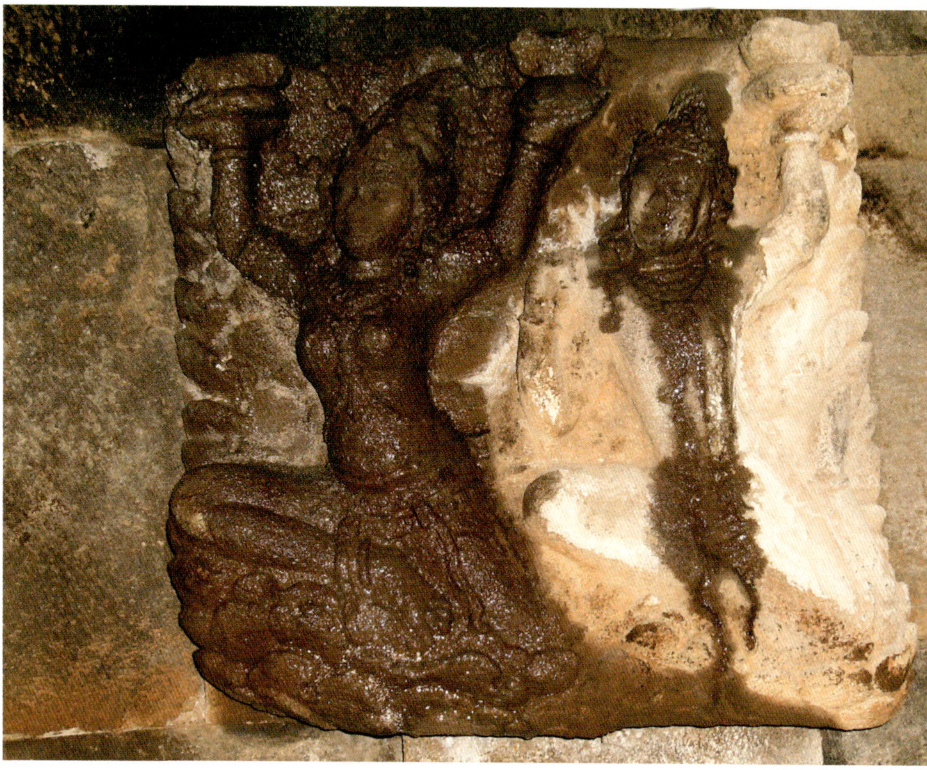

ABOVE: *The goddess Uma riding on a cloud on the wall at right of the lingga-yoni.*
BELOW: *Shiva is also shown riding on a cloud on the wall at left.*

other being Ganesha). Shiva has the reputation of being an ascetic and hermit. He is normally portrayed naked or wearing animal skins; his hair is matted and his flesh covered in ashes. He wears snakes for belts. He remains in a state of silent meditation for aeons at a time and does not like to be disturbed. When he is disturbed, there is danger of his third eye opening—the dread Eye of Shiva that has enormous destructive power.

Yet, Shiva also has the reputation of being excessively sexual. He embodies both extremes of sexuality: complete renunciation and a total, aggressive lust (*kama*). He is often in a state approaching madness and intoxication—that is, when he is not sitting in asana and lost in trance. According to one version of the tale, when Shiva and Uma first had intercourse, that single act lasted for more than 1000 years. The other gods became so anxious over this excessive length of time that they used various means to try to interrupt them. One of these methods involved singing Shiva's praises outside the chamber where he and Uma were in passionate embrace. When Shiva withdrew from Uma in order to see what the singing was about, his seed—which, until then, he had retained—fell onto the ground, making a golden pile. Agni, the God of Fire, saw it and consumed it before Uma/Parvati could seize it. The end result was that all the male gods became pregnant, which was painful for two reasons. In the first and most obvious place, a pregnant male presumably is not a happy male; in the second place, the seed of Shiva burned like fire itself.

Books have been written in the attempt to decipher many of these legends, not only from a historical or religious perspective, but also from Freudian and Jungian perspectives, as well as a wide variety of other approaches. Part of the problem lies in the fact that there is no single, coherent narrative. The *Rig Veda* is one source, the Puranas another. Then there are the Tantras themselves, which are dialogues between Shiva and Shakti that add new material that may be at variance or inconsistent with the older texts. However, once we realize that even the oldest book of the Abrahamic religions, Genesis, contains two separate and conflicting versions of the Creation myth, we are forced to accept the fact that, even though there may be inconsistent versions of the same legend, that does not devalue any particular one of them. Instead, we have to analyze the texts in an attempt to identify both the similarities and the differences, and understand why the differences exist and what they can tell us.

As we have seen, the Javanese versions of the Indian epics are substantially different from the originals. In the case of Candi Ijo—which was built at the same time as the more orthodox Prambanan—we have two reliefs that express a story concerning Shiva and Uma and display emblems for which we have no immediate explanation. The deities seated on clouds are one anomaly; the vessels they carry are another. Authorities are generally in agreement that the reliefs reference the Creation; and where Shiva and Uma are concerned, creation always implies the seed of Shiva.

As we saw in the previous chapter, there was an intense preoccupation with the elixir of life, amrita, at the late Majapahit temple sites. At those sites, the important figures were Bhima, Garuda, Durga, and the Nagas, with some assistance from Semar. Although we know that Durga is Uma and that Uma was cursed by Shiva, we do not see Shiva represented at these later temples except in the form of lingga. The legends depicted at Ceto and Sukuh are concentrated on amrita—immortality—and not on creation. At Ijo, on the other hand, the relationship between Shiva and Uma is more explicit and their presence in the main temple at either side of the large lingga-yoni reinforces the idea that the temple is dedicated to their mystical union. We may say that creation necessarily precedes immortality, and that the unifying characteristic between them is this mysterious substance called amrita, which, somehow, is equated with human sexuality.

As the first "couple," Shiva and Uma are the source of all created beings. While Brahma is usually called the Creator, Vishnu the Preserver, and Shiva the Destroyer, one version of the myth in the *Shiva Purana* has Brahma unable to create until Shiva—who is originally androgynous, a form called *Ardhanarishvara* (from the Sanskrit root *ardha* which means "half")—cleaves himself in half and then mates with his female side, his Shakti who is Parvati and Uma. Thus Shiva bears the connotation, not only of destruction, but also of regeneration. Shiva destroys his original nature in order to reproduce.

The lingga is the symbol par excellence of Shiva. It is the source of the seed of Shiva that—when combined with the yoni of Parvati/Uma—produces the amrita of immortality. The Churning of the Milk Ocean is widely understood to be a metaphor for the sexual act, just as the fire stick—whose friction creates fire—is a sexual metaphor. The aeons-long intercourse of Shiva and Uma was said to create enormous heat, which was one of the reasons the gods did what they could to stop it. That the God of Fire, Agni, consumed the spilled semen of Shiva resonates with this concept.

The enormous lingga-yoni at the main temple at Candi Ijo is easily understood to represent the churn that produced the amrita and, in fact, the water that is poured over the lingga is collected from the spout of the yoni and used as the "water of life." Thus, there is a deliberate attempt to equate the creation story of Shiva and Uma with the lingga-yoni and amrita.

In a Tantric context, this act of creation is replicated in the practice of Kundalini yoga. The goddess at the base of the spine—actually, at the base of the *sushumna* nadi, which is analogous to the spine—rises up the seven worlds (called *bhumi*) or chakras to the sixth chakra at the level of the so-called "third eye" (the cranial vault), where she mates with Shiva, resulting in the spiritual orgasm at the seventh chakra that produces the flow or "rain" of amrita (*amritavarsa*) that descends throughout the body. That the goddess takes the form of a serpent is not as strange as it may seem. The religion of Java, for instance, is replete with serpent-goddesses who mate with human males.

Kundalini yoga, however, is an individual practice designed for yogins who retain their semen and cause it to ascend to the level of the head without the assistance of a female partner. In the Tantric rituals that incorporate sex, semen is also retained, ideally, by the yogin through various means, as we saw in the previous chapter, and made to ascend the same channel, the sushumna. However, great value is also placed on the female excretions, which are considered essential to the production of amrita. The mingling of these two substances is called *maharasa* or "great fluid." What is not usually discussed so bluntly is that the actual physical elements—if produced by trained practitioners—are as valuable as the internalized ones, which is why the vajroli mudra is so critical to the ritual.

While the processes typified by Kundalini yoga are designed to result in an individual's attainment of that intense stage of meditation known as *samadhi*, those that are represented by the Tantric ritual of the Five Ms—the *pancatattva*—may have more mundane applications as well as spiritual ones. The distinction simply may be the distinction between mysticism and magic, as discussed in the first chapter. In the West, we have the tendency to view mysticism as a solitary practice, something that concerns hermits and saints. We do not understand it as a group effort, or as something in which there is a partner. We may accept a guru-chela (disciple) relationship, but not one in which there are two equal partners of opposite gender cooperating in a single mystical effort. Mystics are solitaries, in the Western worldview. They are usually not members of societies or fraternal orders.

Tantra offers a range of options, however. There are dualist and non-dualist sects, Shiva sects and Shakti sects. There are solitary, mystical approaches and those that require a partner. There are those that include sexual intercourse, alcohol, and consumption of animal flesh as well as (possibly) entheogens, and those that proscribe these practices. Yet, in the final analysis, Tantra is all about method and less about dogma. Mantra, mudra, yantra—these are the basic, sensory elements in virtually all forms of Tantric practice, which indicates that the manipulation of reality through what the French poet Rimbaud called the "derangement of the senses" is at the heart of what Tantra is really all about. Whether this manipulation is for spiritual enlightenment or for more mundane, magical goals is up to the users of these systems. We are told that the acquisition of occult powers is a kind of side-effect of the practice and should not be sought after for its own sake. The opposite is probably also true—that the pursuit of magical or occult powers will result in some form of spiritual enlightenment.

At Candi Ceto and Candi Sukuh, it seems likely that the pursuit of amrita was motivated at least as much by real-world concerns as it was by a purely spiritual longing. At Candi Ijo, however, the mundane applications may not be so apparent to the casual observer. It was built, after all, at a time when the Hindu-Javanese project was strong and unchallenged. But fertility and creation have always been concerns, especially to an agriculturally based civilization, and the worship of the forces of nature has always been seen as a necessity. With Garuda and the Nagas so prominent at Candi Sukuh, we can understand that the theft or seizure of amrita from the serpent gods was the operating principle; at Candi Ijo, there is no theft of amrita, but the actual creation of it by Shiva and Uma. For that reason, if for no other, Candi Ijo is sacred ground.

Directly across from the main temple at Candi Ijo is a smaller temple that houses Shiva's mount, the bull Nandi. The photo on opposite page shows the Nandi temple from the doorway of the main temple. Because Nandi is present here, it is assumed that the temple is dedicated to Shiva himself, especially as there is a pedestal next to Nandi that is unoccupied. As at the main temple, the Shiva-Nandi temple has the usual dvarapala head atop the entrance and makaras to the sides.

Inside this temple are the Nandi and the pedestal, as shown opposite.

There is very little space inside this building for both of these objects, so it is a safe assumption that the Nandi is not in its original place. It may have been erected outside this temple, with the pedestal placed in the center with a statue of Shiva on top. As we will see in a look at the newest temple discovery, Candi Kimpulan, it is not unusual to have a Nandi statue outside in the elements.

The photograph on page 218 shows the pedestal and the limited amount of space around it.

Next to the Nandi temple, to the left of it facing the row of three ancillary temples from the main doorway, is another temple with only a yoni present, shown on page 219. If theorists are correct, this would have been the Brahma temple. As we saw at Prambanan, the statue would have been placed on top of the yoni so that the priests could pour water over the feet of the statue. The water then dripped

ABOVE: *Nandi temple as seen from the doorway of the main temple at Candi Ijo.*
BELOW: *Nandi, the bull upon which Shiva rode, is housed inside with an empty pedestal next to it.*

This photograph of the empty pedestal in the Nandi temple conveys a sense of the limited amount of space in the room where it is housed.

Yoni found in the small building that may have been a Brahma temple.

Perforated window may be seen at the rear of this third ancillary temple.

into the yoni and, in that manner, become sanctified. Again, however, the yoni seems quite cramped in this small building.

The third ancillary temple is notable because of the perforated window at the rear. This photograph, taken from the front, shows the window on the rear wall.

On the next page is a closer view of the perforated window.

The purpose of the window was most likely to let out the smoke from a Homa sacrifice, as there is nothing in this temple except what appears to be a fire pit.

ABOVE: *Closer view of the perforated window.*
BELOW: *Fire pit of the Homa sacrifice.*

This outdoor fire pit for the Homa sacrifice is in the shape of a reversed pyramid.

Even here we can see the remains of some incense sticks that were burned in the pit, indicating that it is still in use.

Farther out, and down to a lower terrace level, there is a large pit obviously designed for the Homa sacrifice, for it is in the shape of a reverse pyramid, which is the typical form for a Homa fire pit. Note the difference in style between this fire pit and the one in the ancillary temple.

Thus, the original purpose of these temples is still not completely certain. Except for the main temple building that houses the lingga-yoni quite easily for its size, the designation of the other three ancillary temples as Brahma, Shiva, and Vishnu seems somewhat contrived. There is only a yoni in the Brahma temple, and it is a very tight fit. There is a bull and a pedestal in the Shiva temple, also a very tight fit. And in the Vishnu temple, there is a perforated window that suggests it was designed for the Homa sacrifice, even though its fire pit is not in the traditional reverse-pyramid design, but is rather a simple rectangle. The reverse-pyramid style was known to the builders of Candi Ijo, for there is a large one on one of the other terraces. Thus, we are faced with more mysteries.

ABOVE: *Note the size and sophistication of the terrace ruins of Candi Ijo.*
BELOW: *View of the ruins of the upper terrace where the main temple is located.*

A closer view of the terrace ruins shows the foundation of a structure.

The terraces are in near-total ruin, for the most part. The photographs opposite and above nonetheless give some sense of the size and sophistication of this site. It is well to remember that Candi Ijo is the name given to the site by recent generations because of its location on Mount Ijo. There is no record of its original name, nor of the people who built it.

The photo at top left on page 222 is a view of some of the ruins, as seen from the upper terrace where the main temple is located. Below it is a view of one of the terraces taken from a bit farther down the hill. Above, we see the ruin of the central structure.

As the top photo on page 224 shows, some of the foundations are more or less intact, but the walls themselves collapsed long ago. The restoration project is slow and woefully underfunded. The site does not attract the attention that Borobudur or Prambanan do, yet there seem to be as many as seventeen separate buildings located on at least eleven terraces here. Most of the statues have disappeared, and although there were some inscribed stones that made references to purification ceremonies, these were no longer in evidence when the author was there.

The stone shown at the bottom of page 224 would probably have appeared over the entrance to one of the ruined temples. For now, however, it sits ignominiously on the ground.

ABOVE: *Inscribed stones make reference to purification ceremonies.*
BELOW: *This carved relief would have been above the entrance to one of the temples.*

Some roof ornaments are visible in the background of these ruins, as are remnants of makaras at either side of the makeshift entrance.

This appears to have been a roof ornament with a lingga-like shape

Another perforated window suggest this building was used for the Homa sacrifice.

In the image shown on page 225, there are some roof ornaments visible in the background, and remnants of makaras at either side of the makeshift entrance that are a little difficult to make out due to the erosion.

The photo opposite gives us a closer look at the roof ornaments and at what might have been a lingga-like finial for the top.

The photo above shows another perforated window that suggests that the original purpose of this building was the Homa sacrifice, as the window would have let out the smoke.

And on page 228 is yet another of the many temples in a state of ruin.

Finally, the photo on page 229 shows the rear of the main temple at Candi Ijo. The dvarapala can clearly be seen in relief, as well as the elaborate ornamentation carved into the stone, including pillars like those at Prambanan. What is clearly evident, however, is the attempt at restoration that shows stones of various colors

Another of the many temples in a state of ruin.

and sizes pieced together like a jigsaw puzzle. This is common throughout the restoration work taking place in Java. There are simply too many stones, scattered over too large an area, and it becomes an impossible task to fit them precisely back where they originally belonged. In addition, villagers have taken stones from the collapsed buildings to use in other construction—a practice that is common worldwide.

A view of the rear of the main temple at Candi Ijo.

Postscript

As I was preparing to leave Candi Ijo, I decided to take some video footage of the site. I stood next to the main temple—the one housing the lingga-yoni—and simply panned the entire area around it. When I finished, I found that my camera had stopped working and was frozen in mid-function. I could not turn it off. None of the controls were working. So I removed the batteries, waited, and reinserted them. The camera worked fine after that.

When I got home, I decided to view the video footage. That was when I noticed that, every time the camera panned toward the main temple, there was an electronic stutter, like a minor short-circuit. It only happened when the video camera moved over the surface of the temple from its extensive pan of the surrounding terraces.

This peculiar malfunction has never happened before, or since. It was only at Candi Ijo that the camera acted strangely.

Chapter 7

Candi Kimpulan, the White Temple

On December 11, 2009 workers beginning an excavation for a new library at the Islamic University of Indonesia were startled to find that their backhoes had hit something quite solid. They had already dug down to a level about seven feet below the surface and had begun removing soil when they found that the soil was not as stable as they would have liked. They decided to dig down another twenty inches or so, and that is when they struck what they thought was solid rock. Instead, it turned out to be one of the most important archaeological discoveries of the decade.

The main and ancillary buildings at Candi Kimpulan, the White Temple.

A view of the archaeological site of Candi Kimpulan in the Spring of 2010 with a mosque in the background.

What they found were two completely intact Hindu temples, conservatively dated to the ninth or tenth century CE. What is important about this discovery is that it is the first time a temple from that period has been found in perfect condition, with the statues still standing in their original positions. At the other, more famous, sites like Borobudur or Prambanan—or even Candi Suku, Ceto, Ijo, or any of the others—there had been significant destruction of the buildings and deterioration of the stone reliefs, and the statues and pieces of statues were found scattered all over the landscape. Here, at the newly discovered site are two buildings—a main temple and a smaller ancillary temple—that still had a Nandi bull, an exquisite statue of Ganesha, a lingga-yoni, and some pedestals or altars, all in their original positions. It was as if someone had planted a time capsule almost three meters underground over 1000 years ago.

Another striking feature of this site is the fact that the stones are all com-

A closeup of the main building of the White Temple. Some damage may be seen to the yoni above. Note the convex circles that will be discussed on page 238. The statue of Ganesha was found on the pedestal to the right of the lingga-yoni

pletely white. As you have noticed from the other photographs in this book, the usual coloration of the andesite stonework is dark brown to dark grey. This is odd, because it is entirely possible—even probable—that the volcanic eruption that buried Borobudur in the ninth or tenth century CE was the same eruption that buried this site. Yet, the larger complex shows significant damage from the elements, while the smaller site is unbelievably pristine.

The temple, called the White Temple, is a small one, probably used by a local village. That it was a temple to Shiva is obvious from the Nandi (Shiva's mount), as well as the statue of Ganesha (one of Shiva's two sons). There is the ubiquitous lingga-yoni—one at each temple, which in itself is unusual—as well as some stranger features. In the first place, no statue of Shiva has been found so far at the site. That implies that it was taken into safe-keeping at the time of the eruption, but that is pure speculation on the author's part. Also, the walls of each building are rather high, yet there does not seem to be any means of entering the temples except through some rather narrow doorways that are missing staircases. It is

ABOVE: *A closer view of the main temple showing dvarapala heads at various intervals along the top of the wall.*
BELOW: *This is the smaller building showing two pedestals in front of lingga-yoni*

ABOVE: *A closer view of the smaller temple. Note pit at right that may have been a fire pit or used for the storage of water.*
BELOW: *Another angle of the small building showing the circle placements.*

ABOVE: *Another view of the larger temple building.*
BELOW: *View of the two buildings.*

ABOVE: *A close-up of the lingga-yoni.*
BELOW: *Another angle showing the high walls.*

possible that the staircases were made of wood that presumably disintegrated over the centuries, since the temples are also missing roofs.

In Bali, for example, it is not unusual to see wooden roofs erected over stone temples, so it is possible that this was the practice at this small temple as well. However, it raises the question: Why have no similar temples been found in Java?

On page 232 is a full view of the site as it appeared in the spring of 2010. You can see the imposing Islamic structure behind it, which is the university's mosque. That a temple to the Hindu god Shiva should be located so close to a mosque is one of the things about Indonesia in general that is fascinating and so endearing. University authorities have stated that they will build around the temple site and will attempt to incorporate it into the architecture. After all, they say, it is part of their culture and their heritage.

In the first photograph of the White Temple itself on page 233, you can see some damage to the yoni. It is not certain when this damage took place. The most intriguing elements, however, are the convex circles that dot the floors of both temples. Some are of the opinion that they were supports for wooden pillars holding up a wooden roof. If this were so, however, the circles would be flat. Some of them are, but others are clearly convex and could not have been used to support anything. Moreover, there is a vague sense that the circles were placed in a deliberately symmetrical fashion, which may imply either a more elaborate superstructure than has been imagined, or perhaps the representation of a constellation in stone.

All of this is pure speculation, of course. At this time, we have no way of knowing what these strange circles represent. They are not found at any of the other sites we have so far investigated and, since the general consensus is that this site is the best-preserved in all of Java, it would be very useful to know more about them. The Ganesha statue was found in this temple, in front of the lingga-yoni and facing the entranceway, but it was removed for safe-keeping due to the danger of relic hunters who sell these statues for a hefty profit on the black market.

The photograph at the top of page 234 gives a closer view of the main temple. You can see the dvarapala heads at various intervals along the top of the wall, as well as some small bas-reliefs at the putative doorways. If you look at those "doorways," you can see that they are completely self-contained and are rather more like window sills than doorways. It is still a mystery how anyone managed to get to the top of the temple, since so far there is no evidence of a ladder or stairway. One possible explanation is that the buildings were located in the middle of a body of water and accessible only by means of a small boat, but that may be too fanciful a suggestion.

At the bottom of page 234, the smaller building is shown, complete with the Nandi and another intact lingga-yoni. There are also two pedestals that appear to be lotus pedestals, upon which the statues of the gods would have been placed. There are two in this building, which implies that two statues are yet to be discovered.

At the top of page 235 is a closer view of the same building. Notice the pit on the right that may have been a fire pit, but also may have been used to store water for the temple ceremonics. The strange stone circles are present here as well, but in this case, they seem flat and utilitarian. They are at the four corners of the building, with one oddly placed circle near the main entrance. If it was used to hold up the roof, then someone walking onto the floor from the entrance would have had to walk around the roof support, which seems odd.

On the bottom of page 235 is another angle of the same building, showing the circle placements. As you can see, the circle closest to the entrance is in a problematic position if it is, indeed, a roof support.

The four photographs shown on pages 236–237 were taken from different angles and from positions as close to the buildings as the author was permitted to get. As you can see, the walls are quite high. The number of circular structures on the floor seem to be far in excess of what would have been required to hold up a wooden roof.

Some suspect that there may be two more temple structures yet to be discovered at this site, one on either side of the smaller temple. This would be more in line with the typical Hindu temple arrangements in Java at the time, with a main temple facing three smaller ones. We will have to wait for the excavation to restart before we know any more.

Once the temple was accidentally found in December of 2009, the building of the university library obviously came to a halt while everyone decided what to do. A kind of turf struggle took place between the university, which owns the site, and the government agency responsible for the preservation of antiquities. All work stopped and nothing more was done for months. Finally, at the end of 2010, work was scheduled to begin again, but the eruption of Mount Merapi—oddly enough, probably the same volcano that buried the site in the first place 1000 years ago—stalled work once again.

The temple is called variously Candi Kimpulan (after the village in whose district it was found) or Candi Pustakasala (the Sanskrit word for "library"). Like most Javanese temples, no one really knows what it was originally called. The fact that the structure is so unusual when compared to other Javanese temples indicates that it may have been the center of a spiritual leader or sect that was still Hindu, but different enough that an individual vision determined the style of the temple.

That each building has its own lingga-yoni suggests that the purification rites associated with the production of amrita were just as important here as at the

One of two reliefs on either side of the entrance to the main temple shows a sitting figure next to what appears to be a lotus plant.

other temples. There are no Garudas or Nagas, no stories from the *Mahabharata* or *Ramayana*. The simplicity of the temples may be their strongest point.

There are only two reliefs presently visible, to either side of the entrance to the main temple. One is shown above. They seem to be identical. One is a sitting figure—not in asana or any formal pose, but in a casual position—next to whom there appears to be a lotus plant. Unfortunately, this does not help us to identify the figure, since virtually every Hindu deity has been associated at one time or another with the lotus.

The symbolism of the lotus is based on the unique nature of the plant. Its roots are in muddy waters, but its stem rises high above the surface of the water—sometimes several feet high—and then the actual flower rises still farther. For that reason, it is considered to be a metaphor for the human soul that can rise above the mud and aspire to the heavens.

According to Indian tradition, Vishnu was born from a lotus that grew from the navel of Brahma. Buddha was also believed to have been born from a lotus, and the badly deteriorated relief at Borobudur shows him walking on a series of seven lotus plants at the time of his birth. Lotuses are also associated with the chakras. Their flowers open as each chakra is awakened by the rise of Kundalini.

The popular Indian goddesses Lakshmi and Sarasvati are usually depicted with lotuses, as are Krishna and Vishnu. It is rare that Shiva is associated with a lotus, however, although it does happen. The figure in the relief with the lotus is, as mentioned, seated in a casual way, which does little to enhance its importance as a deity. Even its gender is not determined. As we have seen, the gods are usually depicted as standing, or sitting in a formal meditation asana. We are tempted to say, therefore, that the casual posture may indicate that the figure is not an Indian god, but a human being or even a person from Javanese sacred literature, even though its style is, in all other respects, Indian. The presence of this relief at either side of the entrance to the main temple is just another mystery of the site.

The temple at Candi Ijo was built at about the same time as Candi Kimpulan. To be sure, Candi Ijo is relatively austere and simple when placed against Candi Sukuh (for example) or Prambanan. It therefore has more in common with Kimpulan. Yet the architecture is quite different, aside from some ornamentation in the form of the dvarapalas and, of course, the lingga-yonis. That there would be two such entirely different building styles within a few kilometers of each other, and built during the same period, naturally raises questions and emphasizes once more how little we really know about the history of Indian religion in Java.

Section III

Tantric Practice

Prince Hermes. After so many injuries done to the human race, by God's counsel, and by the aid of art, here I flow, made a healing medicine. Drink from me who can; wash who wishes; stir who dares; drink, brethren, and live.[1]

1 Joscelyn Godwin, trans., *The Chemical Wedding of Christian Rosenkreutz* (Grand Rapids, MI: Phanes Press, 1991), p. 60.

Chapter 8

Sacred Marriage and the Goddess of the Southern Ocean

Da ward ein roter Leu, ein kühner Freier,
Im lauen Bad der Lilie vermählt,
Und beide dann mit offnem Flammenfeuer,
Aus einem Brautgemach ins andere gequält.[2]

Faust 1042–1045

What we have seen in the preceding pages has been the concretization of sexuality in stones and buildings that are centuries old. The sexual references are clear and unambiguous in Candi Ceto and Candi Sukuh—the later iterations of this theme in Java—and somewhat less obvious, but no less present, in the earlier Candi Ijo, Candi Kimpulan, and Prambanan in the form of lingga and yoni that are unambiguously sexual.

We have also analyzed some of the narratives concerning sexuality in the Indian and Javanese epics, so we know that there has been a great deal of mystification concerning the sex act, and concerning gender relationships on other levels—jealousy, celibacy, motherhood, adultery, etc.

That all of this is by no means restricted to Java or even to Asia is clear to anyone who has studied ancient religions. The religions of Sumer, Babylon, Egypt, Greece, Rome, and so many others all expressed sexuality in religious or mystical terms. Perhaps the most interesting of these is the *hieros gamos:* the sacred wedding. In this scenario, either two divine partners marry, or a divine partner marries a human partner, or two humans marry under particularly sacred circumstances.

In any case, the two partners in question are identified as a king and queen. The natural reaction is to associate them with secular rulers, but we must remember that kings and queens had more than a mere political function. They had an additional, spiritual dimension, of which the Western concept of the "divine right of kings" is but one manifestation. There are biological lineage issues—bloodlines—that relate directly to sexuality, and there are spiritual lineage issues that involve the blessing and favor (and sometimes the incarnation) of the gods.

2 "A bold suitor, the Red Lion/in a tepid bath wedded the Lily/both then tortured by an open flame/and forced to another Bridal Chamber."

There is a similar blending of the secular and the spiritual in Jewish religion, where the Messiah is both a political and a spiritual leader, and must come from the appropriate bloodlines. The emperor of Japan is called a "son of heaven" and the secular ruler of Tibet, until the Chinese invasion, was the Dalai Lama, who was also the head of one sect of Tibetan Buddhism. While we may consider Tibet to have been a theocracy, the same is not true of Japan; yet both rulers have spiritual lineages and associations as well as secular ones. Indeed, the idea of the separation of church and state is relatively new.

In Java, this concept managed to survive 500 years of Islamization by the simple expedient of incorporating Islamic elements, like the recitation of appropriate surahs from the Quran, references to Allah and the Prophet, and others. There was a "readjustment" of the existing Hindu-Javanese practices so that they conformed—at least in appearance—to prevailing Islamic theological requirements. This was not unusual for a country that had already accommodated both Buddhist and non-Buddhist Indian religious practices by assigning Javanese characteristics to them. This simply goes to the author's main argument that practice was more important than theory in Java, and Tantra, being more of a practice and somewhat less of a theory, fit well within the Javanese paradigm.

This is particularly true of a very unusual ritual that takes place with some regularity to this day—a ritual that has nothing at all to do with Islam and yet one that the rulers of Yogyakarta and Surakarta (Solo) are expected to observe—the ritual marriage with the Queen of the South, *Nyai Lara Kidul.*

Also known popularly as the Queen of the Southern Seas, Nyai Lara Kidul is a spirit queen who lives in an underwater palace in the ocean off the southern coast of Java. She commands a spirit army. The legends concerning her are extensive and often contradictory, but the basic elements are that she was a human princess who either refused to marry or was exiled from the palace due to a disfiguring skin disease. In either case, she wound up alone in the forest meditating and, one day, either heard the call of the spirit world in the ocean or—according to another version—felt so miserable that she threw herself into the ocean to end it all. In any event, she was embraced by the spirit world that exists under the seas and became its queen.

The second phase of the story concerns a prince, Senapati, who is meditating alone on the beach, trying to find his path, the destiny chosen for him as the leader of a new kingdom. His meditation is so strong that the oceans begin to churn and Nyai Lara Kidul rises from the sea to discover the source of the agitation. To make a long story considerably shorter, the Queen brings the prince to her underwater kingdom, where they make love for a period of three days. The Queen tells the prince that he will become the ruler of a great kingdom and that she will guarantee the continued well-being of that kingdom if every ruler in the future will marry her and continue the tradition begun with him. Senapati goes on to found the Mataram dynasty in the late 16th century CE.

Ever since then, succeeding rulers have sought the advice of the Queen through meditation in caves near the beach at Parangtritis, where it is believed Senapati first encountered the Queen. They also perform various rituals intended to placate or invoke her. What is inescapable is the fact that, even in the present day, the Sultan of Yogyakarta and the Sunan of Surakarta are expected to cohabit with this strange spirit ritually, thus keeping alive a tradition that has been unbroken for more than 400 years. In fact, in recent years, these rulers have affirmed that they have encountered Nyai Lara Kidul on more than one occasion.

The Serpent Queen

Various scholars have suggested that Nyai Lara Kidul may represent an ancient Indonesian serpent goddess, a *nagini.* In Java, snakes are symbols of fertility, as they are frequently encountered in rice fields. This association with snakes and rice gives rise to a host of concepts linking them to the rice goddess, Dewi Sri (the Javanese equivalent of the Indian Sri Dewi), and from there to various mother goddesses and goddesses of fertility. The link between an ocean spirit and a snake may seem tenuous at first, but in this case there is an association on the basis of Nyai Lara Kidul's skin disease. Some have suggested that it resembled the scales of a serpent; others say that the fact that the Queen appears young, whole, and beautiful during the waxing moon and old, ugly, and deformed during the waning moon is a reference to the snake shedding its skin.

That there may have been a snake cult in Java before the advent of Indian religions is postulated as a near certainty, but there is virtually no information about it in documentary sources. However, it is known that these cults did exist throughout Southeast Asia and that, in some countries, the ritual marriage of a king to a serpent was commonplace. It is far too early to suggest that these ancient "weddings" may have provided a template for the concept of a serpent goddess at the base of the spine—the coiled serpent Kundalini—who rises along the body to mate with a god in the cranial vault, but the parallels are arresting, since the metaphor seems consistent. The serpent resides in the watery "Underworld"—i.e., the place where the fluids, semen and menstrual blood, urine and feces are stored—and must leave the Underworld in order to mate with the male divinity at the upper regions of the body. If we view the churning of the ocean as a metaphor for sexual arousal, then even the meditation of Senapati that causes the Southern Ocean, the home of Nyai Lara Kidul, to foam is consistent with this idea, and moreover consistent with the Indian tradition of the Churning of the Milk Ocean that gave us amrita. Further, during that episode, the goddess Lakshmi was produced from the churning ocean.

Lakshmi—as a young, beautiful goddess of good fortune, fertility, and material wealth—is the consort of Vishnu. She appears in the *Ramayana* as Sita, the wife of Rama. Usually, she is also depicted either holding a lotus, or seated or standing on a lotus. She is the daughter of the king of the Milk Ocean, and thus has further associations with Nyai Lara Kidul. Lakshmi is believed to represent the power of Kundalini, as she emerged from the Milk Ocean due to the churning produced by the great Serpent King; when she appeared, she was holding a lotus.[3] The lotus is a symbol of the chakras in the human body that are opened by the rise of the serpent goddess Kundalini; it is also, in a sense, a symbol of the entire process, as its roots are in the mud and its flower high above the waters.

It may be that the Sudamala story that we outlined in the chapter on Candi Sukuh is also relevant here, for in that tale we have the beautiful Uma transformed into the ugly Durga, only to be redeemed and become the beautiful wife of Shiva once again. This certainly parallels the tales told of Nyai Lara Kidul, whose appearance changes with the phases of the moon; in fact, Durga lives in a cemetery surrounded by evil spirits, and Nyai Lara Kidul lives in an underworld palace where she is the queen of demons.

Thus, there are many coincidences between the story of the Churning of the Milk Ocean and that of Nyai Lara Kidul herself. How much of the Javanese legend was directly influenced by the Indian epics and how much is indigenous to Java is difficult to tell. Yet, this fairy-tale-like story of a goddess living under the sea and a human king living on the land, and their annual tryst guaranteeing the prosperity of the kingdom, survives to this day as the aition for a series of official state rituals.

---

3 Woodroffe, in commentary on his translation of verse 12 of the *Sat-Cakra-Nirupana,* references Lakshmi as being identical with Kundalini and the receptacle of the amrita (Sir John Woodroffe, [Arthur Avalon], *The Serpent Power* (New York: Dover Publications, 1919, 1974), pp. 351–353). Further, Kali, in his translation and commentary of the Devimahatmya, alerts us to the fact that Lakshmi is identified with Sri (Shri)—the original Mother Goddess—in the Vedas. (Devadatta Kali, *In Praise of the Goddess: the Devimahatmya and Its Meaning* Berwick, ME: Nicolas-Hays, 2003, pp. 7, 88, where he cites the Srisukta as the first text to mention this identification.) Sri Devi, or Sri Dewi, is the Dewi Sri of Java, a rice goddess of fertility who is often identified with snakes, as well as with Sita of the *Ramayana.* This myth is examined in detail in Robert Wessing, "Sri and Sedana and Sita and Rama: Myths of Fertility and Generation," Asian Folkore Studies, Volume 49, 1990: 235–257.

The first of these, the Labuhan, is performed annually on the birthday or the anniversary of the coronation of the Sultan of Yogyakarta. The term *labuhan* comes from the Javanese word *labuh,* which means "to throw." This is a ceremony in which offerings to the Queen are literally thrown into the sea. The offerings must be of a certain type, and very carefully prepared. They include garments of certain colors and designs, cloth, perfume, lotions, incense, and even currency. Also included are the hair and nail clippings of the sultan, provided in special wooden boxes.

This last seems to be a kind of reverse spell (at least, the way it is understood in the West). As is known through popular literature going back centuries, "witches" cast spells using the hair and nail clippings of their intended victims. They are the link necessary in order for the spell to work. Today, we know that some of these bodily elements may contain an individual's DNA and thus do contain the identity of the person intended. In the case of the Labuhan offerings to Nyai Lara Kidul, the sultan provides his own clippings to the Queen, thus sealing their relationship on an esoteric plane.

The Labuhan offerings are cast into the sea, brought into the waves by a procession of courtiers after the recitation of the appropriate mantras. After a while, the offerings are washed back ashore because of the strong current coming in from the Indian Ocean, particularly in the area of Parangtritis, where many a swimmer has simply disappeared into the waves. The attendees of the ceremony then take what they can, believing these offerings to have been blessed by the Queen of the Southern Ocean.

The Labuhan ceremony is colorful and not a little strange. It takes place more or less simultaneously with two other rituals, one at Mount Merapi (the volcano) and the other on Mount Lawu (the location of Candi Ceto and Candi Sukuh). The offerings there are roughly the same, but made to different spiritual forces. Merapi is the northern part of the north-south axis that runs through the palace—the Kraton—of Yogyakarta and to the sea at Parangtritis. The Kraton is the *axis mundi,* the center of the world, but the spirits in the north and the south must be propitiated as well. Thus, another ritual similar to the Labuhan takes place at Merapi, fixing the axis and ordering the world.

The ritual at Mount Lawu takes place because the present sultan of Yogyakarta is a direct descendant of the last king of the Majapahit empire, Brawijaya V. (We saw the statues of his assistants at Candi Ceto.) Therefore, the ritual of ordering the spatial axis of the Kraton must also include a ritual acknowledging the spiritual and genetic bloodline of the sultans (one may say, the timeline or temporal axis). Once again, the offerings are similar: clothing, incense, etc.

The most astonishing ritual of all, however, is the ceremony that takes place in Yogyakarta (less frequently) and in Surakarta (more frequently), when the sultan has what can only be called a tryst or sexual liaison with the same Queen of the Southern Ocean. This ceremony indicates that the sultan has a "wife" who is a spirit; in fact, the queen of spirits in the Underworld. The fact that, at various times, both the Sultan of Yogyakarta and the Sunan of Surakarta have admitted actually seeing the Queen or being in some way aware of her presence means that this spiritual entity is taken very seriously and the ritual consummation equally seriously. Both leaders are also, of course, Muslim. Therefore, they have been married in some manner to this spirit, otherwise a sexual relationship would be *haram*—forbidden.

This is not as unusual as it may seem at first. Before we go into a detailed description of this ritual, however, a look at how this meme has been observed since time immemorial will help us put this practice into context.

Sex Is Not a Metaphor

One of the earliest written records we have of a sacred marriage is that of the Akitu festival of ancient Mesopotamia (probably dating from the Old Sumerian period, or circa 3000 BCE–2340 BCE).[4] This was the New Year's festival—a time to celebrate fertility and wealth. In the various city-states of what we know as Sumer, these festivals were accompanied by ritual intercourse between the king and a goddess, often the goddess who descended to the Underworld: Inanna.

There is a great deal of controversy over this topic. Scholars are divided as to when the practice known as "sacred marriage" originated, and where. Even the meaning of the ritual has been open to some debate. While it is generally accepted to be a fertility rite, some aspects of it remain mysterious and undefined. There are astronomical features that are little understood, as well as questions about precisely whom the king is supposed to represent. Is the king himself a god, at least for the purposes of the ritual? Or does he represent a human being (and thus representative of the populace) in intercourse with a divine being? In other words, does the king represent heaven in this ritual, or earth? It seems to depend, at least in part, upon the nature of the goddess being invoked. No matter what, it is certain that the ritual is intended to guarantee fertility and protection for the kingdom and, in that sense, its purpose is identical to the Javanese version.

4 The basis for this dating can be found in Samuel Noah Kramer, *The Sacred Marriage Rite: Aspects of Faith, Myth and Ritual in Ancient Sumer* (Bloomington, IN: Indiana University Press, 1969).

Why would this be so? Why would practices in countries as remote from each other as Sumer and Java, and in times as distant as the second millennium BCE and the first millennium CE, have such common—yet very specific—elements?

The first common element is the idea that the goddess represents the Underworld. This is a trope we find in agricultural societies in which the fertility of the earth is a major concern. The goddess represents either the earth or the crops the earth produces, and thus has associations with the power residing under the surface of the earth. The powers that are believed to reside below the earth are known as chthonic and, in Java, the chthonic deities include most famously and importantly Nyai Lara Kidul.[5] While she resides below the seas—which is also a chthonic metaphor—she is represented by a snake or serpent and takes on the serpent's coloration and appearance. Serpents are considered chthonic by their very nature, of course.

Inanna—the Goddess of Love, the planet Venus, and fertility—is chthonic in the sense that she descended to the Underworld through an elaborate ritual that involved seven stages or stations, and then returned to the earth, only to be told that she must spend eternity in the Underworld if she cannot find someone to take her place. She offers her husband, the wild shepherd god Dumuzi, as her stand-in.

Dumuzi has some personal characteristics in common with Shiva. He lives in the wild, meditates constantly, and has a somewhat erratic relationship with his wife, Inanna. He is an untamed figure, while Inanna is the picture of grace and sophistication (and lust).

In the praise poem known as Shulgi X (a text dating from around 2050 BCE), King Culgi (Shulgi) approaches the chamber of Inanna, who greets him with these words:

> When I have bathed for the king, for the lord, when I have bathed for the shepherd Dumuzid, when I have adorned my flanks (?) with ointment (?), when I have anointed my mouth with balsamic oil, when I have painted my eyes with kohl, when he has ... my hips with his fair hands, when the lord who lies down beside holy Inana, the shepherd Dumuzid, has ... on his lap, when he has relaxed (?) ... in my pure (?) arms, when he has intercourse (?) with me ... like choice beer, when he ruffles my pubic hair for me, when he plays with the hair of my head, when he lays his hands

5 See Robert Wessing, "A Princess from Sunda: Some Aspects of Nyai Roro Kidul," *Asian Folklore Studies,* Volume 56, 1997: 317–353. On page 321, he makes a case for the chthonic nature of Nyai Lara Kidul (mentioned here as Nyai Roro Kidul).

> on my holy genitals, when he lies down in the ... of my sweet womb ... when he treats me tenderly on the bed, then I will too treat my lord tenderly.
>
> I will decree a good fate for him! I will treat Culgi, the good shepherd, tenderly! I will decree a good fate for him! I will treat him tenderly in his ...! I will decree the shepherdship of all the lands as his destiny![6]

Thus we have all of the basic elements of the Javanese rite reflected in this 4000-year-old Sumerian practice. A king owes his power, authority, and fate to a goddess who lives at least half of the year in the Underworld. Further, the king is identified with Dumuzi—the husband of Inanna and a Shiva figure in his own right—making the love match represent a divine marriage taking place in the heavens. The Sumerian (and, later, Babylonian) king must re-enact this ritual once a year to ensure the success of his administration.

I should note that there is no pretence of a metaphorical interpretation of these events. Inanna, in the poem, speaks clearly and passionately about sexual intercourse. She refers to her genitals, her pubic hair, her self-adornment, and explicitly to intercourse. Like the core texts of Tantric initiation, this ritual obviously is not meant to be understood symbolically, but actually. The only symbolic elements are the ones we expect from Tantra—that the participants in the ritual identify themselves and their partners with gods. To assume otherwise—that is, to put forward the idea that these rituals and sentiments were not meant to be taken literally, but were intended as poetic language referring to other-worldly matters for which sexuality is only a metaphor—is to remain ignorant of the real intentions (and the real functions) of this ritual complex.

It is entirely possible that the same mistake has been made with reference to the Biblical Song of Solomon, which has many elements in common with this literature. I submit that, in these and other similar rites and texts, sex is not a metaphor. Sex is the process, and the sexual act is necessary for the re-enactment of the process. It's not the language that is metaphorical, but, in a way, the act itself. The language is literal—participation in the ritual as written is necessary if one is to understand the process of which sex is the *method.*

---

6 As translated in J. A. Black, G. Cunningham, et.al., *The Electronic Text Corpus of Sumerian Literature (www-etcsl.orient.ox.ac.uk/),* Oxford, 1998, lines 14–41.

Other examples from the ancient Near East are numerous and what details are available are suggestive. For instance, a cuneiform tablet regarding the city of Isin from between1974 and 1954 BCE gives information about the New Year festival:

> … the king ritually slept with a priestess of Inanna, performing, what has been termed, the Sacred Marriage Rite. This ritual was based upon the original motif of the god Dumuzi marrying Inanna, their union ensuring a year of plenty.[7]

In this case, the information is explicit: a sexual act took place with a priestess of Inanna, the king representing Dumuzi. The reason is the same: ensuring fertility.

Another, first-millennium BCE text has even more detail. In this case, a special chapel for the New Year has been established next to a graveyard. When the king approaches the chapel, a voice summons him from within and he enters. There is a great slaughter of sheep, chanting, the burning of incense, and finally the sacred marriage rite. In this instance, the king waits outside the bridal chamber—the chapel constructed for this purpose, which is also referred to as the "perfumed hideaway." There is singing from the graveyard as the king and the goddess await the right moment. The implication is that the ceremony is taking place at night. Finally, the king turns to the goddess and invites her into the bridal chamber, saying: "My beloved, enter the door into our house. With my mouth, consort of our lord, let me kiss thee." We are then told that the goddess is laid upon an embroidered bedspread.[8]

Here we have the modification of the bridal chamber being erected next to a graveyard. The king retires into the chamber with the "goddess"—presumably a priestess, but this is not specified. When he emerges, he comes with blessings and promises. The goddess in this case is identified as Nana (a shortened form of Inanna and not to be confused with the God of the Moon, Nanna).

In a Sumerian incantation from the Ur III period (the second millennium BCE), we see that the sacred marriage and the consecration of water were inextricably linked:

7 Mark E. Cohen, *The Cultic Calendars of the Ancient Near East* (Bethesda: CDL Press, 1993), p. 235.

8 This episode is from R. Steiner, "The Aramaic Text in Demotic Script: The Liturgy of a New Year's Festival Imported from Bethel to Syene by Exiles from Rash," *Journal of the American Oriental Society,* 111 (1991) pp. 362–363 and cited in Cohen, *The Cultic Calendars of the Ancient Near East,* p. 452.

> As heaven became king, earth became queen,
> Erra became king, Mami became queen,
> then Enki, the king of the Abzu
> in order that heaven should purify the holy water,
> created the virgin water, the holy water ...[9]

Erra was a war-like king of the heavens; Mami was a creation goddess who formed human beings out of blood and clay. Enki was the god of magic who dwelled in the Abzu, a watery abyss. The word *abzu* was used to refer to vessels of water that were kept in Babylonian temples for purification and initiation. Thus, the relationship between magic, water, creation, and the *hieros gamos* is once again reinforced by this ancient incantation. A note to the translation of this text states:

> The assumption by Erra and Mami of the kingship of heaven and earth, which was undoubtedly the mirror of the political kingship, must have reflected a political event. This kingship was also the pattern and the ideological reason for the sacred marriage.[10]

As the eminent Sumeriologist Samuel Noah Kramer has pointed out, one of the roles of the king in the *akitu* ritual was to identify himself with the lineage of kings going back to the very origins of the kingdom. As the husband of Inanna, he was reiterating the role that they both played in the very beginning of the first Sumerian kingdom, when it was believed that Dumuzi was its human king and Inanna its tutelary goddess.[11] This again parallels neatly the Javanese ritual, for the sultan who marries Nyai Lara Kidul is a descendant of the original monarch of the Mataram II dynasty, and this sacred marriage solidifies that ancient relationship.

The first month of the year was known in the Old Babylonian period (2000–1600 BCE) and perhaps earlier as "the throne of the sanctuary."[12] This was also a time when food was distributed to temple personnel, at least at Nippur and probably at other cities as well. The association with the New Year, an abundant harvest, and the sacred marriage ceremony is clear. (The title of the month as "the throne of the sanctuary" also raises important questions about how the sacred precincts of

9 J. Van Dijk, A. Goetze, M. I. Hussey, *Early Mesopotamian Incantations and Rituals* (New Haven: Yale University Press, 1985), p. 35.

10 Dijk, *Early Mesopotamian Incantations and Rituals,* p. 35.

11 Samuel Noah Kramer, *The Sumerians: Their History, Culture and Character* (Chicago: University of Chicago Press, 1963, 1971), pp. 140–141.

12 Cohen, *The Cultic Calendars of the Ancient Near East,* pp. 80–81.

a temple were understood in Sumer and Babylon, and attendant implications for the Temple in Jerusalem, a point to which we will return shortly.)

With these examples as a guide, let us now look at the sacred marriage of the present-day sultans of Java with the Serpent Queen.

The Bedhaya Semang: *The Spirit Dance of Yogyakarta*

The Sultan of Yogyakarta and the Suhunan of Surakarta both claim to be the husbands of the divine consort, Nyai Lara Kidul. As such, both observe—to one extent or another, and often depending on the personality of the ruler involved—the rituals necessary to placate this demanding spirit. The reason for this is that both cities were part of the Mataram II Empire and, in the year 1755, the kingdom was split into two courts as part of Dutch attempts to divide and conquer. Each court then developed its own traditions and rituals, although based, of course, on those of the Mataram dynasty that they both represented. The literature on these rituals is not extensive in European languages, but they have been mentioned in articles or in passing references in books by such experts on Indonesian religion, culture, and anthropology as Robert Wessing, Roy Jordaan, Niels Mulder, and others. In the Indonesian languages, of course, the literature is much more comprehensive, albeit still rather confusing.

The Sultan of Yogyakarta usually commands more attention from the government, because Yogyakarta famously and aggressively supported the independence movement against the Dutch, while the response of the administration in Surakarta was rather tepid by comparison, the latter basically throwing their lot in with the colonizers. Yogyakarta itself is a "special district" answerable only to the president of the republic for this reason. However, the sacred dance to invoke Nyai Lara Kidul is often more intensively and regularly practiced in Surakarta (Solo). Even so, due to the fact that the special district of Yogyakarta commands a much larger stretch of shoreline than Solo, many Javanese believe that the relationship between the sultan and the "Mermaid Queen" is stronger there.

The main ritual in honor of the Queen is a dance called (in Yogyakarta) the Bedhaya Semang, which translates roughly as "spirit dance." This dance involves nine human dancers and one spirit dancer, who is Nyai Lara Kidul herself.

In Solo, this dance takes place at least once a year, on the anniversary of the Suhunan's consecration. In Yogyakarta, it had not been performed in decades prior to a performance in October 2002 due, it is said, to the dangers inherent in its performance. A version of it—known as *Bedhaya Harjunowijoyo*—was performed for the sultan on the occasion of his sixty-sixth birthday, on April 17, 2010 at the

Kraton.[13] In both cases, the dance may be performed only in the Kraton and only before a very select audience. In the old days, the dancers were all young girls or women—usually unmarried and, in some cases, concubines of the ruler, although it is said this is not the case today.[14] They are dressed as brides, an important detail that emphasizes the sacred marriage aspect of the ritual. Today, in Solo, the dancers are princesses and other members of the suhunan's royal household, as long as they are able to perform the slow and intricate movements required and to devote all the time and energy necessary to learning the dance (which may be rehearsed only one day out of every thirty-five). They may not be menstruating during the dance. If a dancer is menstruating, she is replaced in order to keep the total number of dancers at nine. The instructions for the correct performance of the dance are quite severe and the dancers resemble persons in a trance—which is sometimes the case. Before the 20th century (and perhaps for a few decades into it), when it was believed that Nyai Lara Kidul had possessed one of these dancers, she was led to the chambers of the ruler after the dance for the requisite sexual intercourse. To deny the Spirit Queen this special attention was to invite disaster.

The reason the author is devoting so much space to this dance is because this arcane and complex ritual is still performed to this day, and for all the same reasons, by the court of the Suhunan of Solo. The creator of this dance—known in Solo as the *Bedhaya Ketawang*—is said to have been Senapati himself, who was a fifth-generation descendant of King Brawijaya V (whom we last met meditating on Mount Lawu and building Candi Ceto and Candi Sukuh). Indeed, not only this dance, but also the gamelan music that is associated with Indonesia, is said to have been his creation or the creation of his grandson, the famous Sultan Agung.

The music of the gamelan is said to duplicate the sounds Senapati heard while in the palace of Nyai Lara Kidul. If one accepts this, then listening to the gamelan becomes a rather other-worldly experience, for one can understand how the strange timbre, scales, and gongs of the gamelan orchestra might duplicate sounds heard under the ocean. The dance itself is said to be one that Senapati learned while with the Queen in her underwater palace, which may explain the exaggeratedly slow movements of the dancers—as if they were moving under water. Their delicate gestures and attitudes are known as *halus* or *alus*—a word that can mean "grace" or "refinement," but also a term used to describe the elevated status of court personnel, princes, and princesses, and elegance, manners, and etiquette in general.

In order to practice the dance, rehearse the music, or even transcribe the notes of the music, offerings and sacrifices first must be made to the Spirit Queen. She

13 See Tarko Sudiarno, "Bedhaya Harjunowijoyo: Portraying a Sultan," *The Jakarta Post*, 24 May 2010.

14 Clifford Geertz, *The Religion of Java* (Chicago: University of Chicago Press, 1976), p. 283.

will tolerate no mistakes, no sloppiness. The stress on the performers and musicians is such that some have been known to faint, become ill, or even—in one case—go mad.[15] (It is claimed that this is one of the reasons why the Sultan of Yogyakarta has not authorized a *Bedhaya Semang* in quite some time, although the Labuhan ceremony described above is still observed regularly.) If the three-hour dance is performed correctly and without error, however, the Queen is said to become very happy and to bless the court with good fortune and security. This is something that is taken very seriously indeed.

In the old days, the sultan or prince was identified as a god in his relations with the Spirit Queen, who was, and remains, a goddess. It was the same Shiva-Shakti relationship that we know very well from Indian religious tradition and especially from Tantra. Today however, this is not allowed because of the monotheistic framework of Islam. Instead, the rulers are identified as men of faith who submit to God, rather than as gods themselves. The Spirit Queen, however, remains a goddess, a consort, a shakti. She does not aspire to a higher spiritual state, as a human being does. She is, in a sense, imperfectible, whereas humans are—theoretically—perfectible. Nyai Lara Kidul may have been human once, but now she is given over wholly to the realm of spirit. Regardless of the theological distinctions, in practical terms the relationship between the sultan and the Spirit Queen is essential to the well-being of the region.

There are rooms reserved at several hotels in the vicinity of the beach where the Labuhan ceremony takes place and where it is believed Senapati first met the Queen. These rooms are reserved for the goddess and have become places of pilgrimage for Javanese, as well as minor tourist attractions in their own right. The rooms are always decorated in green—Lara Kidul's favorite color—and provided with flowers, incense, and, of course, basins of fresh water. The sultans used these rooms to meet the Queen at various times, but it is not known what transpires there between them.

Nyai Lara Kidul does not restrict herself to these thoughtfully provided rooms, however. It is well-known that she would meet the Sultan of Yogyakarta in what is known today as the Water Palace—more accurately, the Taman Sari, or "Flower Garden"—that is believed to have a secret underground tunnel leading, not only to the Kraton, but also to the sea. It is believed that the Spirit Queen would travel through the tunnel to meet with the sultan at the Water Palace for their private trysts. In addition, members of the sultan's harem of concubines also used Taman Sari for recreation. There was a large swimming pool there, as well as a bathing

15 See, for instance, Jan Hostetler, "Bedhaya Semang: the Sacred Dance of Yogyakarta," *Archipel.* Volume 24, 1982, pp. 127–142.

ABOVE: *An entranceway at Taman Sari, with a restored Kala head above it.*
BELOW: *Another restored entrance showing the Kala in greater detail.*

One of the mysterious underground tunnels through which Nyai Lara Kidul herself is said to walk.

pool and numerous other smaller pools (hence the term Water Palace) and artificial islands. It was built by a an architect using European methods and styles in the 17th century, and probably had a military purpose as well—the sultan and his family could escape the Kraton through a tunnel and wind up in the more easily defended Taman Sari in case of an attack. Most of the complex is in ruin, and what used to be part of Taman Sari is now a village that surrounds the site.

There are underground passages at the Water Palace. The site is in bad shape due to some severe earthquake damage over the years, but parts of it are open to visitors. Opposite and above is one entranceway at Taman Sari, with a restored Kala head above it. In the right foreground of the photo, you can see part of the restored pool.

Oppposite and below is another restored entrance showing the Kala in greater detail.

Above is one of the mysterious underground tunnels, which seems to end in a blank wall. The lighting fixtures are, of course, modern. It is believed that Nyai Lara Kidul herself walks these passages when she moves with her spirit army from the sea, through the Kraton, and to Mount Merapi, stopping off here to commune with the sultan, who retires to a secret room at Taman Sari to meditate.

ABOVE: *Four staircases meet at a central platform above a pool used for ablutions.*
BELOW: *A sleeping platform in one of the private quarters at Taman Sari.*

ABOVE: *A view from the roof of Taman Sari showing a row of ventilation buildings.*
BELOW: *A view from within one of the ventilation buildings.*

A nineteenth century earthquake damaged the structure shown above.

The image at the top of page 260 shows one of the most-often photographed staircases that leads from the underground quarters and tunnels to the pools on ground level. Four staircases meet at the central platform. Below the staircase, you can see what is left of a pool used for ablutions by Muslims, as a mosque was also part of the site.

At the bottom of page 260, we see one of the private quarters at Taman Sari, with its sleeping platform. The brazier underneath the central opening was probably used for heat on cool nights.

The photo at the top of page 261 shows a view from the roof of Taman Sari with a row of buildings that were used as ventilation tunnels for the underground passages and rooms. The white building in the background is the eastern gate.

At the bottom of page 261 is a photograph taken from within one of the ventilation buildings. Again, the light fixture is new.

And finally, at the top of this page, we see a view of some of the damage done to the structure by a 19th-century earthquake. The entire complex was also heavily damaged when the British came through during an invasion of Yogyakarta in 1812—the same year they were also invading the United States.

One of the mysteries surrounding Taman Sari is the identity of the architect who designed it. Known as *Demang Tegis* or *Demang Portegis,* he is said to be the survivor of a shipwreck who turned up on the Parangtritis beach and walked into Yogyakarta like a ghost. He could not speak Javanese, and eventually revealed himself to be Portuguese. Since he had knowledge of construction, he was put to work designing and building Taman Sari.[16]

While this story has been the subject of much discussion and historical debate, what is relevant here is the belief that the man literally walked out of the sea onto a beach sacred to Nyai Lara Kidul, and became a servant of the sultan who had just formed the Yogyakarta sultanate. Thus, as the Kraton itself was being built, this unknown Portuguese sailor who came from Lara Kidul's underwater realm was enlisted in the building of the complex where the sultan would meditate and meet with the Spirit Queen (according to tradition). While the idea that Taman Sari represents Portuguese (or any foreign) architectural influence has been denied by scholars for decades, more recently the allegation has undergone some revival at the hands of both Javanese and Portuguese authorities.

In Modern Times

While much of the above may seem like a fairy-tale or imaginative literature, it is worthwhile to point out to what degree of seriousness this relationship between the sultan and the Spirit Queen is taken by present-day political rulers. The accounts are much more numerous than one may imagine, and involve virtually every modern Indonesian president, from Sukarno on.

Neils Mulder speaks of the intention of President Sukarno, the first leader of Indonesia after independence, to annex Dutch New Guinea as part of Indonesia. Realizing that this would require a major military undertaking, he decided to enlist the aid of Nyai Lara Kidul and her spirit army. So he went to Yogyakarta in an attempt to recruit her to the cause. According to Mulder:

> Through her help, he was successful. However, when Western New Guinea became part of the Indonesian territory, Sukarno failed to pay tribute to the Nyai and, therefore, the spirits that had been recruited to recover the new province could not find their

16 This tale has been told many times. It appears in an old Javanese text at the Kraton entitled *Serat Rerenggan* that is considered suspect on archaeological grounds. See, for instance, Asip A. Hasani, "Taman Sari shows foreign architectural touches," *The Jakarta Post,* 27 April 2002.

> way back to their aquatic origin. Roaming around in the Yogyakarta area, they caused havoc to the rice harvest. Because of this, the mayor of Yogyakarta ordered the performance of the powerful shadow play *Semar Boyong* on the mystically potent beach of Parangtritis.[17]

The ploy worked, the crops recovered, and all was well with the world. It was not the first time a *wayang* (shadow play) would be used to correct a political situation, nor would it be the last. As mentioned previously, the wayang kulit is not merely an entertainment; the puppet master, the *dalang*, is as much a shaman as a performer. Certain plays are selected to be performed according to the needs of the community. Thus, the shadow play is as much ritual as it is theater—if, in fact, the two can be separated.

In 1957, for example, a group of men from Yogyakarta decided to underwrite the performances of all of the episodes of the *Mahabharata* as wayang. As the performances proceeded—one every three weeks, in order—they eventually came to the scene where Karno, one of the heroes, dies. On that same day, November 30, students attempted to assassinate Sukarno with grenades. What is so striking about this episode is that Sukarno was usually known by his nickname, *Bung* (or "Brother") Karno.[18] Thus, it is believed that the wayang is so powerful that it calls into play sinister forces from the world of spirits that impinge on the world of human beings, often with disastrous results. For that reason, selection of the right play to perform at the right time is of utmost importance. In fact, the word *dalang* is often used pejoratively, to refer to someone who is controlling political events from behind the scenes. While the West uses the term "puppet master" in precisely the same way, it does not carry with it the religious and occult overtones that the word *dalang* does in Indonesia.

In 1984, the previous sultan of Yogyakarta, Hamengku Buwono IX, granted an audience with the journalist Paul Spencer Sochaczewski.[19] During that interview, the sultan revealed an incident that took place at the Kraton during the time of the Dutch occupation. One evening, he and his companions heard the sound of soldiers moving about the palace, wearing armor and beating drums. There was no one in the Kraton but himself, his family, and his staff. Yet they all heard the sounds of an invisible spirit army, which they insist was that of Nyai Lara Kidul.

---

17 Neils Mulder, *Mysticism in Java: Ideology in Indonesia* (Amsterdam: The Pepin Press, 1998), p. 55.

18 Mulder, *Mysticism in Java.*

19 Paul Spencer Sochaczewski, *The Sultan and the Mermaid Queen* (Singapore: Editions Didier Millet, 1984), p. 76.

What makes this episode all the more poignant is that Yogyakarta, of course, was the center of resistance against the Dutch in Java. The sultan himself had been Vice President of Indonesia, under Suharto. We are discussing educated, powerful, political leaders with an ancient relationship to a serpent goddess and who, moreover, believe in that relationship and take it seriously.

When the sultan died in 1989 and his son was crowned as successor, the fact that the new sultan's wife did not ride with him in the golden carriage during the triumphal procession was a subject of much gossip. As later reported, the reason was simple: Nyai Lara Kidul had appeared and taken her place next to the sultan. The sultan's human wife graciously remained behind with her family and friends to allow this supernatural wife the honor.[20]

When we think of the *hieros gamos,* or sacred wedding, we usually place it in an ancient context like that of Babylon or Sumer. We rarely understand this to be taking place today, and particularly not in what is usually called the largest Muslim country in the world. Yet, as we have seen, not only is this concept alive and well, it is also largely unchanged from its ancient forms and functions. That the sacred marriage between the Sultan of Yogyakarta and the Queen of the Southern Ocean has been filtered through the Tantric framework of Shiva and Shakti is clear. The association of the Queen with magic, with fertility, and with the protection of the realm, combined with the human agency of the sultan and his careful observation of the rituals ensuring his power and sovereignty—all meeting together in a spiritual wedding that, at least prior to the 20th century if not later, included some form of sexual intercourse—means that the spiritual culture of Java reflects this worldview. A spiritualized concept of power including religion, magic, and sexuality is the core element of the Javanese political structure, as it is of Tantra. There is perhaps no other place on earth where this is understood as clearly as it is in Java, and practiced as deliberately—not only by high-ranking politicos and palace courtiers, but by the people themselves.

20 This was reported widely in the Indonesian press at the time, and remarked upon by Wessing, "A Princess from Sunda," p. 252, fn 6.

Chapter 9

Love and Magic in a Javanese Cemetery

If the worshipper is not married or his wife is unable to participate, the worshipper may ritually marry one other woman for the purpose of the ceremony only.[21]

Probably the most blatant and current expression of Tantrism in Java is the practice of having sexual intercourse—with strangers—in cemeteries. There are so many elements of this phenomenon that are purely Tantric that we are forced to accept that some of the most esoteric aspects of what is popularly known as "left-hand-path" Tantra are virtually common knowledge among the population of this predominantly Muslim country—and not only in theory, but most certainly in practice.

Kemukus is located in the Sragen District of Java, not far from the Sultanate of Solo and the temple complexes of Candi Sukuh and Candi Ceto. It is understood to be the tomb of a Javanese saint, Prince Samudra, who died for love (see photo opposite). Unfortunately, this is not a Harlequin Romance sort of love story. The woman he loved was his own mother.

There are several different versions of the story of Prince Samudra. Most are not as shocking as the popular version that involves incest and palace intrigue. But all versions agree that Prince Samudra is a symbol of unconditional (and illicit) love.

His tomb is at the top of the mountain—*gunung*—Kemukus. There is a steep stone staircase leading up to the tomb itself from a main gate (which is typical of many Javanese shrines). Along the way, there are small houses and shops selling bottles of water and local snacks. The small, concrete houses are used by couples to consummate their relationship—that is, when they do not use the open areas around the tomb. They are also used by local prostitutes to service the men who arrive on certain days of the Javanese calendar to find a stranger for the ritual, since there are usually many more men than women in attendance. As may be imagined, this has contributed to a kind of legalized prostitution at Kemukus.

21 Helen Crovetto, "Bhairavi Cakra: Goddess Mandalas/Rituals in Contemporary Tantra's Nondualism," *Pacific World: Journal of the Institute of Buddhist Studies,* Third Series, Number 8, Fall 2006, p. 241.

The entrance to the shrine at Kemukus.

Sex in a Cemetery

> ... something beyond this seems to be involved in the use of corpses and cremation grounds, for it is often clear that people undertaking these rituals are householders who have not renounced the world, are not engaged in ascetic practices, do not seem primarily concerned with affirming the underlying divinity of the forbidden or the polluted, and are not undergoing initiation into a tantric cult. It is also clear that the desires that motivate this type of spirituality are often worldly: power over one's enemies, kingly authority, eloquence in speech, and so on. ... Corpses and cremation grounds ... seem to function as objects and places of power by ... means of which or in which extraordinary achievements may be accomplished.[22]

22 David Kinsley, *Tantric Visions of the Divine Feminine: The Ten Mahavidyas* (Berkley: University of California Press, 1997), p. 235.

The devotees at Kemukus begin arriving as the sun goes down. Certain days—the Friday Pon and to a lesser extent the Friday Kliwon—are considered most auspicious for the performance of this ceremony These days are calculated according to the Javanese calendar, which uses a five-day week.[23] The ritual specialists say that this ritual must be performed in seven consecutive months in order to be effective.

Couples pair up in the foreground of the shrine, along the walkways. Or, in many cases, men select one of the prostitutes who ply their trade at the shrine. This is not to say that all or even most of the women at the shrine are prostitutes, however. Many women do come to Kemukus because they have business concerns or family issues and have been told that this system works. It is a Javanese form of the Catholic novena in many ways, if the novena included sex.

The couples must then offer incense, flowers (and cash) to the *juru kunci,* the "key keeper" or guardian of the shrine. This is a Muslim man and, some claim, a *dukun,* or shaman, who actually blesses the union of the couple. The couple circumambulates the tomb of Prince Samudra and then retires to a private location to consummate the union. This often occurs in the open air, outdoors in the dark under the trees. In the last few years, however, rows of small buildings have been constructed to house the many couples who come to Kemukus seeking favors from the spirits.

On the author's visit to Kemukus in 2008, accompanied by two colleagues from the university, he witnessed several of these ceremonies. The concern of the women was that the men be circumcised—a necessary Islamic practice, but not one that is normally found among Hindu men. Thus, it seems that this quintessentially Tantric and Hindu ceremony has been Islamicized to an extent. The general atmosphere is solemn, not what a Westerner might expect of a place where temporary sexual liaisons are sanctioned. It is the union that is blessed, and the union has as its purpose the securing of a favorable outcome in the mundane world—an outcome guaranteed by spiritual forces. The sexual act is the second part of the

23 The five days are called Legi, Pahing, Pon, Wagi, and Kliwon, names that we encounter in the extremely complicated Balinese calendar system as well. Recourse to a Javanese calendar (or the traditional almanac known as *primbon*) is necessary for understanding how this five-day week relates to the other calendars in use in Java, and to the greater cyclical calendars also in use by the Javanese. The "Friday Pon" is, as the name implies, when the Javanese day of Pon falls on the Gregorian day of Friday. This occurs once every 35 days (Javanese 5-day week x Gregorian 7-day week = 35 days). Thus, the ritual should be performed once every 35 days on the Friday Pon, for a total of seven consecutive Friday Pons. Perhaps coincidentally, a cycle of five phases of seven days each appears in a Japanese Tantric context as the gestation period of a mystical fetus (see James H. Sanford, "Wind, Waters, Stupas, Mandalas: Fetal Buddhahood in Shingon," *Japanese Journal of Religious Studies* 1997 24/1–2, p. 20).

ritual, the first being the blessing ceremony itself, which imposes upon the act the necessary seriousness and the invocation of the spirit of Prince Samudra.

This is not a concept unique to Java. As Sir John Woodroffe points out, concerning the iconic Tantric ritual of the *pancatattva:*

> As I have said, the ordinary rule is that the wife or Ādyā Śakti should be co-performer (Sahadharminī) in the rite. An exception, however, exists where the Sādhaka has no wife or she is incompetent (Anadhikārinī). There seems to be a notion that the Śāstra directs union with some other person than the Sādhaka's wife. This is not so. A direction to go after other women as such would be counsel to commit fornication or adultery. What the Śāstra says is—that if the Sādhaka has no wife, or she is incompetent (Anadhikārinī), then only may the Sādhaka take some other Śakti. Next, this is for the purpose of ritual worship only. Just as any extra-ritual drinking is sin, so also outside worship any Maithuna, otherwise than with the wife, is sin.[24]

Similarly, the partners in the Kemukus ritual must be blessed before they can proceed to the remainder of the rite. It is not necessary that the sexual act be performed with a stranger, but this has become enshrined in the pilgrimage rite anyway. This fact has prompted Islamic purists to criticize the practice—as well as the pilgrimage itself—but it persists in spite of this.[25]

This may be because the fact of sex with a stranger seems to create a specific type of tension necessary for the ritual to succeed. There is no emotional stake in the relationship, no "baggage" that one carries into the ceremony that comes from a shared history with an individual partner. There is, in short, nothing to deflect attention away from the ritual itself. Both parties are there, ostensibly, for the same purpose—to get the attention of the spirit and to obtain favor. In the case of the prostitute, of course, the goal is different. She is there to facilitate the operation, but does not necessarily share in the desired outcome (improved health, success in business, etc). In this, however, she is not so different from the traditional female participants in some Tantric circles, who were chosen because of their low caste or

24 Sir John Woodroffe, *Shakti and Shakta* (London: Luzac, 3rd edition, 1929), p. 580.

25 As the union is blessed, and as the sex involved takes place only within the ritual context—the sacred time and sacred place—there is a strong argument that this does not support claims of adultery or fornication, which would be against Islamic law. The acceptance of polygamy in Islam, as well as the relative ease of getting a divorce, may also contribute to the somewhat relaxed attitude toward this practice.

outcast status. She is there as an object, to be true, but as an object of veneration. She represents Shakti, the female energy of the universe, just as the male represents Shiva. Quite simply, the fact that she is not her partner's wife may be a source of the power she brings to the ritual.

The need for what would ordinarily be called an "illicit" sexual relationship has a long pedigree in Tantra, a discipline that requires the breaking of a series of tabus. That is one reason why the story of Prince Samudra is so compelling. According to the version understood by the pilgrims, Samudra was involved in a carnal relationship with his own mother; in another version of the story, he stole one of his father's concubines. The Oedipal implications in both scenarios are clear; yet, the emphasis in the stories is on love, no matter what the cost, no matter how disapproving society may be.[26] People go to Kemukus prepared to "love" a total stranger—to worship the idea of love itself as separate from any identification of the actual sexual partner and to attain union with a source of power (Shiva or Shakti) both within and beyond themselves. While the Tantric texts can help illuminate what takes place at Kemukus—and at a few other, similar sites in Java—the rituals of Kemukus can actually help us to understand Tantra better.

The name of Prince Samudra is, itself, suggestive. The Churning of the Milk Ocean, by which means amrita was created, is called in Sanskrit Samudra Manthan, which resonates with the name of the ill-fated Prince of Mount Kemukus. The word *samudra* can mean any body of water, but in this context, the temptation to link the Tantric rituals of Kemukus with the attainment of amrita is very strong, especially when we realize that temples in the same vicinity—Candi Sukuh and Candi Ceto—are also monuments to amrita.

There is prostitution in Java, of course. While many foreigners may not be aware of it in the smaller cities, it is certainly apparent in Jakarta. Local men, however, know how and where to procure prostitutes in the other cities and towns. There is no particular need to go to Kemukus for sex. The difference is that Kemukus is government-sanctioned: it is a religious site where a religious ritual is performed that happens to include sex. Indonesian sensitivity to local spiritual customs is an important hallmark of that society, and has contributed to the reputation of Indonesia as a democracy and a moderate Islamic country—one that understands and accepts the importance of *adat,* or local customs.

26 As we have seen, even the sultans of Yogyakarta and of Solo are expected to maintain an extra-marital "relationship" with the Goddess of the Southern Ocean in an annual ritual that appears to have Tantric roots.

Also, Kemukus is not that easy to reach. It requires something of a pilgrimage and, in many cases, devotees treat it in exactly that way, choosing a more arduous approach across a nearby lake rather than simply driving up the mountain in a four-wheel drive. Anyone going to Kemukus has an agenda in mind that is not necessarily purely sexual. Yet, the allure of anonymous sex in a traditional religious setting, protected by the government and thus not subject to civil or criminal or religious penalties, may be part of the attraction, although certainly not the main attraction. People come to Kemukus with real problems they need to solve, real pain they wish to heal. They resort to this practice because of the consensus view that it works. It is a mundane application of a spiritual practice—the use of a deeply esoteric mechanism to achieve worldly gain. In this sense, it falls within the realm of magic rather than mysticism.

The Anonymity of Bodies

One point that may be important to this discussion is the fact that the corpses encountered either in the cremation or charnel grounds, or in the relatively more pristine Javanese cemetery, are those of strangers to the Tantrikas. The rites that are carried out in sometimes hideous circumstances—sitting atop corpses, kindling a sacrificial fire (a *homa*) in the corpse's mouth, having sexual intercourse next to, or on top of, a corpse—are all performed in proximity to the dead bodies of unknown persons. The intention is to sacralize death, to elevate the corpse to the status of a symbol of all bodies, all corpses, all death. But that is the "enlightened" view. In actuality, people with the best of spiritual intentions must confront the gruesome quality of a decaying body while in a psychologically vulnerable state. All the meditation, self-deprivation, fasting, and chanting does not prepare them for the actual confrontation. Add to this a requirement to perform sexually, and we may be forgiven if the impression we receive is that of a peculiar kind of training—perhaps that of a serial killer or other psycho-sexual monster.

The corpse is a stranger to the Tantrika, just as the victim is a stranger to the serial killer or lust murderer. They are both "stand-ins" for something deeper. In the case of the male serial killer of female victims, the victim is a stand-in for the mother, or a woman who has abused or betrayed the killer, or for womankind in general. To the Tantrika, the corpse is a stand-in for Death itself, but in a grander, more macrocosmic manifestation. The corpse is a stand-in for the Tantrika, as well, for the Tantrika will one day become reduced to that very state, to the charnel ground or the cemetery. It represents the stage in alchemy of the putrefaction of the body, a necessary preliminary to obtaining the Philosopher's Stone. It is also part of the initiation of Siberian shamans, who must experience death and dismemberment and even disemboweling before they can reach spiritual attainments.

What if the corpse in the charnel ground, however, were that of a loved one? Or of someone known to the Tantrika in some other context? The associations—psychological, emotional, perhaps even sexual—would provide a virtually insurmountable obstacle. The concept of death would be more real, more poignant—and would, in this case, threaten to derail the entire ritual by making it an act of pure necromancy. The vivid memories of the life of the body would be recalled in the midst of this intense and extremely focused ritual, and the fundamental purpose of the rite would be forgotten. It is impossible to think of death in the abstract with a corpse in front of you—especially when it is the corpse of someone you know.

The necessary anonymity of the dead body is thus a key for understanding the necessary anonymity of the living body—either the sexual partner of a Tantrika in a rite of pure Tantra, or the "tantroid" rite that is performed at Gunung Kemukus. It is the abstract concept of shakti, of psycho-sexual power if you will, that is the focus of the ritual and not the desire someone has for a loved one. As death is rendered symbolic and abstract, even with the corpse present before the Tantrika, so is love rendered equally abstract, equally symbolic, even as the body of the partner is joined in sexual embrace.

There is a strong tradition in Indian religion—including most especially Tantric forms—of meditation in cemeteries or charnel grounds. The reality can be much more hideous than this simple description seems to convey. In India (as well as in Tibet and Nepal), bodies are either cremated or, in some cases, left in the open air to decay gradually and become the food of carrion birds, jackals, and other predators. This is sometimes referred to in the West as "sky burial." That means that the rituals that are said to take place in "cemeteries" actually take place in some of the most frightening and disturbing places on earth—places littered with decaying bodies and whitened bones, with the eerie sounds of animals and birds feasting on the remains. It is a nightmarish tableau, with similarities to the experiences in the forests and jungles of shamans, who must undergo their own virtual dismemberment and destruction at the mercy of wild animals, demons, and nature. The Western concept of cemeteries does not do this scenario justice.

In the West, a dead body is handled in a discreet and nearly invisible fashion. From the hospital or morgue to the funeral home to the cemetery or crematorium, the body is handled by professionals. It is usually embalmed (unless there is a religious objection) and put in a box, fully dressed, where it may be viewed in a decorous public area like a church or funeral home, and then brought to a cemetery and buried (or cremated from the coffin itself). The point is that Westerners are "protected" from the gruesome facts of death. What is left is grief over the loss of a loved one, but the terror of the charnel ground—the blunt fact of the horror-show image of the decaying body left out in the elements to be devoured by birds and beasts—does not obtain.

The grounds at Kemukus do not in any way resemble the Indian version, of course. Prince Samudra is said to have converted to Islam, and Islamic burial customs do not include "sky burial." But the idea of sex with a stranger at a tomb is as close to the Tantric ideal as one is likely to get in Java, or anywhere else outside the Indian sub-continent.

While reports of Tantric circles meeting in charnel grounds in India and performing intricate sexual rituals there are commonplace in the literature, we rarely come across an analysis of what the psychological or psycho-spiritual effects of this particular aspect of Tantric ritual may be. Imagine, for a moment, the sights, smells, and sounds of a place reserved for the open-air disposal of corpses. Imagine that place at night, in the company of Tantric practitioners, after an appropriate fast and many hours of chanting mantras. The ritual of the five elements takes place; alcohol and perhaps a hallucinogenic drug are consumed.[27] Then the sexual aspect of the ritual—the fifth element—begins. What is the impact of this on human consciousness—which is, after all, the ground of spiritual experience?

One might say that to have sex—to commit an act of creation—in a place of death is to collapse time.

The goddess of the graveyard is Kali, the Black Goddess who appears to the uninitiated as a hideous being with a necklace of skulls and a skull cup (*kapala*) filled with blood. She has a long, lolling red tongue and is often depicted dancing on the inert body of Shiva. Entire volumes have been written about this goddess and her importance to Indian religion generally, including the fact that blood sacrifice is still an essential element of her worship in many regions. Her name is the feminine form of the Sanskrit root *kala,* which means "black," but also "time." We have come across this term before in connection with the sixteen vaginal secretions known as *kalas* that refer to the divisions of the lunar month as well. Thus, the relevance of Kali to Tantric esoteric philosophy consists of these ideas of time,

---

27 The use of datura as an entheogen in Tantric rites and texts is well-documented. See Parker and Lux, "Psychoactive Plants in Tantric Buddhism: Cannabis and Datura in Indo-Tibetan Esoteric Buddhism," *Erowid Extracts,* Number 14, June 2008, pp. 6–11; Parker, R. C., "The Use of Entheogens in the Vajrayana Tradition: a brief summary of preliminary findings together with a partial bibliography," 2008, n.p.

death, and the feminine, in addition to traditional Tantric concepts of fertility for those Tantrikas who view Kali as the Mahadevi, or Great Goddess.

In Java, however, one is hard-pressed to find any evidence of a Kali cult at the various temples we have been investigating. The feminine is usually represented by Uma, Parvati, Sita, or the more fearsome Durga who, in some Tantric traditions, is a manifestation of Kali and is also often worshipped in cemeteries or in other desolate places. Durga worship was certainly known in Java, particularly in the 10th to the 13th centuries.[28] Statues of Durga have been found at various sites, some of them royal temple complexes where it is believed the kings of Java invoked Durga to protect their kingdoms from enemies. These statues are virtually identical in many respects to those of Kali.

Both Durga and Kali are considered feminine aspects of Shiva, representing his less pacific attributes of anger and fierceness, respectively. (Parvati and Uma represent Shiva's calmness.) It is important to remember, however, that each of these feminine aspects of Shiva represent Shakti, or the spiritual power of Shiva. In this instance, then, we may say that Durga is the *shakti,* or power, of Shiva, just as the other goddesses are. Although Durga has a different personality from that of Uma or Parvati, she is nonetheless also a manifestation of Shiva's power. Calmness, anger, and fierceness become normal, acceptable, even expected attributes of divinity, and the goddesses become carriers of these forces. Indeed, Durga is often pictured astride a lion, thereby evoking similarities with the Egyptian goddess Sekhmet (and by extension, with the familiar tarot trump, Strength). To make matters more interesting, both Sekhmet and Durga are considered responsible for epidemics. Yet, even though Sekhmet is considered the personification of anger and fierceness, she is also a benevolent goddess under the right circumstances—yet another similarity she shares with Durga.

The categorization of the feminine as the source of spiritual power was one of the supreme contributions of Tantra to Asian religion, for it elevated the status of women—every woman, of every caste—to equality with men. Female divinities enjoyed equality with male divinities—if not, at times, superiority. This happened in the cult of Shakti, which elevates the female above the male and includes the worship of Durga. As we have seen, it is to Uma that we owe the actual Creation itself, otherwise Shiva would have been content to remain in meditation for eternity. While it is beyond the scope of this work, it is interesting to speculate on

28 See, for instance, Hariani Santiko of the Universitas Indonesia, "The Goddess Durga in the East-Javanese Period," *Asian Folklore Studies,* Volume 56, 1997: 209–226. However, no temple dedicated to Durga has so far been discovered in Indonesia, although other temples contain cella in which her statue may be found.

whether the elevation of women in Tantric theory and praxis was one reason for the vehement opposition of the Brahmins to this discipline, for it upset the social hierarchy and especially the caste system.

That said, no temple to Durga has been discovered in Java so far, leading some scholars to believe that the predominant form of Tantra in Java was the worship of Shiva rather than Shakti.[29] Regardless, the graveyard is still an important locus for Javanese spirituality and specifically for those rituals associated with invoking spiritual assistance in worldly affairs. Durga, like Kali, is often invoked in the graveyard setting, especially when asking for magical assistance in some mundane goal. Further, while no temples specifically dedicated to Durga have been found in Java, statues of Durga in Shiva temples are nonetheless common there, so her worship was normative.

To have sex in a graveyard setting, however, is to take the concept of a magical spell for power a step further. It is an invocation of the feminine power, of Shakti, in the last place one would expect it. If the core of feminine power is fertility, conception, and birth, then a cemetery would seem to be an inappropriate place to worship a goddess, or the power of a goddess. The connection can be found in the iconic image of Kali dancing on the corpse of Shiva.

To Tantrikas, this is a profound revelation of the identity of Shakti. It instructs that the human body is no more than a lump of flesh without the quickening power of the feminine. It is the energy expended in the act of intercourse that is preserved in the human being that results from it. For a male, the energy is dissipated immediately after orgasm; for the female, the energy is preserved in the process of conception and gestation. The male is spent, even falls asleep; the female begins the nine months of alchemical transformation. We may see an analogue to this in the concept of Kundalini, the Serpent Goddess said to reside at the base of the spine. She represents Shakti, and must rise through the chakras of the human body to mate with Shiva, who waits for her, inert, at the highest chakra. All the energy, therefore, is feminine. It is the goddess who must seek out the god, as Uma sought Shiva.

Further, to have sex in a charnel ground drives home an important point that language itself is inadequate to convey. To achieve orgasm in front of a corpse—to create this terrible contradiction—is to experience divine power in a way that is inexpressible in words. The initiate, who has been prepared by intensive periods of meditation and fasting, breaks the five tabus of the *pancatattva,* one by one, until finally the partner is embraced and the sexual act, the maithuna, begins. Seeing the end result of conception before you as you labor to conceive raises basic,

29 Santiko, "The Goddess Durga in the East-Javanese Period."

primal —yet wordless—questions. It puts into a kind of relief the emotional baggage many have acquired in relation to sexuality and neutralizes these "hang-ups" by changing the context in so dramatic and extreme a fashion. While there are no corpses lying on the ground in Kemukus, it is still a tomb and a place of death. Associating the sex act with Prince Samudra's incest removes the practitioner from the social and religious frames in which sexuality is normally contained, while at the same time providing another, equally acceptable albeit very different, context. It is a ritual that provokes, even demands, transcendence. It is an act oddly imbued with implications of compassion, of clarity and revelation.

It is also an act of defiance.

In the West, the nexus of sex and death has taken on hues of rebellion. The famous Black Mass has similarities to Tantric rites. Like the *pancatattva,* it also breaks social and religious tabus in an atmosphere of illicit ritual and sexuality, but it is strangely devoid of any redeeming spiritual dimensions. The Black Mass is almost completely political, designed to repudiate the Church's dogma and organization and to "liberate" its participants from the psychological hold of the Church. There is no pretense of attaining higher spiritual states through the practice of the Black Mass; the very practice itself implies that such higher states are a fiction, since by performing the Black Mass one risks eternal damnation in the eyes of the Church. However, according to some sources, the Mass can be used to obtain worldly benefits if it is used as a means to worship the Church's main opponent, Satan. In this way, the more mundane goals of both Tantra and the Black Mass find common ground.

This is not to say that Tantra was not political, or did not have political overtones. Secret meetings of groups consisting of mixed castes and genders occurring in graveyards at night were *de facto* political. They constituted a challenge to acceptable religious and social behavior and may even have arisen as a response to this behavior. Yet, the main purpose—the organizing principle behind these occult Tantric groups—is not understood as political, but rather as spiritual in nature. The difficulty lies in separating the spiritual from the political in any situation where there are groups of individuals meeting in secret for ideological reasons (as opposed to purely criminal conspiracies). As it says in 1 Samuel, 15:23: "Rebellion is as the sin of witchcraft."

The similarities between Tantra and Western occultism do not end there, however. One can easily interpret the grimoires of the medieval European magicians and sorcerers as Tantras. Books in which the use of occult diagrams, words of power, and ritual gestures—what in Tantra are called yantra, mantra, and mudra, respectively—are recommended for the acquisition of temporal power, and the acquisition of power outside normal channels of endeavor at that, are always a threat to social institutions. According to these sorcerer's workbooks, ideal locations for the summoning of spiritual forces are remote and desolate places, including mountains, caves, forests, and deserted buildings. Thus, the same sites that could be used for conspiratorial purposes are also recommended for ritual contact with spiritual power.[30]

For necromancy in particular, of course, a cemetery is the ideal site.

So we may pose the question: Is the ritual undertaken at the tomb of Prince Samudra in Kemukus, and at other shrines throughout Java, a form of necromancy, of communication with the dead?

Tantric Necromancy

There is considerable evidence that Tantrikas performed rituals that would be considered necromantic by Westerners. One of the most famous of these is the reanimation of a corpse.

One of the texts giving instructions for this procedure is called the *Uddisa-tantra,* but the idea that a dead body can be reanimated is known to Indian literature just as it is in the West.[31] A more important function of cemetery magic, however, is the acquisition of *siddhas,* occult powers, through the agency of the spiritual forces that inhabit the charnel grounds.

The cemetery or charnel ground is a liminal site, a borderland between two forms of existence.[32] The living go there to leave the dead; the dead pass through to another form of existence, eventually even another life in this world (according to Indian beliefs concerning reincarnation and the afterlife). Thus, one can look at the cemetery as a place where the normally impermeable border between life and death is a bit more transparent, a bit more fragile. Charnel grounds are believed to

30 It is, perhaps, the genius of the Indonesian government to accommodate these practices as state-sanctioned, which tends to rob them of their value as a threat to the political status quo and instead keeps them in the realm of the purely spiritual. We will look at this idea—the idea of transgression—in a more detailed way in the chapters that follow.

31 See, for instance, references in David Kinsley, *Tantric Visions of the Divine Feminine: The Ten Mahavidyas* (Berkeley: University of California Press, 1997), p. 138.

32 See Victor Turner, *The Ritual Process: Structure and Anti-Structure* (Harmondsworth, UK: Penguin, 1969) for the seminal work on liminality. Also Kinsley, *Tantric Visions of the Divine Feminine,* pp. 237–238 for the application of this concept to the Indian charnel ground, and Robert Wessing, "Spirits of the Earth and Spirits of the Water: Chthonic Forces in the Mountains of West Java," *Asian Folklore Studies,* Vol. 47, 1988: 43–61 for similar references specific to Java.

be filled with strange creatures, ghosts and vampires, demons, and otherworldly forms of life that can be contacted by Tantrikas for purposes mundane as well as lofty. Rituals are performed before decaying or burned corpses or, at times, on top of them. There are even rites in which a sacred ritual fire is lighted in the very mouth of a dead body.

In Java, cemeteries are considered to be full of shakti that is derived from the ancestors who are either buried there or who are deemed to be in some sort of sacred relationship with that particular spot. People who died violent deaths—either in that spot or buried in that spot—are good sources of this type of shakti. Their spirits are called *siluman,* and are invoked by those looking for wealth who offer sacrifices to them for that purpose.[33] This is in line with Tantric thinking on the subject, which values the skulls of people who have died violently for use as sacrificial vessels (*kapala*). Skulls of criminals and the insane are valued for this purpose as well.

In addition, it is not uncommon to hear of those who marry the ghosts and spirits that frequent these cemeteries, including a snake spirit called an *ipri* that takes the form of a beautiful woman. The *ipri* arrives at midnight and has intercourse with her "husband," then leaves him money. The marriage is usually arranged by a shaman local to the haunted site; he may even be the caretaker of the cemetery, the *juru kunci.* This theme of marriage to a beautiful snake spirit has become enshrined in one of Java's most famous rituals, in which ideas of power, fertility, and transgression are interlaced. This is mentioned to emphasize the fact that the beliefs and practices we are discussing do not represent the actions of a marginal community in Java, but rather reflect general attitudes that extend to the sultans themselves. We discussed the phenomenon of the Goddess of the Southern Sea, Nyai Lara Kidul, and her marriage to the sultans of Yogyakarta and Solo in the previous chapter. For now, it is enough to understand that these facets of the Javanese belief system may be remnants of Tantric rituals that were introduced to the island from India as early as the sixth or seventh century CE.

A serpent goddess is a familiar meme to those who study Kundalini yoga, in which the shakti of a human body—the Kundalini—is represented as a snake goddess coiled at the base of the spine. The goal of Kundalini yoga is to raise the serpent goddess up the chakras of the body to mate with Shiva, who rests at the level of the sixth chakra, analogous to the pineal gland in the brain, or what some devotees refer to as the "third eye." Just as the snake goddesses are chthonic entities who dwell below the earth, so Kundalini is a snake goddess who dwells at the

33 See Wessing, "Spirits of the Earth and Spirits of the Water." A *siluman* may also be a water spirit, and may also appear in the form of a snake.

lowest extremity of the torso.[34] Both are "married" in occult rites, resulting in the acquisition of *siddhas*—paranormal and other abilities.

For Western readers, the image of the serpent goddess Kundalini rising up the spinal column calls to mind the familiar scene of the serpent in the Garden of Eden. The serpent's promise to Eve—"ye shall be as gods" (Genesis 3:5)—is reflected in the expectations of yogins who intend to attain enlightenment through this practice. The same image is used frequently in Western alchemy, as a serpent crucified to a wooden cross, which symbol is usually understood as representing fixed mercury (an iteration of the same concept in a *seemingly* different context).

As we saw in a previous chapter, the connection of the serpent with divine knowledge, even immortality, is an essential part of the Indian belief system. The churning of the cosmic ocean takes place with a serpent wrapped around Mount Sumeru, which results in the production of amrita, the elixir vitae. In Java, the serpent spirit (the *siluman*) gives wealth. In Kundalini yoga, the serpent spirit gives immortality (amrita). In this, the beliefs are virtually identical to those of Western alchemy, which strives to produce both the elixir of life and the Philosopher's Stone—immortality and the transformation of base metals into gold.

In both systems, it is necessary to proceed through the stage known to the alchemists as *putrefactio:* putrefaction, the decaying corpse. In Tantra, this stage is embraced in actual practice through rituals in charnel grounds, but also in the use of skeletal material for ritual objects. As mentioned above, one of these is the *kapala*—a cup made from the skull of a person who died a violent death. The photo on page 280 shows an example of one of these that is in the author's possession.

The interior is made of silver, and the rim is decorated with a series of silver skulls around the circumference of the skull. Liquids like blood, wine, milk, and other substances are poured into this vessel. Examples of the kapala are found in many Tibetan *tangkas,* particularly those of wrathful deities like Kali, when it is usually depicted as full of human blood.

The photo on page 281 shows the heavily carved crown of the skull, depicting a god and goddess in the embrace known as *yab-yum.* As can be seen, the deities are trampling on two corpses. The god wears a tiger skin and a belt of skulls, and one of his arms is holding a trident—all of which indicates that the god in question is Shiva, in erotic embrace with his Shakti.

That the skeletal material for these kapalas comes from unfortunate souls who died violently or had horrific lives is born out by the memoire of a contemporary traveler in Northern India and Nepal, Andrea Loseries-Leick, who writes:

34 Wessing, "Spirits of the Earth and Spirits of the Water."

A kapala, a ritual cup made from the skull of a person who died a violent death.

> For certain Tantrik practices the use of particular skulls is indicated. For instance all offering rites (*gser skyems*) for female protectors such as Palden Lhamo (*dPalldan Lha mo*) and Ekajati should be performed with a skull of a 25-year-old woman who has died during childbirth. In the Yamanataka-Tantra used in the Drikung lineage a black skull (*thod nag*) as an offering vessel is mentioned, ideally derived from a promiscuous woman, as well as a skull of an incestuous person.[35]

She also writes concerning an object known as the kangling, a trumpet made from a human thighbone, noting that "... a Kangling made of the left thighbone of a sixteen-year-old Brahmin girl is valued highest."[36]

The photograph on page 282 shows a typical kangling. As can be seen, silver is used at both ends of the device, as in the kapala.

Another instrument made of human skeletal material is the *damaru,* or sacred drum, shown on page 283. The damaru is made from two skulls bound together

35 Andrea Loseries-Leick, *Tibetan Mahayoga Tantra: An Ethno-Historical Study of Skulls, Bones and Relics* (Delhi: B.R. Publishing Corp., 2008), p. 93.

36 Loseries-Leick, *Tibetan Mahayoga Tantra,* p. 77.

The heavily carved crown of the skull showing two deities in the yab-yum embrace.

A kangling, a trumpet made from a human thighbone.

at the crowns with silver, with animal skin stretched across each one to make the drum's surface.

Concerning the *damaru,* Loseries-Leick writes:

> Ideally, one skull should be from a sixteen-year-old girl born in the Year of the Dragon, while the other half may derive from a sixteen-year-old boy born in the Year of the Tiger ... In any case, the two skulls should be of different gender.[37]

She goes on to write that certain Tantric sects, like the Kapalikas and Aghoris, use human fat to anoint the skulls to keep them from drying out.[38] This fat is obtained from the cremation grounds themselves, as it drips from the bodies. She claims she personally used this substance on her own collection of ritual skulls, but they were confiscated at a border crossing.

The intention of this author is not to shock or titillate his readers but to convince them of the seriousness with which this type of morbid ritual activity—involving death, putrefaction, and the direct confrontation of the absolutely worst facts of human existence—is taken by the Tantrikas. As we saw previously, the use of every type of human excretion and remains is a commonplace among some Tantric sects. Indeed, their incorporation, either symbolically or in reality, is central to many otherwise benign-sounding initiations—for instance, the famous Kalachakra initiation of the Dalai Lama that has been conducted as part of his global spiritual program, involving at times thousands of participants, in many

37 Loseries-Leick, *Tibetan Mahayoga Tantra,* p. 82.

38 Loseries-Leick, *Tibetan Mahayoga Tantra,* p. 95.

A damaru, or sacred drum, made from human skeletal material.

countries around the world. It is safe to assume that very few of these initiates are aware of the language of the core texts of the Kalachakra Tantra, like the *Sekoddesa* commentary on the *Paramadibuddha.*[39] This commentary uses language so explicit that it bears a warning by the editor:

39 Edward A. Arnold, ed., *As Long as Space Endures: Essays on the Kalachakra Tantra in Honor of H.H. the Dalai Lama* (Ithaca, NY: Snow Lion Publications, 2009), p. 51. The *Paramadibuddha* is the root Tantra of the Kalachakra system, which, according to tradition, was taught by the Buddha himself one year after his enlightenment. There is no complete text of this document in either Sanskrit or Tibetan, although portions of it do exist in various forms. While the core text can be reliably dated to the first years of the 11th century CE, it is believed the Kalachakra initiation is much older and can be dated to the seventh century CE. An abridged form of the *Paramadibuddha* became known as the *Sri Kalachakra,* which is the Tantra in regular use by Tibetan Vajrayana Buddhists today.

> Please judge yourself and the material wisely, recognizing your own limitations and respecting the text if you find parts of it incomprehensible at this time.[40]

Without devoting too much time to an analysis of this text, with its description of the "descent of semen" and the necessity of maintaining "the vajra erect," it will be enough to quote the commentary on stanzas 83–85:

> With the stanza that begins "The ambrosia of the moon" ... the Blessed shows that, during sexual union, beings meet in an unmistakable situation, as also occurs at the moment of death.[41]

This enigmatic statement equating sexual union with death is an appropriate one with which to end this discussion of the fascinating sexual ritual that takes place at Gunung Kemukus at the tomb of a prince who fell in love with his mother, and was slain.

40 Arnold, *As Long as Space Endures,* p. 52.

41 Arnold, *As Long as Space Endures,* p. 73.

Chapter 10

Kabbalah, Tantra, and Sexual Gnosis

Prelude

> Surely one of the most influential forces in the rise of modern sexual magic was the complex body of texts and traditions that make up Jewish Kabbalah. … Erotic symbolism is pervasive throughout Kabbalistic literature …[42]

To many students of Kabbalah, it will come as something of a shock to realize that there is a Tantric thread running through the tapestry of Jewish mysticism. Yet modern Kabbalah scholars, from Moshe Idel to Elliot Wolfson to Rafael Patai, have all pointed out the Tantric element of Jewish mystical writings and practices. Patai in particular emphasizes the possible identity of the Shekinah—the feminine aspect of the Jewish deity—with none other than the Hindu goddess Kali. These are the conclusions of respected scholars, not the wild speculation of armchair anthropologists. What this means for any student of religion—or, indeed, any Kabbalist or Tantricist—is profound. Patai himself goes so far as to speculate that there was a historical connection between Kabbalah and Indian Tantra, perhaps to the extent that one influenced the development of the other.

This uniting of two separate esoteric strains—one from India, the other from Israel by way of Spain and North Africa—is evidence of a phenomenon that is already well-known to Western occultists—that the secret teachings of all places and times share a basic fundamental understanding of the created world. This concept has come under tremendous pressure and criticism from postmodern sources that insist on the uniqueness of every culture and deny the relevance and accuracy of what they term "universalism," which they characterize as just another relic of the colonial era.

Far from denying the uniqueness of individual cultures or religions, the esoteric approach recognizes that there are basic elements of human biology and psychology that find unique forms of expression from culture to culture, but that nonetheless point to a deep commonality. Social organization differs from place to

42 Hugh B. Urban, *Magia Sexualis: Sex, Magic and Liberation in Modern Western Esotericism* (Berkeley: University of California Press, 2006), p. 42.

place and from time to time, and is dependent on a wide variety of environmental factors. Thus it is a mistake to draw too fine a parallel between the religion of the ancient Teutons (for instance) and that of ancient China or Mexico. The esoteric approach insists, however, that certain basic elements of human consciousness are identical across racial and culture boundaries. The most obvious of these elements is human sexuality.

Regardless of whether a culture views the sun as male or as female, for instance, the sexual polarity of sun and moon is recognized in many cultures that have had little or no contact with each other. The role of parents, the raising and initiation of children into society, the sex act itself—all of these are experienced everywhere, in every culture, and often have drawn about them a cloak of tabu and mysticism. The association of human fertility with the fertility of crops or the availability of game is another phenomenon worth mentioning, as is the mysticism associated with war, disease, and death.

Thus, although this is a study of the Tantric temples of Java, the author feels it is useful to provide a look at Western ideas of Tantra in order to promote greater communication between the two approaches. Many people in the West believe they know of what Tantra consists, especially those who have engaged in a study or practice of what is sometimes (disparagingly) called "neo-Tantra." Just as many people in the East take it for granted that there is nothing worthwhile in Western ideas about Tantra, since they are formulated by those who have no direct knowledge of the Asian versions, do not speak any of the languages, and do not have a grounding in the culture or literature. Indeed, it seems to the most casual observer that what passes for Tantra in the West is a glorified excuse for sexual license. In other words, some of the same recriminations that are directed against Tantrikas by the Brahmins in India may find their parallel in those aimed at the Western "Tantrikas" by its genuine practitioners.

Without coming down on one side or the other, the author will try to describe various aspects of Western Tantra—in particular, those elements that are common to ceremonial magic and alchemy—in order to give a more solid platform for discussion and investigation. In the past thirty years or so, the field has become much more sophisticated, as a growing number of scholars have attempted to analyze Western Tantra within their own disciplines.

Among the names one encounters in any serious study of the subject are Paschal Beverly Randolph and Aleister Crowley, who are related via the teachings of an esoteric European society known as the Ordo Templi Orientis. However, the tradition of what we call Western Tantra goes back much farther than that, to at least the time of the Florentine Academy, if not to the Jewish mystical tradition that inspired some of its leading lights. It also includes the field of alchemy, long considered to be the ancestor of modern chemistry, but which, in fact, reflects a different worldview in which no element is static. Rather all are part of an ongoing process of evolution and transformation.

In this chapter, we'll consider how these Western forms of mysticism and magic relate to Tantra, and especially to their Javanese "tantroid" manifestations. The idea is not to prove that Javanese practices somehow influenced—or were influenced by—Middle Eastern and European forms, but rather to point out that the Javanese approach to Tantra is mirrored in the Western approach as a way of reducing the enormous cultural and religious structures of Indian Tantra to their basic, functional components. Hopefully, we will learn something about Western Tantra in the process, of course, but we will also gain a deeper understanding of Tantra itself.

The Bridal Chamber of God

The early history of the Jewish people and their religion includes references to an *Asherah.* Although this term appears forty times in the Tanakh, there is the usual academic controversy over what it means. To be sure, Asherah is not clearly identified in any of the books of the Bible, and perhaps with good reason. The inferences are startling—the Asherah can be nothing less than the consort of the Jewish god, Yahweh.

In 1929, an archaeological discovery in Syria of Ugaritic texts yielded some artifacts that offered the first non-biblical references to Asherah and enabled Biblical scholars to begin identifying her. The later excavation at Kuntillet 'Ajrud in the eastern Sinai (1975–1976) gave scholars more clues to her identity. Citations in the books of the Old Testament were vague and ambiguous. In some cases, the Asherah was believed to represent a cult object of some sort rather than a deity. That assumption was in error for several reasons, not the least of which is the idea that a cult object can exist independently of the deity for which it was created or identified. The 1929 Ugaritic inscriptions gradually made it clear that Asherah was probably referred to as both a deity and a cult object. The object, in this case, is believed to be a wooden post or pillar that was placed near the altar in the sanctuary.

To understand this, it is necessary to realize that the early, pre-exilic (pre-sixth-century BCE) form of Judaism was not identical to the form of the religion we know today. There was a purely monotheistic, Yahweh, branch of the faith, as well as a more syncretistic form that incorporated elements of the Canaanite and

Phoenician religions of the area. The Bible as we know it is largely the result of the Yahweh cult extirpating the syncretisic cult, both politically and in the books of the Bible (although references to these other practices are well-known to Biblical scholars, as well as to careful readers of the texts).

That Yahweh would have a consort, then, is understandable in light of the fact that the other gods of the region had consorts, much in the way we have already noticed in the Indian religions. Asherah may, in fact, have begun life as a consort of El, the local god with whom Yahweh was eventually identified or amalgamated.

Recently there has been considerable interest in the idea that Asherah may be linked to, or even identified with, the goddess Qudshu. Qudshu was known throughout the Middle East, from Egypt to Babylon, as a goddess of fertility. She was often depicted standing on a lion nude or partially nude—*en face,* fully facing the observer—holding lotus flowers in one hand and snakes in the other. This iconography is very similar to the bas-relief of Lilith or Ishtar that we saw in the chapter on Candi Sukuh, but the added presence of lotus flowers, lions, and serpents brings to mind a host of associations with the goddesses of India that eventually made it to the religion of Java, including Durga, who is often shown riding a lion and holding lotus flowers. In fact, one of the epithets of Asherah is "Lady of the Sea," which recalls Nyai Lara Kidul.[43] Another is "Lion Lady," which recalls Durga, who has been identified with the same Nyai Lara Kidul and, possibly, with Sekhmet in Egypt.[44] Both Asherah and Nyai Lara Kidul are ladies of the sea, goddesses of fertility and eros who are associated with serpents, and the consorts of rulers. Scholars have pointed out that one of the epithets for Asherah may be "She who treads on the Sea Dragon," which is eerily reminiscent of the Queen of the Southern Seas.[45] This is not to insist that there is an identification between the two, but only that they reflect a similar concept and do so employing similar symbols.

Asherah/Qudshu was characterized as a goddess of extreme eroticism. In her Akkadian incarnation as Ashratum, she is described as the "bride of the king of heaven," as well as "mistress of sexual vigor and rejoicing."[46] As Qudshu, her name is translated as "holiness" or "sanctuary," a concept that will bring us closer to one

43 John Day, "Asherah in the Hebrew Bible and Northwest Semitic Literature," *Journal of Biblical Literature,* Vol. 105, No. 3 (September 1986), pp. 385–408.

44 William G. Dever, "Asherah, Consort of Yahweh? New Evidence from Kuntillet 'Ajrud," *Bulletin of the American Schools of Oriental Research,* No. 255, Summer 1984, pp. 21–37.

45 Day, "Asherah in the Hebrew Bible," pp. 388, 396.

46 Day, "Asherah in the Hebrew Bible," p. 386.

of the most mysterious aspects of pre-exilic Judaism—the secret of the Holy of Holies in Solomon's Temple in Jerusalem.[47] As Rafael Patai points out:

> ... the Biblical notion that the tabernacle was built in order to service as a dwelling place for Yahweh is transformed in Talmudic literature into the idea that both the desert sanctuary and the Solomonic Temple were the earthly abode of the Shekina.[48]

One of the Gnostic gospels found in the Nag Hammadi corpus in 1945 is the Gospel of Philip. This document, which has been dated to the third century CE, is concerned with ideas of androgyny and sexuality in a sacred context and makes repeated references to the "bridal chamber," which is seen as a means of uniting the split between humans and God. The separation of woman from man in Genesis (with the creation of Eve) is a metaphor for the exile of humanity from the divine, an exile that can only be ended in "the bridal chamber." In fact, it very specifically states, with reference to the Temple in Jerusalem:

> The Holy of Holies is the bridal chamber. Baptism includes the resurrection [and the] redemption; the redemption (takes place) in the bridal chamber.[49]

The theme of the sacred water (baptism) and the image of the bridal chamber are repeated constantly in the Gospel of Philip. The identification of the Holy of Holies with a bridal chamber is arresting; it calls to mind the other temples of the region, those of Babylon and Sumer that had chambers built at the top where the king or the high priest met with the goddess once a year at the New Year festival. Similarly, the Jewish high priest was only allowed into the Holy of Holies on the

---

47 Day, "Asherah in the Hebrew Bible," p. 388. The Hebrew word *qadosh* ("holy") comes from this root, as well as the name of the Masonic degree "Knight of Kadosh," which is based on the Hebrew. The term "holy spirit"—which appears in Isaiah 63:10–11—is *ruach qadosh,* with the word ruach rendered variously as spirit, wind, breath, etc. In Gnosic texts, the Holy Spirit is considered feminine and the power that "quickened" the womb of Mary. It is thus a fertilizing power, which is in line with ideas concerning the goddess Qudshu.

48 Rafael Patai, *The Hebrew Goddess* (Detroit: Wayne State University Press, 1990), p. 100. This is also true of the Kabbalistic literature. For instance, we read in the Sepher ha-Zohar: "Moses fashioned the Dwelling in the desert to bring Shekinah down to earth. . . ." (2:143a) See Daniel Matt, *The Zohar: Pritzker Edition,* Volume 5 (Stanford: Stanford University Press, 2009), p. 309.

49 The Gospel of Philip (II, 3) in James M. Robinson, ed., *The Nag Hammadi Library in English* (New York: Harper and Row, 1977), p. 142.

Jewish New Year. If the God of the Jews had a consort, then the depiction of the Holy of Holies as a bridal chamber is perfectly consistent with other Middle Eastern religions of the same era. We remember, in fact, the vision of Ezekiel (8:11–18), in which it is pointed out that women cry for Tammuz in front of the Temple. Tammuz is, of course, Dumuzi, the shepherd king whose consort was Inanna/Ishtar, who spent months in the Underworld every year, and whose ritual was accompanied by mourning. It is possible that, by the time of the post-exilic period, the idea of Asherah had been repressed to a certain extent and become less a concrete image of a goddess than an ambiguous wooden pole that was planted next to Yahweh's altar to represent the power Yahweh had to manifest in the created world—a pole that was decorated as a tree, as in the Tree of Life.

One of the problems with Asherah and identifying her definitively as the consort of the Jewish god lies in understanding the role of the consort in Middle Eastern religion. Is Asherah a goddess in the sense that El, Baal or Yahweh are gods? If not, then how to define her?

We find a clue in an article by B. A. Mastin, in which the author gives us an intriguing possibility in a passing reference.[50] In citing the work of P. K. McCarter, Mastin says that the "asherah of Yahweh" may refer to "the Effective/Active Presence of Yahweh," which then became personified in the wooden pole and identified as Yahweh's consort.[51] This raises the possibility that the goddess represents the power, or shakti, of the Jewish god. If so, this would solve the problem of Yahweh and "his Asherah" quite neatly, for there would be no reason to justify or defend the notion that early Jewish religion was polytheist if we see Asherah as an "emanation" of the "active presence" of God.

This idea has been put forward by Simo Parpola of Helsinki University, who published translations of some of the Assyrian oracles in 1997. For Parpola, the Assyrian goddess Ishtar—with whom Asherah has sometimes been identified—is best understood as the "breath" of the god Asshur:

> Ištar, who in the oracles addresses the king as her child, *is Aššur revealed in his mother aspect.* In speaking through the prophet, she, however, is at the same time also an entity distinct from Aššur: a divine power working in man and thus bridging the gulf between man and god. ... Accordingly, Ištar can be viewed as the "spirit"

50 B. A. Mastin, "Yahweh's Asherah, Inclusive Monotheism, and the Question of Dating," in John Day, ed., *In Search of Pre-Exilic Israel* (New York: Continuum, 2006), pp. 326–351.

51 Day, *In Search of Pre-Exilic Israel,* p. 338.

> or "breath" of Aššur (= God)—a concept well-attested in Neo-Assyrian texts.[52] [emphasis in original]

This concept of the masculine divine manifesting as a female quality is one we encounter in Kabbalah and most specifically in the personality of the Shekinah, of whom the *Zohar* speaks as the Matronita.

The Matronita—Kabbalah and the Shakti

Undeniably, one of the great contributions of Kabbalists to the history of Judaism is the explicit utilization of gender images to depict the nature of God and the consequent application of erotic symbolism to characterize the divine-human relationship.[53] The most famous—if not the earliest—text of Jewish mysticism is the *Sepher ha-Zohar,* the Book of Splendor. Composed as a commentary on the books of the Torah and in the frame of a dialogue between famous rabbis, it made its first appearance about the 13th century CE in Spain, in a region near Barcelona where there was an active and influential community of Jewish mystics. The Spanish environment of the author(s) of the Zohar can explain the use of the Spanish word *Matronita* to refer to the Shekinah, although the word is rendered in Aramaic. *Matronita* is the diminutive form of the word matron, which means "matron" or "wife." Applying a diminutive—essentially saying "little matron"—implies that the person being described is young or inexperienced, even virginal. Although the root of *matron* is the same as for "mother"—*mater* in Latin, or *madre* in Spanish—the idea of motherhood is not necessarily implied. Instead, it may mean a young woman with elevated status.

The idea of the Shekinah as a young bride is a constant theme in Jewish mysticism. The respected scholar of Kabbalah Moshe Idel has gone so far as to identify two "consorts" of God in Kabbalistic texts: the Shekinah, and a divine concubine or mistress.[54] That there is a feminine aspect or power to the Jewish God is taken for granted in the Kabbalah. Shekinah is perceived as representing the people of Israel in exile from God; she is also considered to be a personification of *Malkuth,* the last, or lowest, sefirah on the Kabbalistic Tree of Life. As such, she also rep-

52 Simo Parpola, *Assyrian Prophecies* (Helsinki: Helsinki University Press, 1997), p. xxvi.

53 Elliot R. Wolfson, "Shekinah" in Margaret Schaus, ed., *Women and Gender in Medieval Europe: An Encyclopedia* (New York: Routledge, 2006), p. 758.

54 His *Kabbalah and Eros* is a classic in this regard. See especially chapter 3, "God's Wife and Concubine: Paths of a National Myth," in *Kabbalah and Eros* (New Haven: Yale University Press, 2005).

resents the created world and the first stage in a process of spiritual illumination. Without putting too fine a point on it, we can say that there is a rough analogy between Shekinah as *Malkuth* and Kundalini at the *muladhara chakra* at the base of the spine. Both are spiritual feminines representing the first step in the attainment of cosmic consciousness. The goal of both is to unite with the spiritual masculine in the bridal chamber. Shekinah seeks union with God in Kether, the very first sefirah at the top of the Tree of Life. For Kundalini, it is union with Shiva at the level of the sixth chakra, usually identified with the thalamus or hypothalamus in the human brain—thalamus being a Greek word that means "chamber." Both of these ascents are templates for an individual's quest for union with the divine.

> According to other Kabbalists, at the moment of sexual union, the mind of the husband is in fact elevated to the supernal realm and draws down the divine light and the Shekinah herself. These spiritual forces descend into the drop of semen, infusing spirit into the seed.[55]

The Zohar frequently uses marriage and sexual metaphors to describe the relationship between God and his Creation, a fact that has not escaped the attention of a new generation of Kabbalah scholars like Moshe Idel, Elliot Wolfson, Melila Hellner-Eshed, and many others.[56] A complete discussion of this topic requires a book in itself, so, for the moment, we will have to be content with a few examples that help frame the argument for a Tantric interpretation of Kabbalah.

One of the most important prayers in Judaism is the *Shema.* It derives from a verse in Deuteronomy (6:4) and reads "Hear, O Israel! The Lord is our God, the Lord is One" (*Shema Yisra'el YHVH Eloheinu YHVH Ehad*). The prayer is an affirmation of monotheism and, as such, is used in liturgical observances in the synagogue and also by pious Jews upon going to bed and in many other situations.

According to the Zohar, when the Shema is uttered "with perfect intention," a spark flies down from the heavens and illuminates the Tree of Life:

> Then that Tree wafts fragrances and aromas, and all the trees of the Garden of Eden waft fragrances and praise their Lord, for then *Matronita* is adorned to enter the canopy with her Husband. All

55 Urban, *Magia Sexualis,* p. 43.

56 Elliot R. Wolfson, *Through a Speculum That Shines: Vision and Imagination in Medieval Jewish Mysticism* (Princeton: Princeton University Press, 1997); Melila Hellner-Eshed, *A River Flows from Eden: the Language of Mystical Experience in the Zohar* (Stanford: Stanford University Press, 2009).

> those supernal limbs unite in one desire, in one aspiration, to be one with no separation. Then Her Husband is arrayed for Her, to bring Her to the canopy in single union, to unite with *Matronita.* ... At that moment, *Matronita* prepares and adorns Herself, and Her attendants escort Her to Her Husband in hushed whisper, saying "Blessed be the name of His glorious kingdom forever and ever!" (Zohar 2:133b)[57]

This is clearly a *hieros gamos,* a sacred marriage, and is only one of many such references in the Zohar. There is a husband and a wife, the trees in the Garden of Eden, a canopy, and a "single union." Here, the sacred marriage of Inanna with Dumuzi has been re-imagined to reflect, not only the relationship of the people with their national God, but that of an individual with the divine. By saying the words of the *Shema*—with perfect intention—the individual assists in the act of bringing the people of Israel closer to God and, at the same time, increases his or her own state of grace. Through a process of internalization, the individual becomes an active participant in the sacred marriage and not merely an observer. The reference to the Garden of Eden implies that the husband and wife represent Adam and Eve, and that the sacred marriage performed in the Garden is a way of redeeming the Fall.

There is evidence that this internalization process began about the time of the administration of King Herod in the first few years CE (although it could have begun much earlier, as the Book of Ezekiel suggests). At that time, there were conflicts between various religious and political factions in Jerusalem over the conduct of the high priests at the Temple and the way in which Jewish law should be interpreted. The famous account of Jesus throwing the money lenders out of the Temple is one example of how some Jews saw their sacred spaces being polluted. The records left behind by the Qumran sect offer further evidence of the tensions that existed between Jews who were supporters of the Maccabean dynasty in Jerusalem and those who considered themselves purists in a kind of self-imposed exile on the shores of the Dead Sea. The Song of the Sabbath Sacrifice is one example of how the outsiders at Qumran "spiritualized" the Temple of Solomon, creating a "virtual" temple to replace the one that would soon be destroyed by the Romans.

When the rituals and sacrifices normally associated with the Temple of Solomon could no longer be performed due to its destruction, a process of re-interpretation of these rites took place in an effort to retain their spiritual power. This was seen in the texts of the Jewish mystics who relied on the Vision of Ezekiel as a template for how one could "visit" the "virtual" temple. This method is known

57 Matt, *The Zohar,* pp. 237–238.

to us as the "Descent to the Chariot," and as *Merkavah* mysticism. It is a process of visualization of various levels of spiritual understanding until one arrives at the Throne of Heaven. We remember that the high priest was allowed into the Holy of Holies at the Temple of Solomon only once a year, on New Year's Day. This tradition was kept alive by some mystics, who used New Year's Day as the occasion to "descend to the Chariot," thus reinforcing the idea that there is a link between the Temple of Solomon and Jewish mystical practices.[58]

This concept also extended to the sacred marriage. As we can see through a close reading of the relevant mystical texts like the Zohar, the idea of sacred marriage was expanded to involve individuals, not only kings or high priests. Once the physical Temple had been destroyed, its spiritual counterpart became accessible to everyone—and that included the rituals associated with it, properly internalized through the methods of mystical trance and intense visualization. However, not all of these methods were purely mystical.

Sexual relations between a husband and wife were seen to replicate the union betweeen Shekinah and God. In referring to one of the oldest Kabbalistic texts, the *Sepher ha-Bahir,* Elliot Kiba Ginsburg writes:

> In terse, allusive fashion, the *Bahir* has created the basis for imagining the Sabbath as the time of *hieros gamos,* the union of the divine king and bride.[59]

Indeed, the Sabbath was considered an ideal time for a husband and wife to engage in sexual intercourse, for it was the time when God and Shekinah were in union; thus, intercourse between a husband and wife shared in that divine intimacy. In other words, we see once again that sexuality is not a metaphor, but was meant to be taken literally as a practice and a process. The external elements of temple, god, goddess, and sacred marriage were internalized through mental and biological processes, in much the same way that Tantra internalized the cosmic creative process and made it accessible to individuals of all castes or genders. Indeed, noted historian of Jewish religion Rafael Patai has even insisted that there exist direct *his-*

58 The founder of Hasidism, Rabbi Israel Baal Shem Tov, was known to do this on several occasions, according to letters he wrote to his brother-in-law. See Moshe Idel, *Kabbalah: New Perspectives* (New Haven: Yale University Press, 1988), p. 94, where these letters are quoted.

59 Elliot Kiba Ginsburg, *The Sabbath in the Classical Kabbalah* (Albany: State University of New York, 1989), p. 108. Ginsburg devotes an entire chapter to this concept.

torical links between Indian Tantra and Jewish mysticism, going as far as to suggest that Kali and Shekinah are cognates.[60]

This type of thinking was castigated in the postmodern era as representing universalism, a theory of anthropology and comparative religion related to the doctrine of diffusionism. Briefly, diffusionists believe that many of the world's cultures influenced each other in remote antiquity. As an example, this is considered to be the reason why Mayan ruins resemble Egyptian pyramids or the Javanese temples on Mount Lawu. This same point of view is used to argue that the Native American culture had links to ancient Phoenicia, for instance, or to Welshmen from the time of the Round Table, or to Chinese Buddhist monks—to name just a few of the more popular theses.

Many commentators regard diffusionism as inherently racist— such as the implication that the Native American population could not have built the famous "burial" mounds of the North American continent or the Mayan or Aztec temples on their own without outside help. Opponents of diffusionism are called "independent inventionists," because they believe that individual cultures grew and evolved on their own without influence from the outside, especially in any discussion of Native American cultures. This is, of course, the postmodern view that has superseded the universalist theory that all cultures have elements in common and may come from a common source or sources—an "Ur-kultur."

The amount of epigraphic and other evidence in North America (particularly) that suggests the presence of European and North African missions in North America long before Columbus is problematic for independent inventionists, however. Be that as it may, the opprobrium with which any hint of diffusionism is greeted means that some evidence will have to wait until new theories emerge that allow us to accept that these two perspectives are not mutually exclusive.

Until then, we can draw interesting and educational parallels between Indian Tantra and Jewish mysticism, and between these and European alchemy, that bridge the gap between the two and demonstrate that there is an underlying methodology understood by disparate cultures that permits individuals to attain union with the divine and to take part in the ongoing act of Creation.

60 Patai, *The Hebrew Goddess,* p. 150; see also his *The Jewish Mind* (Detroit: Wayne State University Press, 1996).

The Chemical Wedding

The rituals and religions of other cultures, other places, and other times are a kind of Rorschach test. They provide outlines, colors, and even drama, but often the real core of the system evades us because we project onto it what we already know from our own culture. Thus our analysis of these cultures tells more about who we are than about who they were. In a nutshell, this is the argument that postmodern anthropologists have with the universalist approach to comparative religion of the late 19th and early 20th centuries.

There have been stories of lights in the sky and gods coming from the heavens for thousands of years, at least since the beginning of written language. In the 20th century, this was interpreted as aliens from other planets. What in ancient India they saw as flying chariots we, in this period, call flying saucers. In another 100 years, we can expect that there will be another technology and another paradigm, and we will interpret those lights in the sky as something completely different.

But the lights will not go away. They will continue to demand an interpretation.

Somehow, the authors of Western alchemical texts understood the value of this kind of approach. They realized that there was more than one way of looking at a phenomenon. Explanations that were too specific robbed the phenomenon of its meaning and of its relationship to other phenomena, cutting it off from the rest of creation and making it something singular and isolated.

While alchemy has a long and fascinating pedigree, there is no space here to go into historical detail. What the author proposes is to take one particular and famous example of the alchemical literature as a starting point—the enigmatic *Chymical Wedding of Christian Rosenkreutz.* While there may be doubt that the *Chymical Wedding* is a true representative of alchemical texts, popularly understood—since there seem to be no formulas or recipes for preparing metals for transformation, etc.—it has had tremendous influence on the growth of Western secret societies, who have adopted its hero, Christian Rosenkreutz, as a symbol of a person on a spiritual quest of personal transformation.

Briefly, the story is that of Christian Rosenkreutz, a Christian knight who receives an invitation to a wedding at a castle. He receives this invitation on the eve of Easter Sunday—i.e., Holy Saturday, which represents for Christians the time that Jesus was in the tomb before the Resurrection. It is also, according to some Christian traditions, the day that Jesus descended to the Underworld to free the souls that had been trapped there since the time of Adam's sin. (It is worthwhile to remember that one of the earliest recorded deities, Dumuzi, also spent time in the

Underworld. The mourning for the death of Tammuz/Dumuzi recorded in Ezekiel is paralleled in the mourning for the death of Jesus on Good Friday.)

Christian receives this letter while he is in the midst of meditation. As he is sitting in silent prayer in his home, a great storm rages outside. He ignores the storm, as he is used to this phenomenon while he is meditating. At this time, a beautiful woman appears who hands him an invitation to the wedding.

We can see that this single image resonates with our Javanese hero, Senapati, meditating on the beach. A great storm rose up then, the ocean churned, and out of the storm appeared Nyai Lara Kidul, a "beautiful woman." Both experiences bring the meditator to an other-worldly kingdom—Senapati to Nyai Lara Kidul's palace beneath the waves, and Christian Rosenkreutz to the castle of the king and queen. In the former, it is Senapati himself who marries the Queen of the Southern Ocean; in Christian's case, he will witness a strange wedding in the castle.

The author has covered this text in some detail elsewhere, so will not dwell too much on its convoluted plot.[61] Instead, we will focus on a few elements that reflect our theme. The *hieros gamos* takes place on the fourth day of a seven-day event. In this wedding, however, the bride and bridegroom are slain—in fact, two other Kings and two other Queens are slain as well, along with the executioner, who is identified only as "the Moor." This brings the total number of dead to seven. The constant reappearance of the number seven throughout this text is remarkable, indicating some of the same concerns as those of the Qumran sect in the document known as the *Song of the Sabbath Sacrifice,* which invokes a "virtual" temple through the repeated use of the number seven, as well as of the Book of Revelation—The Apocalypse—with its repeated "seven" imagery. The author has identified this preoccupation with "seven" as an indication of deeper significance than the seven planets or days of the week, etc. He argues, rather, that it represents the idea that the constellation of seven fixed stars known as the Big Dipper or the Chariot (Ursa Major) was the subject.[62]

It is interesting that a Moor is singled out as the executioner. Moors in European literature meant Muslims and North Africans, members of the Arab armies

---

61 Peter Levenda, *Stairway to Heaven: Chinese Alchemists, Jewish Kabbalists, and the Art of Spiritual Transformation* (New York: Continuum, 2008), pp. 191–208.

62 Levenda, *Stairway to Heaven.* Briefly, the seven stars of the Dipper revolve around the Pole Star and thereby represent seven levels in the approach to immortality (the seven stages in alchemical operations; the seven palaces in *merkavah* mysticism, etc.). Since the Pole Star represents north, and the Dipper is circumpolar and never rises or sets, the association of this constellation with ideas of immortality and centrality—the *axis mundi*—is certain.

that had invaded Europe in the eighth century CE and who remained in power in Spain until 1492. That a Moor would execute members of a Christian royal household may be a gloss on European history. In alchemical terms, however, a Moor has other associations, so the juxtaposition of Moor and King and execution in the *Chymical Wedding* is perfectly tuned.[63] To be sure, it was the arrival of the Moors (Muslims) in Central Java in the 15th century that signaled the end of the Majapahit Empire and the beginning of Mataram II, at about the same time as the period in which the *Chymical Wedding* is set.[64]

The sacred wedding and massacre take place on the fourth day; on the morning of the fifth day, Christian Rosenkreutz comes upon a tomb beneath the castle where "Lady Venus" is kept. She lies, naked and beautiful, on a bed draped around with curtains. This is another reference to Ishtar/Inanna (Venus) in the Underworld (the tomb). She is motionless—not dead, but dreaming in her underground crypt.

An enigmatic poem on a tablet next to the bed reads:

> *When the fruit of my tree has completely melted, I shall awake and be the mother of a King.*[65]

Again we note the association with royalty and fertility. We will return to the tree motif shortly. Adam McLean, in his commentary to the *Wedding* and specifically to the Venus episode, notes that Lady Venus represents "the powerful passions of the feminine side of human nature," while the masculine side represents "lofty

63 A common instrument in the alchemist's laboratory was a cold still, called a "Moor's Head." But there are also references to a "man, black as a Moor" (*Schwarz wie ein Maure*) in the "Fourth Parable" of the *Splendor Solis* of Solomon Trismosin, dated 1582 (British Museum, Harley MS 3469). This figure represents one of the phases of the alchemical process. The accompanying plate shows a man whose torso is black, whose head and right arm are red, and whose left arm is white. Ascending out of a muddy pit is a beautiful woman, white, who stands waiting for him with a red cloak. She wears a crown and has wings, and a star hovers over her head. Like all alchemical illustrations, this one seems to be designed to elucidate the obscure prose, but succeeds rather in tempting us with a range of possibilities.

64 On the sixth day, according to the text, Christian Rosenkreutz finds an urn on which the date 1459 is inscribed, which refers to the year the Wedding takes place. The meaning is uncertain. We know from other sources, including a code within the Wedding, that Christian was born in the year 1378, so while 1459 may have other esoteric associations, it is within reason (barely, perhaps) that Christian would be alive and 81 years old at the time of the Wedding. In 1459, the Islamic Sultanate at Granada in Spain—site of the famous Alhambra—was still in existence and thus there were still Moors in Europe.

65 Joscelyn Godwin and Adam McLean, *The Chemical Wedding of Christian Rosenkreutz* (Grand Rapids: Phanes Press, 1991), p. 74.

abstractions" such as the "Arts and Sciences."[66] The meeting between the two forces "must result in inner struggle and death. Thus the wedding of the King and Queen can only be achieved in this castle through a death process."[67] The Queen is thus identified with Lady Venus or, at least, with the forces that Lady Venus represents.

However, what if death, in this case, was not meant literally, but rather metaphorically? What if the death of the King and Queen at the time of the sacred wedding, or *hieros gamos,* is a reference to *le petit mort* of the human orgasm? After all, the death of the two royals was required in order for the elixir vitae and the Philosopher's Stone—the amrita of the Tantras—to be produced. The bizarre juxtaposition of marriage and massacre may be a reference to this basic biological fact in an appropriately "hermetic" context, with the added instruction that both partners are slain—i.e., both attain orgasm. If we remember that we are dealing with twilight language—just as we were with the Tantric texts—we can begin to read the *Chymical Wedding* with different eyes.

This is not to insist that the entire allegory can be understood sexually in all of its detail; but the sexual allegory is one level of the tale, which represents, after all, transformation and transmutation through the union of opposites. That is why it is entitled a "Wedding" and not a "Massacre" or an "Execution." The *Wedding* is filled with allusions to male-female polarity; they are inescapable and take place on each of the seven days and often multiple times on each day. When we add to that the set piece on the sixth day of the ascent up a tower of seven levels that is accomplished by means of ladders, ropes, or wings, we have before us a hermetic representation of the ascent of Kundalini, which is understood here, not in its purely Indian aspect of a psycho-biological process, but in terms of a spiritual-chemical process, referencing the seven steps in the alchemical transmutation of base metals into gold. Keep in mind, however, that these processes are manifestations of the same basic process as it appears in different realms. Acknowledging this, we can use the one to interpret the other.

The metaphor of the tree is constant in alchemical literature as well. We find illustrations of trees in many alchemical texts, from the *Splendor Solis* of Trismosin (1582) to *The Pleasure Garden of Chymistry* (1624) by Daniel Stolcius, the appearance of which, eight years after the publication of the *Chymical Wedding,* presents us with material that helps to illuminate, somewhat, the narrative of the *Wedding.* Often, the tree is referred to as "the Tree of the Philosophers," and the allusion to

66 Godwin, *The Chemical Wedding,* p. 129.

67 Godwin, *The Chemical Wedding.* As we will see in the next chapter, this theme of sex and death is echoed in the 20th-century work of French author Georges Bataille.

the Tree of Knowledge in the Garden of Eden is sometimes implicit, sometimes explicit.[68]

Eve was tempted in the Garden by a serpent who bade her eat of the fruit of the Tree (Genesis 3:1-7). In the *Wedding,* Venus lies in the tomb beneath the castle, waiting for the fruit of the tree to melt so that she can be freed. There are two Trees in Eden: the Tree of Knowledge is the one from which Eve took the infamous apple (or, possibly, pomegranate) and the Tree of Life—i.e., immortality. We are accustomed to interpreting these episodes in a moral or ethical framework: humanity sinned against God and was denied immortality and hence has been suffering ever since. The language of Genesis makes that clear.

In other cultures, however, this is interpreted differently and, indeed, Eve is called by Adam the Mother of All Life (Genesis 3:20). Her name comes from the Hebrew root *hawwa* meaning "life." If we stand back from the Biblical account a little, however, and look at Eve as a Mother Goddess—at least, as representative of the Shekinah or the shakti of God—we can see this story in another way. We know, for instance, that Eve was created by being split from Adam's body. Thus, Adam and Eve were originally one person, one being. This androgyny is reminiscent of how the primordial Shiva is often represented in India. Uma is Shiva's feminine nature, his shakti and creative power. In this way, we can see Eve as Adam's shakti. Their "marriage" takes place after they have eaten of the fruit of the Tree of Knowledge, when they first realize they are naked in the Garden. Yet, according to Genesis, they have forfeited immortality, for they have not eaten of the Tree of Life.

The story of humanity then becomes a quest for the Tree of Life, hidden behind the walls of the Garden. In India, as in Java, this is the quest for amrita, the elixir vitae that is produced by the churning of the cosmic ocean, snatched from the possession of the Nagas, the serpents. The Tree of Life itself—the *etz chaim*—becomes a potent symbol of spiritual progress in Kabbalistic circles. It can be considered the Tree of Eve, an *etz hawwa.* Both refer to the word "life" and they are both linked with the serpent.

Indeed, the symbol of Asherah, the consort of Yahweh, was a wooden pole or tree. Groves of trees were also sacred to Asherah. This identification of a primordial or divine female figure with a tree in ancient Jewish religion may give us a way to comprehend the story in Genesis a bit better.

68 As in the *Philosophia Reformata* (1622) by Johan Daniel Mylius, a colleague of Stolcius mentioned above.

To those who object that this turns Adam into some kind of god—if Eve is the Mother Goddess—one only has to point to the Kabbalistic tradition of Adam Kadmon, the "Primordial Adam." Adam is here identified as the Perfect Human, representing the source of all human souls. Far from the view we have of Adam as the man who docilely followed Eve's example and ate of the forbidden fruit, to the rabbis and later the Kabbalists, Adam represented something far more powerful and sublime. Kabbalists, comparing the two seemingly contradictory statements in Genesis concerning the Creation, understand that Adam was first created both "male and female"—that is, androgynous—and then was split from his female nature to produce Eve. Until that moment, Adam was the perfect "image and likeness" of God, the closest we can come to experiencing the Divine directly. It is this bringing back together of Eve and Adam to re-create the Androgyne that is the meaning of *teshuva,* or redemption, a word that also means "return."

In alchemy, the androgyne is represented by another constant symbol, shown in the two images at the top of page 302. The two woodcuts are both taken from different versions of the famous alchemical treatise *Rosarium Philosophorum.* In both, we find the symbol of the androgyne in the center and a Tree of Life to the left. Both androgynes are winged, holding serpents in their left hands.

In the second woodcut, we see the figure standing on serpents in a way that is reminiscent of the Garuda figures from Candi Sukuh (shown again at bottom right on page 302). It bears an uncanny resemblance to the alchemical woodcuts above.[69]

The figures in the two woodcuts at the top of page 302 are holding a cup with three more serpents in their right hands. This image of the elixir vitae being secured from serpents by a creature that is a winged human is so specific that it is striking to find such a parallel between a 16th-century European text and a 15th-century Javanese sculpture. We can only suspect that the connective tissue, in this case, must be India.

The first woodcut represents the perfection of Luna, and the second that of Sol. In alchemical terms, Luna, or the moon, represents silver and Sol, or the sun, represents gold. Of course, there are also layers of associations, correspondences, and meanings attached to these two concepts, foremost among them that of Luna as feminine attributes and Sol as masculine. The androgyne or hermaphrodite is a symbol of the *hieros gamos* perfected, shown at bottom left of page 302. The two halves of the human personality—the Shiva and the Shakti, the male and the female—have been united, returned to a pre-lapsarian state in which Adam had

69 From *De Alchimia opuscula complura veterum philosophorum,* Frankfurt, 1550.

TOP LEFT: *The Androgyne is a constant symbol in alchemy.*
TOP RIGHT: *An androgynous image from the* Rosarium Philosophorum.
BOTTOM LEFT: *The* hieros-gamos *rite of the sacred marriage from an alchemical manuscript.*
RIGHT: *The serpents at the base of the Garuda statue at Candi Sukuh recall the serpents in the* Rosarium *woodcut above.*

not yet been split from Eve and was still in direct communication with God. The return to this state is the goal of the alchemical mystics as well as of the Indian and Javanese Tantrikas. In both cases, this state is attained through a "refined"—in the sense of metals— version of sexuality, of the *hieros gamos,* the sacred marriage that is nonetheless enacted with real elements, real flesh-and-blood elements.

In the Catholic Church, the term "elements" is used to indicate the bread and wine that are transformed into the body and blood of Christ and consumed by the faithful during the Mass. The technical term for this transformation is transubstantiation, a term that only came into general use in the Church in the 12th century. The concept involves recognizing that the substance of the bread and wine has changed into the body and blood of Christ, but that the appearance —what are called the "accidents"—have not changed.

In alchemy, there is transmutation rather than transubstantiation. Elements are changed both in substance and in accident, or appearance. Lead becomes gold, truly. However, in a more Tantric approach, the idea of transubstantiation has merit, for the body is not outwardly changed. We can still recognize the Tantrikas as the same human beings who started the Tantric process, but they have been changed inwardly and attained a degree of spiritual transformation. The alchemical transmutation of the elements is considered a physical sign of the inner transformation—or transubstantiation—of the alchemist.

The physicality of the Catholic Mass —the elevation of body and blood into sacraments and the consumption of them as a requirement for every Catholic—has lent itself to occult manipulations. Several grimoires, notably that of Pope Honorious, require some contact with these elements to enhance the magical operations. Others recommend stealing them from a church or having a priest consecrate them especially for the rituals. That there is occult power invested in the transubstantiated bread and wine has been a common belief for centuries. Without trying to make too sharp a point about it, the vaguely cannibalistic or theophagic nature of the Mass has similarities with some Tantric rituals involving the flesh of corpses and the consumption of forbidden foods. The very idea of the Mass is horrifying to a pious Jew or Muslim—the idea that God can be, and should be, eaten verges on the savage and surely can have little to do with monotheism. Thus, the Protestants of the Reformation insisted that the Mass was more of a memorial service commemorating the Last Supper of Jesus, rather than a magical rite involving changing the substance of bread and wine into the spiritual body and blood of God.

The actual transubstantiation is carried out through the grace of the Holy Spirit, the third member of the Holy Trinity that also includes God the Father and

God the Son. The Holy Spirit is usually depicted as a dove, and is also identified with water via the sacrament of baptism.[70] It was the Holy Spirit that was responsible for the Virgin Birth, i.e., the impregnation of Mary with the divine essence of God. This combination of ideas is remarkably similar to those of the elixir vitae and the action of Garuda, the winged deity, in securing the water of life. It is Garuda who is depicted many times at the temples on Mount Lawu, where amrita was collected and dispensed to the faithful.

The author mentions this to demonstrate that Tantric or tantroid elements—ideas and rituals involving the elevation of spirituality through the manipulation of matter—can be found everywhere, even in the West and even in the most sacrosanct of Western religious thought and practice. Magic is the Western form of Tantra, as Francis King has pointed out, and the Catholic Mass is considered by many to be a form of the highest magic.[71]

70 1 Corinthians 12:13, which states that the Holy Spirit is present at baptism and that the believers are "made to drink of one Spirit," and Matthew 3:16, which describes the Holy Spirit descending over Jesus at the moment of his baptism.

71 Francis King, *Tantra: the Way of Action* (Rochester, VT: Destiny Books, 1990).

Chapter 11

Tantra, Magic, and the West

> ... Apollonius ...carries with him a commendatory letter to the Brahmins ... Here these admirable eastern magicians present him with such rarities as in very truth he was not capable of. First of all they shew him—as Philostratus describes it—a certain azure or sky-coloured water, and this tincture was extremely predominant in it, but with much light and brightness.... Apollonius confesseth how the Brahmins told him afterwards that this water was a certain secret water and that there was hid under it or within it a blood-red earth.
>
> Thomas Vaughan, *The Fraternity of the Rosy Cross* (1652)[72]

As mentioned in the previous chapter, two of the most influential occultists of the West in the last 100 years are P. B. Randolph (1825–1875) and Aleister Crowley (1875–1947). While other names may be better known—H. P. Blavatsky, Manley Palmer Hall, Krishnamurti—Randolph and Crowley were interested less in repeating or revising the hermetic and occult writings of the past than they were in blazing new paths and developing an entirely new esoteric paradigm. It is from studies of Randolph and Crowley that a generation of both practitioners and academics has arisen in the last thirty years, a generation that is re-evaluating Western occultism and making it a field of serious study and respect. Much of this has to do with the interest generated by Kabbalah studies on the one hand, and by Tantric studies on the other.

The interpenetration of these two fields has provided us with a means of appreciating the richness and depth of a literature and a praxis that has been dismissed too often by mainstream scholars. The relevance for Javanese studies rests in the pragmatic integration of sexo-magical practices from diverse sources that characterizes Western occultism. Many of these sources are identical to those that helped form the Hindu-Javanese experience. Hindu and Buddhist forms of Tantra are foremost in this Western phenomenon, which developed hundreds of years after a similar approach took root in Java. Indeed, the blending of Islamic and Hindu esoteric philosophies and practices that we find in Java are duplicated to some

72 Arthur Edward Waite, ed., *The Works of Thomas Vaughan, Mystic and Alchemist* (New York: University Books, 1968), p. 353.

extent in Europe and the Americas, and in particular in the modern secret society, the Ordo Templi Orientis or OTO.

As this chapter's epigraph illustrates, the belief that the famous Greek magician of the first century CE, Apollonius of Tyana, visited India where he learned the secrets of alchemy and the amrita was current at the time that the Rosicrucian Fraternity was being introduced in the 17th century. The author of the quotation is Thomas Vaughan, a Welsh alchemist whose works are thinly veiled descriptions of the Tantric aspect of alchemy. Vaughan is believed to have perished due to "unguided autonomous nervous system experiments," according to Kenneth Rexroth in his Foreword to Vaughan's collected works—certainly a bizarre claim if Vaughan's alchemy had been strictly of the chemical or mineral kind.[73] What makes this all the more interesting is the fact that this reference to Apollonius, India, and the "secret water" takes place in an essay on the Rosicrucian Fraternity.

The 19th and 20th centuries were rife with organizations claiming a Rosicrucian lineage. These include groups founded by Randolph and Crowley, as well as the Golden Dawn. With Randolph and Crowley, we have substantial and irrefutable evidence that their focus was on precisely this "biological" aspect of magic and alchemy, and on the "autonomous nervous system experiments" that it is said killed not only Vaughan, but also his wife.

The history of Randolph, Crowley, and their colleagues has been told in several places in greater or lesser detail, so we will not spend too much time on it here.[74] Rather, we will focus on the element of their work that most concerns us and that has attracted the greatest attention from specialists and casual observers alike—the interpretation of sexuality within spiritual and esoteric contexts.

---

73 Waite, *The Works of Thomas Vaughan,* p. 10.

74 For Randolph and his occult activities, see Joscelyn Godwin, Christian Chanel, and John P. Deveney, *The Hermetic Brotherhood of Luxor* (York Beach, ME: Samuel Weiser, 1995) and T. Allen Greenfield, *The Story of the Hermetic Brotherhood of Light* (Beverly Hills: Looking Glass Press, 1997), as well as John Patrick Deveney, *Paschal Beverly Randolph: a Nineteenth Century Black American Spiritualist, Rosicrucian, and Sex Magician* (Albany: State University of New York Press, 1997). For Aleister Crowley, there have been many biographies over the years, including his autobiography. See Aleister Crowley, *The Confessions of Aleister Crowley,* John Symonds and Kenneth Grant, eds.(New York: Penguin, 1989), as well as Martin Booth, *A Magick Life* (London: Hodder & Stoughton, 2000); John Symonds, *The Great Beast* (New York: Rider & Co., 1951); Richard Kaczynski, *Perdurabo: The Life of Aleister Crowley* (Berkeley: North Atlantic Books, 2010); Lawrence Sutin, *Do What Thou Wilt: A Life of Aleister Crowley* (New York: St. Martin's Griffin, 2002); Kenneth Grant, *Remembering Aleister Crowley* (London: Skoob Books, 1991).

The Brotherhood of Eulis

> One night—it was in far-off Jerusalem or Bethlehem, I really forget which—I made love to, and was loved by, a dusky maiden of Arabic blood. I of her, and that experience, learned—not directly, but by suggestion—the fundamental principle of the White Magic of Love; subsequently I became affiliated with some dervishes and fakirs of whom, by suggestion still, I found the road to other knowledges; and of these devout practicers of a simple, but sublime and holy magic, I obtained additional clues—little threads of suggestion, which, being persistently followed, led my soul into labyrinths of knowledge themselves did not even suspect the existence of. I became practically, what I was naturally—a mystic, and in time chief of the lofty brethren; taking the clues left by the masters, and pursuing them farther than they had ever been before; actually discovering the ELIXIR OF LIFE; the universal Solvent, or celestial Alkahest; the water of beauty and perpetual youth, and the philosopher's stone ...[75]

We begin with a look at Pascal Beverly Randolph, certainly one of the most enigmatic figures of the 19th century, and one who wielded enormous influence over the growth of secret societies in the 20th century. Randolph, an African-American spiritualist, became involved in more extreme forms of occultism while visiting Europe and the Middle East. It is the knowledge—and, perhaps, the initiations—received abroad that led him to create his own secret society, the Brotherhood of Eulis. The Brotherhood was based on his system of occultism, which included sex, drugs, and a method of communication and divination through the use of magic mirrors. The term "Eulis" is problematic, and seems to have been Randolph's own creation.[76] At times, he connected it with the Eleusinian mysteries, an ancient (circa 1500 BCE) form of worship that was based on the story of Demeter, Persephone, and Hades, the lord of the Underworld.[77] Like the annual festival of Inanna and Dumuzi, this was an agriculturally based celebration commemorating the time of the year when Persephone was held in the Underworld and the land

75 P. B. Randolph, *Eulis! the History of Love: Its Wondrous Magic, Chemistry, Rules, Laws, Modes, Moods and Rationale; Being the Third Revelation of Soul and Sex* (Toledo: Randolph Publishing, 1874, 1896), p. 48.

76 Deveney, *Paschal Beverly Randolph*, p. 228.

77 Deveney, *Paschal Beverly Randolph.*

above lay fallow. The celebration of the Eleusinian mysteries took place annually in Greece for nearly 2000 years, until the fourth century CE, making it one of the longest-lasting initiatory cults in history. It allowed men and women, slave and free, to become initiated into its secrets, which to this day have never been discovered or revealed. This rite became the basis for a theatrical presentation by Aleister Crowley known as the Rites of Eleusis.

Another possible meaning for "Eulis" is grounded in the Greek root *eos,* meaning "dawn."[78] Regardless of the ultimate meaning, the Brotherhood of Eulis was based on a spiritualized interpretation of human sexuality and the application of sexuality to magical power. The Brotherhood became the source for several other societies that were spun off from Eulis or inspired by it. As we have seen, Randolph claimed to have discovered the secret of the elixir vitae, the amrita of the Indian Tantricists, which he calls the "water of beauty and perpetual youth." That this was somehow connected with sexuality and with drugs leads us to the impression that he was dabbling in a form of Tantra, with all the transgressive ritual that this implies. At the same time, his discussion of sexuality is always very conservative and respectful of the married state and of "soul union."

Whether Randolph discovered the elixir vitae or not, his obsession with it has fueled Western esotericism for hundreds of years.[79] At least since the days of the *Fama Fraternitatis* in the 17th century, when the Rosicrucian Society first made its appearance, the quest for immortality has been linked with the transmutation of metals. Alchemy and immortality go hand-in-hand, and not only in the West. Chinese alchemy, for instance, shares the same dream. In Java, the temple of amrita at Candi Sukuh also depicts the ironworker manufacturing the sacred kriss. There is an association between transmutation and immortality that at first seems contrived, until we realize that the ancients believed that metals evolved over the course of thousands of years.

Long before Darwin and his study of human and animal evolution, the belief in the evolution of metals and souls dominated alchemical thought and practice.

---

78 Deveney, *Paschal Beverly Randolph.*

79 If he had, it did not do him much good. He is reported to have committed suicide at the age of 50, although some insist that he was murdered. Unfortunately, this is not unusual in the history of Western esotericism. Edward Sellon (1818–1866), who could be credited for having introduced Tantra to the West in the mid-19th century through a series of books that were deemed borderline pornographic, committed suicide nine years earlier at the age of 48. Sellon had lived in India and his books on Tantra did much to create some of the mystification around the Shakti and Kaula cults and their sexually oriented practices. James Webb, an author of serious investigations into the history of occultism, committed suicide in 1980 at the age of 34. Ioan Couliano, the brilliant historian of religion and protégé of Mircea Eliade, whose words open this book, was murdered at the University of Chicago in 1991 at the age of 41.

Gold, according to this theory, is the highest form of metal and all metals are gradually turning into gold; it is their apotheosis. The Philosopher's Stone, mentioned above by Randolph in the same breath as the elixir of life, is a substance that accelerates the process of evolution and enables the alchemist to change lead (the least evolved metal) into gold (the most evolved), the symbol of perfection, both of metals and of the human soul. Those who can control the process of evolution become immortal. Disease and sickness are traits associated with the lesser metals, while control over the evolutionary process indicates an active role in Creation itself. Lead is metal in an imperfect state that is eventually destroyed as it transforms into higher and higher forms of metal. Gold alone is indestructible—i.e., it cannot evolve into a higher metal. It has reached its state of perfection and is immune to disease and decay.

Sexuality, then, is a biological function in service to human evolution; hence the wide range of sexual metaphors and analogies we find in alchemical texts (as well as in Kabbalistic literature). It mimics on a human plane what takes place on the plane of metals and plants. Randolph called this process "affectional alchemy."

In the Randolph scheme, the affectional alchemical process required the commingling of both male and female essences in the sexual act. That means that the act required both a man and a woman, excluded the use of condoms or other birth control devices, and required that ejaculation take place within the female's vulva so that specific male and female secretions would take place and mix. This composite mixture, called "magnetic" in Randolph's phraseology, fulfills "God's purpose in bi-sexing man."[80] The secretions were identified in Randolph's work as those from Cowper's Glands (source of the pre-ejaculate fluid in men) and from the Glands of Duvernay (actually Bartholin; the Duvernay glands were discovered in cows), which provide some lubrication for the vagina during intercourse. Neither of these two fluids has any function known to science other than as lubricant for the sex organs during intercourse, but to Randolph, they were elements of the water of immortality and were possessed of secret, "magnetic" properties that lead to a "bi-sexing" of the human organism.

To Randolph, as to most alchemists, Kabbalists, and Tantricists, the androgyne is a symbol of perfection. Each one of us possesses elements of both genders to a greater or lesser extent. As we will see in the section on Crowley, this concept was elevated to the status, not only of doctrine, but also of ritual.

80 Randolph, *Eulis! the History of Love,* p. 7.

Aleister Crowley and Tantra

> ... I would suggest that the key differences between traditional forms of Tantra and Crowley's system lies not in the details of sexual union but rather in *the emphasis that is placed on sex in the first place.* (Emphasis in original)[81]

A search through the book that can arguably be called Crowley's most famous—*Magick: in Theory and Practice*—reveals references to Hindu mysticism and yoga in nearly every chapter. Terms like *asana, prana, pranayama, samadhi,* and *nirvana* abound, and many of the practices prescribed for followers of Crowley's unique form of ceremonial magic include yoga and meditation. This is certainly not what one would find in an examination of the European grimoires that form the basic texts of magic, and it is not something he would have learned from his time with the British secret society, the Golden Dawn.

It is therefore equally surprising to realize that there is virtually no mention in this text of Tantra itself. The references to sexually based occult practices are there, of course (this is Aleister Crowley, after all), but in a predominantly Western context in the form of the Rose and the Cross, or the Gnostic Mass, etc. What Crowley does do is refer his students to a handful of texts translated from Sanskrit and Pali that can be found in the *Sacred Books of the East* series that was virtually the only source of Hindu, Buddhist, and Daoist scriptures at the time (the early 20th century). The texts he recommends include the *Shiva Samhita* and the *Hathayoga Pradipika,* as well as the *Yoga Aphorisms of Patanjali* and the *Dhammapada.*

While Crowley's emphasis is clearly on yoga and the intensive training of the mind in meditation for the attainment of mystical illumination, the *Shiva Samhita* in particular can be considered a Tantric text, as it connects the practices of asana, mudra, and pranayama with the attainment of supernatural powers, and also provides a brief discussion of Kundalini and the pathways known as ida, pingala, and sushumna. Indeed, the *Shiva Samhita* is in the form of a dialogue between Shiva and Parvati and, in that sense, is consistent with other Tantric works.

The sources for Crowley's education in matters Indological can be identified easily enough. The Theosophical Society began as a Western-oriented occult society when it was founded in 1875 in New York City, but its creator and spiritual guru, Madame Helena Blavatsky, quickly abandoned Euro-centered occult litera-

81 Hugh B. Urban, *Magia Sexualis: Sex, Magic and Liberation in Modern Western Esotericism* (Berkeley: University of California Press, 2006), p. 127.

ture for an approach that was largely Asian. Her emphasis switched from Kabbalah and Hermeticism to Buddhism and Hinduism, leaving the field open to groups like the Golden Dawn and the Societas Rosicruciana in Anglia (and its associated Societas Rosicruciana in America) to concentrate on the Western esoteric tradition. Crowley was quite familiar with both areas of study, and was proud to notice that his birth year and that of the Theosophical Society were the same. The Society was, in fact, the best-known occult society in the West for many years, and has survived to the present day with branches throughout the world. Its headquarters were moved to India during Blavatsky's lifetime, and it became influential in the Indian independence movement, as well as in the independence movement of other Asian countries. At one point, Crowley even attempted to gain control of the Society—an attempt that was never in any real danger of succeeding, but that demonstrates the extent to which Crowley identified with the organization and its Asian-centered approach to esoteric matters.

Other than the Theosophists, Crowley's other real contact with Asian religion and mysticism came in the form of his good friend and colleague—one would even say mentor—Allan Bennett, who was one of the first Englishmen to be ordained a Buddhist monk and who introduced Buddhism to England. Bennett's role in promoting Buddhism has never been forgotten; Theravadin monks of the author's acquaintance from Sri Lanka (where Bennett studied under Sri Parananda in the early years of the 20th century) still revere his memory under his religious name, Bhikku Ananda Metteya.

Bennett was a member of the Golden Dawn, the British secret society that has produced such notable figures of modern occultism as Crowley, Arthur Edward Waite, MacGregor Mathers, and even Nobel Prize-winning poet William Butler Yeats. The Golden Dawn's origins are controversial. The claim that they were the British branch of a German Masonic society was regarded as a hoax for many years, until recent scholarship has suggested that these claims may be true. Regardless of the society's actual origins, the organizers were members of the Societas Rosicruciana in Anglia, a putative Rosicrucian order that was formed by Freemasons.

Crowley joined the Golden Dawn in 1898, received his revelation concerning the Law of Thelema in Cairo in 1904, and then joined the Ordo Templi Orientis (OTO) in 1910, receiving a charter for the OTO in Great Britain and Ireland in 1912. The dates are deceptively simple, for the impact that the Golden Dawn and OTO initiations had on both Crowley and on Western occultism since those years has been far-reaching.

The Golden Dawn taught an organized system of ceremonial magic based on the Kabbalistic Tree of Life and Egyptian mythology. This system includes an initiated version of the tarot cards, of astrology, and of the Angelic Tablets of Dr. John Dee and Edward Kelley, two Elizabethan-era magicians who claimed to have received, not only a system of magic directly from the angels, but also an angelic language with a grammar, syntax, and vocabulary all its own. The Golden Dawn system was nothing short of brilliant, for it brought order into the messy world of grimoires, talismans, and occult ritual of the Middle Ages and beyond. Crowley easily climbed the grades of the Golden Dawn and married the sister of one of its members, taking her on a honeymoon to Cairo where, in April of 1904, he received the *Book of the Law,* a testament that became his sacred scripture and the core document of the movement that grew up around it: *Thelema* (Greek for "will").

It is important to note that there was nothing overtly Tantric or sexual about the magic that was taught at the lodges of the Golden Dawn. It was all very Victorian and very proper—to the extent that ceremonial magic can be considered "proper." There was no nudity, no real or mimed sexual acts, no suggestive language. That said, the Golden Dawn did admit members of both genders and did acknowledge the role of goddesses as well as gods in the Egyptian pantheon they adopted.

Crowley's own *Book of the Law,* however, did contain material that was Tantric in tone, if not in nature. The *Book* is divided into three chapters, the first of which contains the words of the Egyptian goddess Nuit. Her admonitions concerning "wine and strange drugs" and her overtly sexual language about how she should be worshipped are evidence of a tendency toward the Tantric—or "tantroid"—that became increasingly shrill in Crowley's *ouevre.* The second chapter is that of Hadit, the male counterpart of Nuit, with more suggestive language and sexual references. The third and final chapter contains the words of Ra-Hoor-Khuit, the "Crowned and Conquering Child" of the New Aeon, or New Age. This, the most controversial chapter, contains militant language and rather vile imprecations concerning the world's religions. The transgressive nature of the *Book of the Law* so upset Crowley himself that he put it away and ignored it for years, while continuing to practice magic and occultism and maintaining his friendship with other occultists like Alan Bennett, who had since retired to Asia to become a Buddhist monk.

It is entirely possible—though so far not proven—that Crowley's knowledge of Tantra came from his travels in India and other parts of Asia, and from his conversations with Bennett. This is the kind of narrative with which scholars of religion have become all too familiar: the European who goes to the mysterious East and comes back with arcane knowledge. Although this may be said to have begun with Marco Polo, it includes personalities both real and mythical like Christian

Rosenkreutz, Apollonius of Tyana, and even Prester John. Since the 19th century, when Sir Richard Burton gave us his famous travelogues among the mysterious shamans of India and Arabia, all sorts of adventurers, spies, mercenaries, soldiers, mystics, and adepts have found themselves on the Journey to the East with greater or lesser success. This phenomenon was roundly criticized by Edward Said, who deplored the archetype of the civilized European gentleman who dips his toe into the brackish waters of the Ganges and comes back with tales alternately thrilling and disgusting of exotic lands, savagery, and beauty—tales that revealed more about the English imagination than it did about the foreign lands themselves.

This was precisely the image conjured up by the founders of the Ordo Templi Orientis—the Order of the Temple of the East. Their narrative includes the origins of their Order in the travels of their founder, Carl Kellner, who spent time in the Middle East and came back with the sexual secrets of Sufi and Indian mystics (a story that runs parallel to that of Randolph).

According to tradition, Crowley's occult writings up to that point (c. 1910) contained several veiled references to sexuality in a Rosicrucian context that attracted the attention of the OTO. The Order decided to initiate Crowley into its membership with the aim of preventing him from revealing any more secrets, however innocent or inadvertent the previous revelations had been. When Crowley realized the sexual aspect of his work up to that point, he felt illuminated and energized and set to work creating a comprehensive approach to magic and spirituality that would raise human sexuality to its rightful place. It also enabled him to revisit the *Book of the Law* and to accept the openly transgressive element of the more offensive passages as being essential to his unique process of genuine spiritual attainment. What Crowley had done—perhaps without being aware of it—was to write a peculiarly Western Tantra.

As noted previously, the Indian Tantras are written in the form of a dialogue between Shiva and Parvati (Shakti). The goal of the dialogue is to reveal certain secrets of the universe through myth, ritual, and occult instruction. In Crowley's *Book,* there are three chapters, each dictated by one of three Egyptian gods: Nuit, Hadit, and Ra-Hoor-Khuit. Nuit is the quintessential female goddess, while Hadit is her male counterpart. The presence of Ra-Hoor-Khuit, however, brings the traditional form of Tantra into a new dimension. The focus moves from the female-male polarity of Indian Tantricism to a third party: the Crowned and Conquering Child, the product of the *hieros gamos.* The third chapter repudiates all other existing religions and insists on replacing them—all of them—with a new vision and a new form of spirituality of which magic is the tool.

Egyptian religion is not the sole reference point for the *Book of the Law,* however. The very first chapter mentions the Beast and the Scarlet Woman, personalities famous from the New Testament's Book of Revelation (Book of the Apocalypse).[82] This infamous couple, who are signifiers of great evil in the Bible, become identified with the prophet of the New Aeon—Crowley himself—and his Bride. It is important to note that Crowley had a succession of these Brides, called Scarlet Women, whose function was purely ritualistic. By any metric, these women can be understood to have served as the shaktis in Crowley's unique system of magic and Tantra.

We now enter what is probably the most problematic aspect of Crowley's life work—his relationships with a string of Scarlet Women and other sexual partners, male and female, who were involved with him in his pursuit of the Great Work. The fact that some of these partners fared rather poorly in the process is well-documented, beginning with his first wife, Rose Kelley, who was committed to an asylum for alcoholism in 1911 (eight years after their marriage and the ensuing birth of their two children, one of whom died less than two years after she was born).

That Crowley had a succession of mistresses and wives and also frequented prostitutes is well-known. That this seemed scandalous in Victorian England is understandable, but we often observe the same behavior among Tantric adepts in India. On the one hand, it is too easy to claim that Crowley's sexuality was that of an initiate of the great mysteries and therefore beyond our ken, that we are incapable of judging him or his behavior because we have not attained the same level of initiation. On the other hand, it is also too easy to take at face value the stories that were printed about him in the tabloid press and condemn him outright for them.

Crowley's biographers—and there have been many—have done their best to separate the lies from the truth, a task made more difficult rather than easier by the publication of Crowley's own diaries and autobiography. His references to prostitutes, mistresses, homosexual encounters, masturbation, animal sacrifice, and drug use (hashish, opium, heroin, etc) are legion; what is remarkable is that most (if not all) of these references are within the context of magical workings and rites of divination. Clearly, this can be interpreted as Crowley justifying his actions by appeal to a higher, occult purpose. Perhaps there is no reliable way of understanding the truth of Crowley's career without following in his rather moist footsteps, but that is a subject for another book entirely.

What we will do here, instead, is look at some of what he has written specifically on the subject of occult sexuality and interpret it using what we know of Tantra, and especially of the syncretistic form of Tantra we have uncovered in Java.

82 Aleister Crowley, *The Book of the Law* (New York: Magickal Childe Publishing, 1990), I:15, p. 39.

Probably the most blatant expression of Crowley's ideas concerning sexuality and magic is a short pamphlet of twenty pages usually entitled *De Arte Magica* that was first published in 1914.[83] In this text, he writes of the elixir of life and uses primarily alchemical symbols like the Red Lion and the White Eagle. However, he also includes references to prana as well as to the sefirot of the Kabbalistic Tree of Life, and both thinly veiled sexual allusions and more blatant references to semen, menstrual blood, and other bodily fluids. The usual claim is made that this is the great secret at the heart of magic and occultism, and those who possess it have complete power over nature and the elements and can bend the universe to their will. In all of this, we can see similarities to the form of Tantra we find in Java—the syncretism, the importance of the elixir of life, the sexual allusions, and even the occasional references to prana and other Indian concepts.

Crowley goes somewhat further in this text, however, by gradually abandoning the "twilight language" and expressing the ideas and the technology more openly. In one place, he openly advocates the consumption of the "elixir"—the bodily fluids generated by sexual intercourse—and in another he extends the discussion to a form of deliberate sexual exhaustion he refers to as "eroto-comatose lucidity."[84] In chapter 16 of *De Arte Magica,* which is entitled "Of certain Hindu theories," we find what may be Crowley's first mention of the word "Tantra" when he refers to the *Shiva Samhita.* In this chapter, he also refers to the practice of the vajroli mudra (see chapter 5), but without mentioning it by name. He seems focused on the idea that the male Indian Tantrika does not ejaculate, but retains his semen. While this is true for some Tantric practices, it is not true for all. It was, however, a common perception among the scholars of Crowley's time, and to some extent remains so.[85]

Crowley's reference to the *Shiva Samhita,* certainly one of the most explicit of the Tantras, is interesting, because it contains an admonition to retain semen at all costs in its fourth chapter, the section dealing with the vajroli mudra. An edition dedicated to the Theosophical Society that was published in 1887 contains

---

83 See Aleister Crowley, *De Arte Magica* (Edmonds, WA: Sure Fire Press, 1988).

84 Crowley, *De Arte Magica,* p. 13–15, Chapter XIV, "Of the Consummation of the Element Divine, whether Quantity be as important as Quality, and whether its waste be Sacrilege."

85 This understanding is also reflected in the remarks of Moshe Idel (2005) who states, in reference to Kabbalistic views of sexual intercourse, that it is "not an aim in itself or one that is intended to attain personal perfection. The main and final goal or goals are procreation and preparation of appropriate substrata—human beings—to serve as residences for the Shekinah, quite unlike the Hindu ideal of attaining a moment of sublime consciousness by halting the ejaculation of semen" (p. 220). For competing views, see the works by Tantric scholar David Gordon White listed in the Bibliography.

the clear language of the original.[86] The more recent edition by James Mallinson claims to have restored some text excised from the Sris Chandra Vasu translation that specifically concerns the vajroli mudra. While the two translations are not identical, however, there does not seem to be anything missing in that regard.[87]

The *Shiva Samhita* contains the phrase: "Death arises through the falling of semen."[88] It urges adepts to retain semen at all costs—thus the recommendation to practice the vajroli mudra, the "vacuuming" of the seminal fluid from the vagina after ejaculation if, indeed, ejaculation has taken place. *De Arte Magica,* however, speaks clearly about the consumption of the mingled male and female fluids and goes so far, in the chapter on "eroto-comatose lucidity," as to recommend complete sexual exhaustion. This seems to be the antithesis of the practices recommended in the Shiva Samhita.[89]

One thing is clear, however; for Crowley, as for the Indian Tantrikas, the sex act itself represents the essence of magic. Variations of the sex act—positions, fluids, partners—are different elements of a complex technology of spiritual attainment. Each variation produces a different effect. The fact that some groups emphasize abstinence, others the avoidance of ejaculation, and still others the ejaculation and consumption of fluids does not indicate levels of moral or ethical superiority, but different paths leading ultimately to the same end—transformation of human consciousness into something resembling cosmic consciousness.

That sexuality and magic are inextricably linked is underlined by the Kabbalah—not only in the general way that the Shekinah is understood as a female quality of Godhead, but in some specifics as well.

Moshe Idel points out, for instance, that the Hebrew term *shimmush* designates "magical operations" as well as "copulation." Another term, rendered by the Hebrew letters ZQQ, "denotes both having a sexual relationship and making some form of invocation."[90] This meme seems to be at the heart of Western magic, as it is of Tantric practices. Tantra, for all its emphasis on sexuality, is also the most occult of the Indian religious practices. It is often identified with the acquisition of supernatural powers (the siddhis), as well as with spiritual attainments. Because of the use of mantras (which are considered magic spells in the West) and yantras (the

86 Srischandra Basu (Sris Chandra Vasu), *The Esoteric Philosophy of the Tantras Shiva Sanhita* (Calcutta: Heeralal Dhole, 1887).

87 James Mallinson, *The Shiva Samhita: A Critical Edition* (Woodstock, NY: YogaVidya.com, 2007, p. xi.

88 Mallinson, *The Shiva Samhita,* p. 97.

89 It could be argued that the vajroli mudra offers one method of "consuming" the mingled fluids.

90 Moshe Idel, *Kabbalah and Eros* (New Haven: Yale University Press, 2005), p. 43.

equivalent of magic seals and talismans), Tantra is both magical and sexual. There should be no surprise that a magician with the scientific approach that Crowley promoted would be as drawn to Tantra as he would be to Kabbalah and Egyptian magic. One holds the key to the other.

Crowley's use of alchemical imagery in *De Arte Magica* was relatively rare in his other published work, however. While he correctly understood the sexual aspects of alchemical terminology, it is doubtful whether he was able to interpret alchemical texts successfully from a purely (or largely) sexual perspective while maintaining the chemical (and psychological) levels of interpretation at the same time.

In another text, the outline of what he called the Cephaloedium Working that was conducted at the end of 1920, we have sexual references that are so explicit they verge on the humorous:

> Aiwaz is spelt Ayin, the Eye, i.e. that of Shiva or Horus, the Meatus Penis and the Anus: Yod, the Phallus, Spermatozoon, and Hand; Vau the Fertility of the Testes and Uterus as well as the Nail of the mentula, being Taurus the Cow Isis and the Bull Apis or Shiva, the Son in Tetragrammaton, the Redeemer by Reproduction, the Mithraic Bull of Resurrection and Initiation in the strength of the Body. .. And spelt fully Ayin is the Erection and Leaping and Extension of the Phallus; Yod is the Spermatozoon, the Solitary Boy Hermes, the Virgin; while Nun is the Eagle of sexual Ecstasy ...[91]

You get the picture.

The above would be viewed with horror by modern religious studies scholars and anthropologists as the worst sort of universalism. We have Hebrew letters mixed with Indian and Egyptian terms and gods, Mithraism, and so many sexual references that the insistence seems deliberate—an attempt to convince oneself. For instance, the Bull is simultaneously that of the Egyptian god Apis, the Indian god Shiva, and the bull of the Mithraic initiation process—not to mention the "Fertility of the Testes and Uterus." However, we should not allow ourselves to be dismayed by what appears to be a flagrant disregard for scholarly rectitude. What Crowley is doing is decoding the twilight language in which the esoteric texts were written. While we may suggest that sometimes a cigar is just a cigar, in the context of this ritual, the biological references are appropriate.

91 Aleister Crowley, *The Cephaloedium Working*, (n.d., n.p.).

In this same spirit of excessive transgression, Crowley describes the female partner or shakti—the Scarlet Woman—in these terms:

> ... Léa my concubine, in whom is all power given. sworn unto Aiwaz, prostituted in every part of her body to Pan and to the Beast, mother of bastards, aborter, whore to herself, to man, woman, child and brute, partaker of the Eucharist of the Excrements in the Mass of the Devil ...[92]

The shocking mention of something called the "Eucharist of the Excrements" has its parallel in the Kalachakra initiation ritual, where a vase of urine and a vase of feces occupy positions in the "pristine consciousness" mandala, as Jeffrey Hopkins, translator and editor of the definitive text on this Tibetan Buddhist initiation written by the Dalai Lama himself, tells us:

> The two vases in the east are filled with purified marrow; those in the south, with purified blood; those in the north, with purified urine; those in the west with purified excrement. Above and below, there are also vases filled with purified semen and menses respectively. They are on lotuses and are covered with lotuses.[93]

This initiation, again according to Hopkins, had its origins in Java with the initiation by Atisha of Pindo Acharya, the "famous Kalachakra master."[94] While the scatological references in Crowley may be due more to Crowley's own desire to be as extreme as possible in pursuit of forbidden knowledge rather than an insight into the more scandalous forms of Tibetan Tantrism, it is possible that the basic impulse is the same in both cases—a desire to overcome dualistic ideas of purity and filth, of what is acceptable and what is automatically rejected. Transgressive sexuality is followed to its logical conclusion: the sexualization (and hence sacralization) of all human biological emissions and substances.

This approach has been solidified in what is perhaps Crowley's longest-lasting (or best-known) legacy, the secret society known as the Ordo Templi Orientis, or OTO. The higher degrees of this society are known to embody secrets pertain-

---

92 Crowley, *The Cephaloedium Working,* (n.d., n.p.).

93 H.H. The Dalai Lama, *Kalachakra Tantra: Rite of Initiation,* Jeffrey Hopkins, ed. (Boston: Wisdom Publications, 1999), p. 85.

94 Dalai Lama, *Kalachakra Tantra,* p. 61.

ing to sexuality in its spiritual manifestations. The rituals for the VIII, IX, and XI degrees are not written down, but are believed to represent solitary sexuality, sexual intercourse, and anal or possibly homosexual sexuality, respectively. That this is a gross oversimplification is certain. The VIII degree may as easily represent abstinence and celibacy as self-gratification, for instance. The IX may represent the alchemical secret of the Rose and Cross, etc. When we are dealing with occultism, however, we are speaking in "twilight language," in which one set of symbols can be used to encode analogous processes in other systems. Recourse to Crowley's own writings reveals the practical application of some of these sexual secrets, so failing an actual initiation into the OTO or a similar order, it is up to the reader to make what use of it he or she is able.

Crowley lived at a time when serious research into Tantra had only just begun. Many of the most important texts had not yet been translated, or had been translated inexpertly. Moreover, Crowley was not fluent in any of the Indian languages, so did not have access to the deeper levels of meaning hidden within the texts that were available. It required scholars like David Gordon White and Hugh Urban—decades after Crowley's death in 1947—to reveal the close relationship between alchemy and Tantra, and to provide scholars and magicians alike with the context for understanding the alchemical process as a biological one, while not abandoning the other levels of interpretation (and praxis) that are equally relevant and important. The tools that are available today for a serious re-evaluation and rejuvenation of Western esotericism are many and powerful, and we can expect that a 21st-century version of the Golden Dawn may yet take advantage of these developments.

Sex, Magic, and Politics

In Javanese history, many of the Hindu-Buddhist kings were Tantrikas; those that were not often had Tantric priests as members of their courts. This open consolidation of esoteric with political power is unusual. In the West, we have the occasional example of a king or an emperor with an avid interest in occultism, alchemy, or hermeticism who brings experts in these fields to his court. Sometimes the goal is purely mercenary: hiring alchemists to make gold, for instance. In other cases, however, the hermetic arts had actual patrons in the royal houses of Europe. Still, it was rare to find a monarch that openly practiced magic or alchemy. Remember that Europe was the scene of the Inquisition and the witchcraft trials and, later, the wars of the Reformation. The Church had such a hold on the spirituality of the people that any deviation, no matter how benign, was punishable by imprisonment and death. One only has to remember what happened to Giordano Bruno or Galileo Galilei to understand that even scientists and philosophers were not exempt from this persecution and could find themselves sharing a prison—and a stake—with illiterate peasant women accused of witchcraft or poisoning their neighbors' cows. Even a powerful entity like the Knights Templar was disbanded, its members arrested, its lands confiscated, and its leaders executed.

In Java, there was (and still is) room for spiritual experimentation. At the time the Templars were being persecuted in Europe, Tantra was enjoying tremendous support in the courts of the Javanese kings. Perhaps this was due to a Javanese perception that there exists in the world a "hidden force" that is represented equally by the world of politics and by the world of spirituality and magic, and that one factor connecting these worlds is sexuality.[95]

The relationship between charisma and sexuality is an interesting one, a field that is little understood because it is so controversial. We have seen, in the West, how a politician's sexuality can destroy his career, particularly if it is of a "transgressive" nature—extra-marital affairs, homosexuality, pedophilia, etc. Some of our most attractive politicians—the most charismatic and dynamic—have been womanizers or have been accused of being so: Jack Kennedy, Robert Kennedy, Bill Clinton, Martin Luther King. The tension, especially in America, between sexuality and public life, and thus between politics and religion, is such that no calm and objective approach is possible. It is virtually heretical (in a secular way) to suggest that Jack Kennedy's sex life might have been an integral part of his personality as a charismatic and visionary leader. While Americans applaud the separation of church and state that is guaranteed by the Bill of Rights and the Constitution, they still apply strict religious perspectives to their political leaders and expect them to be "spiritually" pure as well as politically astute—a state of affairs that those in other nations find somewhat humorous or, at the least, confusing.

Adultery and homosexuality are viewed by pious Americans as threats to the sanctity (or spiritual integrity) of marriage. Marriage is considered to be a union so fragile, so tenuous, that assaults upon it are legion—especially those we cannot see. There is a raging discourse in America concerning the rights of homosexuals

95 See L. Couperus, *The Hidden Force,* Alexander Teixeira de Mattos, trans. (Amherst: University of Massachusetts Press, (1900) 1985). This colorful novel by a Dutch expatriate living in Indonesia during the colonial period emphasizes the Javanese belief in a "hidden force" behind politics, religion, and life and is a good introduction to some of the themes explored in this book. For those who are skeptical that such a belief does, in fact, exist in Indonesia, you only need to see the plethora of books on the spiritual activities and beliefs of such important Indonesian leaders as Suharto.

to marry, the argument being that allowing homosexuals the same rights as heterosexuals somehow undermines straight marriages. The logic is hard to follow, but may have more to do with how marriage and sexuality were understood by America's European ancestors than with religion itself.

Since the history of love and marriage in the West has been shown to be a topic worthy of several large volumes, I will not attempt to duplicate the efforts of other authors in these pages, but will instead suggest that the central, legal concern of marriage in the West is property and inheritance. Any study of European history will show that succession—of kings and queens—was a constant obsession in the courts. There had to be a legitimate heir; the bloodline was more important than competence or capability. An outsider (a commoner) could not hope to ascend the throne, no matter how brilliant. Thus, love was irrelevant to the condition of sexual reproduction and the manufacture of legitimate heirs.

In the life of everyday people, property was still an issue. Deciding who would inherit property after the death of a parent became a jurisprudential obstacle course. Different cultures and different religions had widely differing opinions and laws on inheritance. An illegitimate child could not hope to inherit, thus implying that bloodline and community sanction was necessary for the peaceful transfer of real estate. This may be among the many reasons why cultures have forbidden homosexuals to marry, for their children would almost certainly not be their own or, at the very least, not the product of both parents, even if artificial insemination came into play. Without a "legitimate" heir, property ownership could not be determined. If the children of homosexual couples were permitted to inherit, then illegitimate children of heterosexual couples could be considered viable heirs as well.

That this was true, not only for monarchs, but also for the citizens of the realm is underlined by the typical marriage ceremonies of India, Malaysia, Indonesia, and even Eastern Europe and Greece. In these ceremonies, the wedding couple is considered king and queen for the duration of the ceremony. They are treated as royalty. In the Russian Orthodox Church, the couple wears crowns of gold. In the Greek Orthodox Church, the crowns may be of flowers, but they are nonetheless crowns. The association of marriage with political power and rule—with the monarchy—is thereby acknowledged, and the association of marriage, political power, and sexuality is made manifest. Even in the *Chymical Wedding of Christian Rosenkreutz,* the married couple at the heart of the mystery are a king and queen.

This demonstrates the nexus between power and sexuality. The rules concerning ownership of a farm are mirrored in those of the ownership of a country. A lawful marriage is a prerequisite; but the state's involvement in married life does not end there. As Michel Foucault has pointed out:

> Up to the end of the eighteenth century, three major explicit codes—apart from customary regularities and constraints of opinion—governed sexual practices: canonical law, the Christian pastoral, and civil law. They determined, each in its own way, the division between licit and illicit. They were all centered on matrimonial relations: the marital obligation, the ability to fulfill it, the manner in which one complied with it, the requirements and violences that accompanied it, the useless or unwarranted caresses for which it was a pretext, its fecundity or the way one went about making it sterile, the moments when one demanded it ...its frequency or infrequency, and so on. ...The sex of husband and wife was beset by rules and recommendations.[96]

Thus, what a man and woman do together, even on the matrimonial bed, is subject to proscriptions and prescriptions, inhibitions and prohibitions. What is transgressive in this environment is not only the standard "crimes" of adultery and homosexuality, but virtually any sexual act that does not have reproduction—the creation of property and an heir to property—as its goal. An adulterous liaison does not produce a legitimate heir; nor do homosexual liaisons. This idea was extended to oral intercourse and anal intercourse as well, which were condemned because they were not capable of producing a human child. This relationship between sexuality and property has been the dark shadow behind all public discourse about marriage, sex, deviation, etc.—no less in the civil arena than in the sacred spaces.

Is it any wonder, then, that the Tantric circle was vilified, not only by British colonialists, but by Indian Brahmins as well? The type of sexuality honored and practiced in the rituals of the Kaula Tantrikas and the Vama Marg practitioners was a physical and material repudiation of the idea that sexuality is purely for the purpose of producing more children—boys to inherit the land, and girls to be sold off into virtual slavery as wives of men they had never met. Love is suspect in this equation; it is a wildcard element that has to be contained, controlled, and directed toward an appropriate end. Love is volatile and unpredictable, and its sudden phosphorescent appearance in a stable and society-conscious family can be perceived as a threat to the community. This is especially true when the emotion of affection is accompanied by sexual attraction.

Sexuality, however, is considered contained once the bond of matrimony is sealed. The matrimonial commitment is made, not only to one's spouse, but (and

---

96 Michel Foucault, "The Repressive Hypothesis," in *The Foucault Reader*, Paul Rabinow, ed. (New York: Pantheon, 1984), p. 317.

probably most importantly) to the community at large. It is a statement that each partner has now accepted the rules and regulations of the community where sexuality is concerned, and that it is expected that viable heirs to whatever property may exist will be safely produced. One defies these expectations at one's peril, as the archetypal example of Romeo and Juliet informs us.

Là-Bas

Tantra, however, calls all of our preconceived notions about sexuality into question. The Tantric circle is, in Western eyes, a Black Mass. There is ritual, there is illegitimate worship, there is secrecy and the unsettling environment of the cemetery, and there is sexuality. Most important, there is also power and the attainment of that power by those not legitimately entitled to it. The Tantric circle implies the creation of an alternative system of religion and government, an alternative culture, and an alternative sexuality. Tantra, in its purest form, is an act of rebellion.

This was also true of the Black Mass, which is said to be performed by defrocked Catholic priests and to feature a nude virgin as the altar. This Mass represents the ultimate rebellion against the Church, which also means against the state. It is a denial of everything that both ostensibly stand for. The control and suppression of sexuality as noted above by Foucault results in its expression in violent images and extreme behavior—a condition that is still with us today.

As Georges Bataille (1897–1962) has noted, reproduction is opposed to eroticism.[97] Bataille speaks of the idea of continuity and discontinuity—that we, as discontinuous beings, yearn for continuity. He notes that we are born alone and die alone, as individuals, and that this is at the heart of our feeling of discontinuity. Community cannot solve that problem effectively.

Eroticism, on the other hand, does provide the sensation of continuity, of being at one with another person and, by extension, with the cosmos itself. He calls this state of being *dissolution*—a term revealing for the way it resonates with alchemy and with Tantra and the amrita:

> The whole business of eroticism is to strike to the inmost core of the living being, so that the heart stands still. The transition from the normal state to that of erotic desire presupposes a partial dissolution of the person as he exists in the realm of discontinuity.

97 Georges Bataille, *Erotism: Death and Sensuality* (San Francisco: City Lights, (1957) 1986), p. 12. Emphasis appears in the original.

> Dissolution—this expression corresponds with *dissolute life,* the familiar phrase linked with erotic activity. ...for the male partner the dissolution of the passive partner means one thing only: it is paving the way for a fusion where both are mingled, attaining at length the same degree of dissolution.[98]

The term "dissolution" is used in alchemy to refer to the second step in the alchemical process of transformation. This step involves dissolving a solid substance in a liquid; one of its symbols is the bath. There are many illustrations of this in alchemical texts; often, they depict a king and queen together in the bath as if it were a wedding bed or a coffin. The process requires repeated steps of dissolution and coagulation, and is often referred to by the Latin phrase *solve et coagula.*

In the quotation above, Bataille is referring to a dissolution of consciousness in which both the male and female partners are "mingled" in the sexual act. It could just as well refer to the alchemical process or to the Tantric process. The mingling is an essential step in the creation of the amrita, the elixir vitae. Indeed, Bataille's study of eroticism is subtitled "Death and Sensuality." The connection between eroticism and death is, in Bataille's view, a necessary one. As humans, we are made mortal and subject to death as "discontinuous" beings when we are "created" through the process of a sexual act. We seek continuity, and do so through eroticism—an eroticism that does not avoid or negate death, but that provides a sense that death is not final but part of (or an extension of) the erotic experience. As we noted in a previous chapter, the connection between death and orgasm—*le petit mort*—is common to many cultures.

Bataille's work was often banned, thus showing once again the sensitivity of governments to open discussions of sexuality. His short novel, *The Story of the Eye,* has a Black Mass as its climactic scene, with elements of fellatio, the consumption of urine and semen with the sacrament, and ritual murder.[99] This story echoes that of J. K. Huysmans' famous novel of Satanism, *Là-Bas* (1891), which also ends with a Black Mass and contains references to the notorious mass murderer, Gilles de Rais.

While the prototype of the Black Mass was, as noted, anti-Church as well as anti-state, by the time Bataille was writing, the notion of the Black Mass had taken on a general anti-establishment, anti-cultural signification. While the desecration of a church and its sacrament may be considered scandalous and even horrifying today, for many 21st-century Christians, pious and otherwise, the idea

98 Bataille, *Erotism,* p. 17.

99 Georges Bataille, *The Story of the Eye* (San Francisco: City Lights Books, (1928) 1986).

of the Black Mass has gradually lost its ability to shock. With the ready availability of pornography and the boundary-testing programs of commercial television and film in the areas of extreme violence and sexuality, it is reasonable to expect that the Western psyche has become desensitized to what was once considered blasphemous and transgressive. The ongoing, highly publicized scandals involving pedophile priests have also meant that many Catholics—and non-Catholics—no longer feel that the Church is as sacrosanct as before.

Instead, we have another figure, another unholy icon, in the character of the serial killer. Previously known as the "lust killer," the serial killer represents a fusion between violent murder and sexuality. As I have suggested in an earlier work, the serial killer may be, for the West, a shamanic symbol.[100] Serial killers are known not only for murder itself, but for the grisly elements that accompany their kills—dismemberment of the body; torture; sexual acts before, during, or after the murder; the retention of souvenirs; etc. These are ritualistic kills in the broadest sense of "ritual," as an act that is repeated in exactly the same way as a kind of compulsion that has meaning for the ritualist. These elements are often present in the development stage of the Siberian shaman, but they occur internally as part of a psychological (and perhaps psycho-biological) process. The popularity of books and movies in the West that romanticize this figure is evidence that the close association of murder and sex has resonance with the general public. There is a sense that the idea of the serial killer represents something sacred or at least something secret and encoded. It is the Minotaur in the Labyrinth, perhaps. The Shadow in the Machine. Isn't the theme of "death and sensuality" present in the Tantras themselves? Even in the Kalachakra Tantra, which is the core text of the initiations carried out worldwide by the Dalai Lama? As suggested previously, the time has come for a Foucaldian interpretation of the Tantras with an assist from Bataille and Derrida, perhaps.

This modern fascination with sex and death may be early evidence, therefore, that the Tantric practices of today may have to undergo a kind of transformation. Does the need still exist for rituals that break tabus in their preliminary stages? If so, what tabus are left to break? How will modern Western seekers approach Tantra and tantroid practices in their effort to attain higher degrees of spiritual awareness and gain siddhis in the process, when they have been inundated with sexually oriented media since birth? Where will the break between normative reality and an alternate reality occur? Where is the liminal boundary between a modern man or woman and the Unknown, the Forbidden, the Other?

100 Peter Levenda, *Sinister Forces, Vol. 3: The Manson Secret* (Walterville, OR: Trine Day, 2006), pp. 52–58.

It may simply be different for each person. While society at large may have disposed of many of the tabus that once loomed so large that the breaking of them was a dangerous spiritual act, on an individual basis, many tabus still remain. Society has not suddenly attained higher spiritual states because the tabus have been lifted. On the contrary. It is possible, then, that for modern Westerners to make effective use of this spiritual "technology," they will have to revisit old neuroses, to chant the forgotten hymns, to become reacquainted with the world as it was known only a century or so ago. Only then will the illusion that the tabus have been broken become the accepted wisdom. As conservative forms of religion become more dominant in Western society, we may find that what we thought had been discarded now returns with a vengeance. When that happens, Tantra will show a way out, and a way up.

Conclusions

The survival of Tantra and of tantroid practices and beliefs in the largest Muslim country in the world provides us with an argument against monolithic expectations where religion and spirituality are concerned. Spirituality is not determined by dogma or doctrine; individual spiritual seekers are not theologians. They are practitioners, and as practitioners, they accept what works and discard what does not. That does not mean that the discarded rites and values are worthless; at any time, they may be revisited. The needs of spiritual seekers change as their level of understanding changes, and as their needs in the world change.

Tantra is a way of action, a magical approach to spirituality that is eclectic and dynamic. That we find syncretism in the religious life of Java should, therefore, come as no surprise. While the West is still struggling with evaluations of sexuality and its place in religion, politics, and spirituality—and confronted by increasingly blatant expressions of sex, violence, and criminal behavior (both real and fictionalized) in the media—Tantra acknowledges the power of transgressive behavior and channels it into areas conducive to psychological development.

In Java, this approach to life and to power has never been denied or suppressed for very long. It may have reached its heyday during the Hindu-Buddhist dynasties that lasted for 1000 years on the island, but it managed to survive throughout the later Islamic period and up into the present day as an integral part of Javanese culture. There were Tantric kings on Java, just as there are innumerable temples that enshrine—literally—the principles of amrita, of Kundalini, and of siddhi. We have seen that these sites are often still the loci of worship and ritual. The rulers of modern Indonesia have acknowledged the importance of these beliefs in their own lives. The Islamic sultans of Yogyakarta and Solo still recognize the power and importance of the Queen of the Southern Seas, and offerings are made to her regularly.

What the West can learn from Java and the Javanese is tolerance and acceptance—but also something deeper. Javanese religious and cultural life is a demonstration of the way in which an individual's spirituality can be accommodated by the community, even in (or because of) the apparent discontinuity of a culture in which monotheistic Islam is merged with Hindu and Buddhist beliefs and practices as well as indigenous religious ideas and rituals. This is a phenomenon that has been remarked upon by anthropologists like Clifford Geertz, Neils Mulder, and Robert Hefner among others, and that has attracted a steady stream of academics and researchers since the 1950s. What the Western academic community often decries as "universalism" is a fact of life among the Tantric temples of Java, where common ground is discovered and celebrated in common—spiritual—denominators.

That is not to say that there is no religious or sectarian violence in Indonesia. Far from it. There are old wounds in the archipelago that even enlightened political and religious discourse cannot eradicate overnight. The Chinese in particular have been the object of racial and sectarian violence; so have some of the Christian communities there. The ugliness of these attacks, which leave innocent people dead and maimed in the name of ideologies, cannot be ignored or swept under the rug. The famous tolerant attitude of the citizens of Indonesia can become undone in an instant, depending on the stressors involved. Yet, in the West, we have witnessed and still witness similar incidents of racial violence directed at entire communities. Somehow, when it happens in a tropical "third-world" country, it seems worse. Colonial ideas about savages and unholy rites rise to the foreground like old ghosts intent on haunting new houses.

It should be remembered, however, that the Republic of Indonesia is only about sixty years old. When the United States was of a similar age, Americans were killing Native Americans with reckless abandon, held slaves, and were on the verge of a civil war. We can argue that times have changed and expect the rest of the world to catch up to what Americans consider normal or acceptable behavior, but that is naive. Instead, we should focus on the tremendous strides that Indonesia has accomplished in those sixty years since independence, and especially in the years since the Reformasi ("Reform") movement brought down the government of President Suharto and ushered in an era of national soul-searching and the lifting of sanctions against other religions and races. The resurgence of popular expressions of Hinduism and Buddhism in Java is another example of the willingness of the Javanese to make room for alternate forms of religious practice and belief.

This is not without controversy. The famous Pancasila edict of Sukarno made it mandatory that every Indonesian profess membership in one of six (originally only five) state-approved religions: Islam, Catholicism, Protestantism, Hinduism, Buddhism, and Confucianism. The state insisted that a belief in one god and the possession of a sacred scripture were mandatory requirements for a religion to be considered acceptable. Also, the religion must be accepted world-wide— it must be a "world religion." This has had the effect of marginalizing those Indonesians who are considered "animists" or "pagans" by Westerners, and has created a broad category of "nominal," or abangan, Muslims who still practice many rituals that are considered kejawen or "Javanese." It has also created some discomfort among Buddhists (who have many scriptures and who are not believers in one God) and among Hindus (whose have as many scriptures as the Buddhists and who embrace the worship of more than one God). Confucians are another problematic category, for some of the same reasons. And are Jehova's Witnesses considered "Protestant" under this law? For a long while, they were not.

This requirement of belonging to one of the six approved religions has its parallel in the imposition of Bahasa Indonesia, a derivative of the Javanese language, as the national language. This is another means of trying to create a national identity—insisting on one language for all, even if it is not native to millions of Indonesians. Was the motive behind this proclamation an attempt to de-emphasize or devalue the cultures and languages of Indonesians other than the Javanese (who are in the majority)? Some have thought so. By creating a somewhat artificial national language and insisting on membership in a limited number of approved religions, the new government is attempting to bring order into chaos and to create a sense of nationalism. The goal is certainly to eradicate potential pockets of resistance and nonconformity, and to get everyone marching in the same direction. Considering the Cold War mentality of the time, we can approve or disapprove of these measures, but certainly now, they can be revisited and they probably will be.

The Javanese attitude toward Tantra and tantroid ideas and practices is one indication that Indonesia may provide a blueprint for tolerance that is not based on a sterile legalistic approach to the phenomenon of multi-culturalism, but one that is the result of a common-sense, pragmatic attitude toward what works and what does not. That an enlightened view of sexuality that cuts across denominational and sectarian lines will be one of the factors influencing such an approach is suggested by the fallout from the recent Mount Merapi eruption of October 2010.

As thousands of villagers were forced to flee their homes and set up temporary housekeeping in shelters throughout Yogyakarta—a situation that lasted for weeks and then for months—an unusual request was made to the Indonesian authorities. Married couples were unable to have sex because of the crowded, public conditions of the shelters. They asked that special accommodations be built so that they could still enjoy a sex life even though they were living in exile from their villages.[101]

The government acquiesced to their request.

---

101 Antara, "Merapi Evacuees Yet To Take Advantage of Stress-Busting Sex Shacks," Jakarta Globe, 24 November 2010.

Glossary

Language key:

A = Arabic
B = Babylonian (also used here for Akkadian and Sumerian words)
C = Chinese (Mandarin)
D = Dutch
E = Ancient Egyptian
F = French
G = Greek
H = Hebrew
I = Bahasa Indonesia (Indonesian)
J = Javanese
P = Pali
S = Sanskrit
T = Tibetan

Please note: There are many ways to spell Javanese and Indonesian words. There has been a movement to standardize Bahasa Indonesia, but many older works use different spellings. Thus, the name of the first President of Indonesia may be spelled Soekarno or Sukarno; Yogyakarta may be spelled Jogjakarta or even Ngayogyakarta (in its older designation as Ngayogyakarta Hadiningrat or Yogyakarta Sultanate). Where logical, I will offer variant spellings of the same word to make the transition between older and newer source material easier for the reader.

The same is true for Chinese. While Pinyin has standardized Romanization of Mandarin words, older texts use different orthography. Thus, Tao in the old system equals Dao in the new.

To complicate things further, many words in Indonesian come from Sanskrit, Arabic, and even Dutch and Portuguese sources. Often, the word survives unchanged, such as the word for "teacher": *guru* (from the Sanskrit). In this glossary, priority is given to the original with the understanding that the same word may also be used in Indonesian with its original spelling intact.

abangan (I) Nominal, as in *abangan Muslim* or "nominal Muslim."

Abhinha Jataka (S) A Buddhist text: one of the stories of the life of Buddha before his incarnation as Prince Siddartha. In this case, the story of the Elephant and the Dog.

abhaya (S) Lit. "fearless"; it is the name of a mudra that protects from fear.

abzu (B) Abyss; also the name for a large basin of water for ritual purposes found in Babylonian temples.

Adam Kadmon (H) From the Hebrew *Adam ha-Kadmoni*, the "Original" or "Primal" Adam. The Perfect Human. In Kabbalah, since "man is made in the image and likeness of God" (Genesis 1:26-27), the ideal of Adam Kadmon represented divine perfection in human form.

advaita (S) Non-duality, a Buddhist concept.

Adya Shakti (S) Adya or Adhya means "first creator"; as Adya Shakti it is another name for the goddess Parvati or Uma, as the consort of Shiva and co-creator of the universe. In Tantra, it is sometimes used as a term for the female partner in the pancatattva ritual.

Agastya (S) Lit. "mountain thrower," the name of one of the Seven Sages of India, and the one who swallowed the cosmic ocean to trap demons who fled there.

Aghoris (S) A Tantric sect in India.

Agni (S) Fire; also the name of the God of Fire in Hinduism.

Agnihotra (S) The most basic form of the Homa ritual, it is translated as "healing fire."

Akitu (B) The Babylonian New Year festival.

aliran kebatinan (I) General term for Javanese esoteric or mystical groups.

alus (J) See "halus": graceful, refined.

amaroli mudra (S) In Tantra, the use of the penis to re-absorb into the male's body the ejaculated seminal fluid as well as vaginal fluids from the female partner's vagina.

amitabha mudra (S) Also known as the dhyana mudra or meditation mudra.

amrita (S) Literally "no death," the elixir vitae, the water of life and immortality. Often confused with *soma*, which probably had a botanical origin as an entheogen.

amrita kumbha (S) A container to hold the amrita (q.v.).

amritavarsa (S) The "rain of amrita" that flows from the seventh chakra down through the entire body at the moment when Kundalini has risen to the cranial vault and a "spiritual orgasm" is achieved.

anadhikarini (S) "Incompetent," in the Tantric sense: incapable of fulfilling the role of Shakti in the pancatattva ritual.

anatta (S) No-soul; a Buddhist concept.

andesite A type of volcanic rock very common in Java, and used as the base material for temples, statues, etc.

antardasha (S) In Vedic astrology, a sub-dasha: i.e., a component of a dasha (q.v.).

apophatism A theological position that says God can be defined through negative statements: i.e., what God *is not* as opposed to statements about what God *is*.

ardha (S) Lit. "half," as in ardha padmasana (q.v.).

ardha padmasana (S) The "half-lotus" asana or yoga position.

Ardhanarishvara (S) A form of Shiva that is androgynous, i.e., half-man, half-woman.

argotique (F) Lit. "slang" or "alternate language," i.e., a form of communication incomprehensible to those outside a certain group. The alchemist Fulcanelli used it as a play on the phrase *ars gotique* or "Gothic art." A form of twilight language or green language.

Arjuna (S) Lit. "bright," "shining," or "silver," from which the Latin word *argentum* ("silver") is derived. The name of one of the Pandava brothers of the Mahabharata. One of the sons of Kunti and the friend of Krishna from whom he heard the famous Hindu text *Bhagavad Gita*. Usually shown with a bow, as an archer.

Arupadhatu (S) The Sphere of Formlessness, the goal of the Buddhist devotee, represented at Borobudur by the three top—circular—levels.

asana (S) In yoga, a position that is held by the body for a length of time, as an aid to meditation or to stimulate a specific psycho-biological response.

Asherah (H) A controversial term found in the Bible and in non-Biblical sources referring to a post or pillar placed next to the altar, to a stand or grove of trees, or to a personality believed to be the consort of God (El).

Ashratum (B) Akkadian form of the Hebrew Asherah (q.v.).

Asshur (B) The main deity and creator god of the Assyrian pantheon, usually shown holding a bow (similar to Arjuna and Rama). One possible etymology of his name is AN.SHUR or "the entire sky." Asshur was also the name of the principle city of Assyria, circa 3000 BCE.

Asura (S) Usually refers to a member of a group of supernatural beings who become demonized in the Bhagavad Gita and in some earlier Hindu texts as the counterparts to the Devas. The Asuras appear in the Churning of the Milk Ocean holding one end of the Serpent while the Devas hold the other, their "tug of war" churning the ocean and producing the amrita. In the Zoroastrian religion, however, the Asuras are given divine status and the Devas become "demonized." There is also the possibility that the word asura is related to the Assyrian god Asshur (q.v.).

Atharva Veda (S) The fourth or "last" of the Vedas, commonly associated with magic.

Atisha (S) A famous Buddhist teacher (980-1054 CE) who studied in Sumatra and/or Java in the eleventh century and brought the teachings back to India and Tibet. He is regarded by the Tibetans as one of the Three Precious Gems of Tibetan Buddhism.

Atum (E) The Creator God of the ancient Egyptian religion, his name is said to derive from the Egyptian word *tem*, meaning "complete." As such, he is considered to represent creation, perfection, and completion. It is tempting to connect *Atum* with *Adam*, especially in the latter's form as Adam Kadmon (q.v.) or the Perfect Adam, but there is insufficient evidence to support this idea. Adam, however, was the "first man" in Jewish religion, and Atum was the "first god" in Egyptian religion.

Avadana (S) A collection of stories of famous Buddhist saints.

Avalokitesvara (S) The Buddha of Mercy. The Dalai Lama is said to be the incarnation of this Buddha. In China, Avalokitesvara is the goddess Guan Yin.

bahasa (I) Language.

Bahasa Indonesia The Indonesian language.

Bahasa Malaysia The Malaysian language, formerly known as Bahasa Melayu.

Batara Guru (J) A Javanese deity analogous to—or in some cases identical with—Shiva. Considered the "supreme God"—who nonetheless derives power from a higher deity, Sang Hyang Wenang who is the source of all divine power—he is an important figure not only in Javanese religion but also in the wayang kulit (q.v.). The name translates as "Teacher God," the word for "teacher"—*guru*—obviously derived from the Sanskrit.

batin (A) Secret, esoteric. Used to refer to the esoteric side of Islam. The root of the Indonesian term kebatinan (q.v.).

Bedhaya Harjunowijoyo (J) A version of the Bedhaya Semang (q.v.) honoring the Sultan of Yogyakarta.

Bedhaya Ketawang (J) The Solonese version of the Bedhaya Semang (q.v.).

Bedhaya Semang (J) The sacred dance honoring the Queen of the Southern Seas, Nyai Lara Kidul (q.v.).

bhasa (S) Language.

Bhima (S) A military commander in the *Mahabharata*, and one of the Pandawa brothers. He is represented amply at Candi Sukuh.

Bhre Daha (J) Prince Daha, a rebel commander during the last days of the Majapahit empire; believed to have consecrated a lingga at Candi Ceto.

bhumi (S) The earth; the world.

Bhumi Devi (S) The Goddess of the Earth; mother of Sita in the Ramayana.

bhumisparsa mudra (S) Lit. "touching the earth"; a Buddhist mudra.

Bima (J) See *Bhima*.

Bimasakti (J) The Milky Way. Lit. "Bima Power."

bodhicitta (S) Lit. "awakening of consciousness" or "awakening of the mind" as a Buddhist term, also used in some Tantras to refer to an initiate's semen during the rituals.

Brahma (S) The Creator God of Vedic India. One of the Trimurti, along with Shiva and Vishnu.

Brahmajala Sutta (P) In Theravedic Buddhism, an important text sometimes translated as the "Net of All-Embracing Views of Perfect Wisdom."

brahmin (S) The highest, priestly, caste in the Indian caste system.

candi (I) Pronounced "chandi"; the word for an ancient religious building such as a temple or monument, usually used with reference to pre-Islamic or non-Islamic buildings.

candi apit (I) Term for a "flanking temple" in Javanese temple architecture, one of (usually) two smaller temples at either side of a central, larger temple.

candrasangkala (J) Lit. "chronogram." A hieroglyphic representation of a date.

chakravartin (S) One who "Turns the Wheel" (of the Law, or Dharma). An epithet for a ruler or monarch who is an upholder of Buddhism.

chela (S) A student or disciple of a guru.

Chinnamasta (S) In Indian religion, a fierce goddess who cuts off her own head.

dalang (I) The puppeteer in traditional Javanese *wayang*.

dalit (S) A member of the "untouchable" caste in India.

damaru (S) A drum made of two human craniums in an hourglass shape.

Dao (C) "The Way": the central concept of Chinese Daoism (Taoism).

dasha (S) In Vedic astrology, a division of time identified with a planetary period. Thus, there is a Sun dasha, a Moon dasha, etc. of varying lengths, with their corresponding sub-divisions known as *antar-dashas*.

desa (I) A village.

Deshawarnana (J) Lit. "description of the districts," a chronicle of the Majapahit dynasty written in 1365 CE and almost destroyed during a Dutch military action.

deva (S) Lit. "god" from which we get the word "diva" as well as, paradoxically, "devil."

devavatara (S) "Descent from the sky," or "descent of the god." To some scholars, Borobudur is a *devavatara* device: i.e., designed to bring devotees up to the heavens and also to bring the gods down to earth.

Dewi Sri (I) The Javanese form of the Indian Sri Devi. A mother goddess.

Dhammapada (P) A famous Buddhist scripture from the Pali canon. *Dhamma* is the Pali form of the Sanskrit *Dharma* (q.v.).

Dharma (S) Lit. "doctrine" or "truth." A central Buddhist concept, and often used to denote Buddhism itself.

dharma chakra mudra (S) The mudra of the Wheel of Dharma.

dharma chakra pravartana (S) Lit. "Turning the Wheel of Dharma."

dhikr (A) In Islam, the repetition of the name of God as a mantra.

dhyana mudra (S) The mudra of meditation or contemplation.

Dhyani Buddha (S) A form of the Buddha in contemplation.

dorje (T) The Tibetan form of the Sanskrit word for thunderbolt, *vajra*.

dukun (I) A general term for shaman, healer, or ritual specialist, in the indigenous Javanese or *kejawen* tradition.

dukun sihir (I) Sorcerer. A "black magician" or "black *dukun*."

Dumuzi (B) The shepherd god of ancient Sumer and Babylon, and the husband of Inanna/Ishtar.

Durga (S) An evil or frightening goddess, usually associated with cemeteries and charnel grounds.

dvarapala (S) A guardian at the gate to a temple, usually shown with only a head.

Enki (B) A Sumerian god, lord of magic and of the Abzu (i.e., the Abyss or Underworld).

Ereshkigal (B) Sumerian goddess of the Underworld and sister of Inanna.

eroto-comatose lucidity A term coined by the British magician Aleister Crowley to refer to a state of heightened consciousness immediately following a series of intense, physically depleting orgasms.

Erra (B) A powerful Akkadian god of plague and pestilence.

etz chaim (H) The Tree of Life.

etz hawwa (H) The "Tree of Eve."

Feng Shui (C) Lit. "Wind Water," sometimes called Chinese geomancy, is a method of determining the best site and orientation of buildings to take advantage of geographical and astronomical features and data. It is related to the Indian art of Vaastu.

Gajah Sena (J) The son of Batara Guru who eventually becomes incorporated into Bhima (q.v.).

gana (S) One of the servitors of Shiva; an imp that is usually shown holding up the created world, much as Atlas is depicted in the West.

Gandavyuha (S) A Buddhist sutra that tells of the quest of Prince Sudhana in search of enlightenment.

Ganesha (S) One of the two sons of Shiva represented by an elephant's head on a human body.

Gelugpa (T) A branch of Tibetan Buddhism, popularly known as the "Yellow Hat" School, of which the Dalai Lama is the head.

gematria (H) In Kabbalah, the practice of reducing words to their numerical equivalents, and then finding words with the same equivalent and associating them thereby. The word has Greek roots, probably from *geometria*.

grimoire (F) From *grammaire*, a magician's workbook or spellbook.

Guan Yin (C) Sometimes spelled "Kuan Yin," the Goddess of Mercy. In India and Tibet, the form is male and is called Avalokitesvara.

gunas (S) The three basic processes of the universe: creation, preservation, and destruction, known as *rajas*, *sattva,* and *tamas* respectively. In Hinduism, these are further referenced by the gods Brahma, Vishnu, and Shiva, respectively.

gunung (I) Mountain.

gunungan (I) The word used to describe one of the devices used in the shadow puppet play, depicting a mountain (such as Mount Meru) or sometimes a tree or other type of axis mundi.

guru kebatinan (I) A teacher of Javanese esoterica; the leader of a Javanese mystical sect.

Hadit (E) Greek form of the Egyptian Heru or Horus. In the Thelemic religion, one of the three speakers of the Book of the Law, along with Nuit and Ra-Hoor-Khuit.

halus (J) Refined, gracious, delicate.

Hanuman (S) The monkey king. In the Ramayana, Hanuman is the loyal friend of Rama and Sita (Sinta).

hawaki ra ya hilangi (J) Lit. "the disappearance of the body." An inscription found at Candi Ceto.

Hayam Wuruk (J) A famous Javanese king of the 14th century CE Majapahit empire.

Hevajra Tantra (S) A Tantric text central to Tibetan Buddhism, it is believed to have originated in India sometime between the eighth and tenth centuries CE.

hieros gamos (G) Lit. "sacred wedding."

Homa (S) The fire ritual of Vedic India. There are many forms of this ritual, some simple and some quite complex, depending on the purpose.

ida (S) One of the three main channels of energy in the human body, according to Indian tradition, specifically yoga. The other two are pingala and sushumna (q.v.).

ilmu hitam (I) Black magic.

Inanna (B) A mother goddess of ancient Sumer, often associated with the planet Venus. Inanna's descent into the Underworld is a well- known myth of the ancient Middle East.

ipri (J) A snake spirit that takes the form of a beautiful woman.

iprit (J) Same as *ipri* (q.v.).

Ishtar (B) A later Babylonian variant of the Sumerian Inanna (q.v.).

Jambi (J) A 13th-century Islamic kingdom in Sumatra.

Jataka (S) Stories of Buddha's previous incarnations.

Jawa (J) "Java," in the Javanese language.

jinn (A) A kind of spirit in Islamic tradition, and the root of the English word "genie." The jinn have families and procreate. Some have converted to Islam. So they are not the same type of ethereal creatures known as spirits in Western culture. They seem to occupy a dimension close to ours.

jnana (S) Knowledge.

juru kunci (I) Lit. "key keeper." A guardian, often a shaman, in charge of a shrine, temple, cemetery, etc.

Jyotish (S) The system of Indian—i.e., Vedic—astrology.

Kailash (S) A sacred mountain, the abode of Shiva and Parvati in the Himalayas

Kakawin Ramayana (J) A Javanese version of the Indian *Ramayana*.

kakayon (J) Another term for *gunungan*, a device used in the shadow puppet theater. In this case, in the form of a tree (*kayu*) rather than a mountain (*gunung*). Both, however, represent the axis mundi.

Kala (S) A wrathful or monstrous figure, usually guarding the entrance to a temple.

Kalachakra (S) Lit. "wheel of time." The name of an important Tantric text and initiation, favored by the Dalai Lama in his many initiations worldwide.

Kalanjaya (S) A giant, servant of Durga with his twin Kalantaka. Both reside in a cemetery and have a role in the *Mahabharata*.

Kalantaka (S) The twin of Kalanjaya (q.v.). A form of Yama, the God of Death.

kalas (S) A complex term referring to sixteen female "essences." The word is also used to mean "time," and "unguent." The sixteen kalas are essences that the female genital organ secretes at various points in the lunar cycle, which is itself divided into sixteen "digits" or kalas. Each of the kalas is believed to have a different quality or property.

kalash (S) A water pot, suspended over the lingga in a Hindu temple from which water or oil or other liquids drip onto the lingga-yoni.

Kali (S) In Indian religion, the Black Goddess, usually shown with skull cups, a necklace of human skulls, and dancing on a corpse.

Kalika (S) A female demonic servant of Durga.

Kalpataru (S) The Tree of Life.

kama (S) Desire.

Kamadeva (S) The God of Love and Desire.

Kamadhatu (S) The world of desire. At Borobudur, represented by the lowest level of the structure.

Kamajaya (J) The God of Love and Desire, same as the Sanskrit Kamadeva. In Javanese history, the second king of Kediri was believed to be his incarnation.

Kamaratih (J) The Goddess of Lust and Passion, same as the Sanskrit Rati. Believed to have been incarnated as the wife of the second king of Kediri, who was himself the incarnation of Kamajaya.

kame'a (H) Lit. "amulet," a word that comes from a root meaning "to bind." It is used in English to refer to the magic squares of the seven "planets" according to medieval grimoires.

kampung (I) A hamlet or village.

kangling (S) A trumpet made from a human thighbone, used in shamanistic and Tantric rituals.

kapala (S) Lit. "head." Used to refer to the skull-cup which is an integral part of some Tantric rituals.

Kapalika (S) A Tantric sect of India that met in cemeteries and charnel grounds.

Kartikeya (S) Also known as Skanda: one of Shiva's two sons. The other son is Ganesha.

Kaula Chakra (S) One of the schools of Tantra that emphasizes the body, sexuality, and the cremation ground. The definition of the word *kaula* is problematic, and may refer to "tribe" or "family." There are, or have been, Kaula sects throughout India at various times.

Kawi (J) Old Javanese script.

kebatinan (I) Based on the Arabic word *batin*, or "hidden": an inner-directed mystical practice, as opposed to *kejawen* (q.v.).

Kediri (J) A Javanese kingdom that lasted from c. 1045–1221 CE. The Kediri kingdom was ruled by a series of monarchs who considered themselves the incarnation of Hindu gods.

kejawen (I) Based on the word for Java—*Jawa*—a more outward-directed, magical practice than *kebatinan*. Care should be taken, though, not to use these definitions in their strictest sense, as they are used sometimes loosely in other texts.

keris (I) See *kris*.

Kertanegara (J) A Tantric king of Java, of the Singhasari dynasty, and an initiate of the Hevajra Tantra.

kinnara (S) A half-male, half-bird creature.

kinnari (S) A half-female, half-bird creature.

kitab (A) Lit. "book."

kliwon (J) One of the days of the five-day Javanese week.

krama (J) A formal form of the Javanese language.

kramatan (J) A place or site believed to be imbued with supernatural power, such as a cemetery or a shrine.

kraton (J) A palace, here used to refer to the Sultan's palace in Yogyakarta and the Suhunan's palace in Surakarta (Solo).

kris (I) A knife, often with a wavy blade, considered sacred and imbued with supernatural power. Also spelled *keris* and *kriss*.

kshatriya (S) The warrior caste in the Indian caste system.

Kuan Yin (C) The same as Guan Yin (q.v.).

kumara (S) A suffix meaning "prince" or "young, unmarried male."

Kundalini (S) Lit. "coiled." In Kundalini and Tantric yoga, the serpent goddess coiled at the base of the spine. Yoga and Tantra are methods of raising the Kundalini to the cranial vault, at which point the amrita is said to be created.

Kunti (J) In the Sudamala epic, the mother of Sadewa.

Kyai Poleng (J) A Naga, or serpent spirit, inhabiting Candi Ijo in Java.

Labuhan (J) From the Javanese "labuh"—to throw—the name of a ceremony of offering to the Queen of the Southern Seas that consists in throwing the offerings into the sea.

lahir (A) The exoteric form of Islam, as opposed to its esoteric form, *batin*.

Lakshamana (S) In the *Ramayana*, Rama's loyal friend.

Lakshmi (S) A Hindu goddess of wealth, prosperity, and beauty.

latihan (I) Lit. "exercises" referring to the mystical practices of *kebatinan* (q.v.).

Legi (J) One of the days of the five-day Javanese "week."

Lilith (H) From the root *layil*, meaning "night." According to medieval Jewish tradition, Lilith was Adam's first wife. Lilith appears in the Babylonian Talmud as a class of demons known as *lilittu* (q.v.).

Lilittu (B) Female demons of the night. A kind of succubus according to some sources, and demons who preyed on women and children according to others.

linga (S) See *lingga*.

Linga Purana (S) One of the Puranas, which focuses on Shiva's lingga and the correct way of worshipping it. It also speaks of the origin of both Brahma and Vishnu, and thus emphasizes Shiva's pre-eminence.

lingga (S) A word with many meanings and associations, it usually refers to the male reproductive organ. Also spelled *linga*.

Loro Jonggrang (J) Lit. "slender virgin," a story that is associated with Candi Sewu.

madya (S) Wine. One of the five tabus to be broken during the *pancatattva* ritual.

Mahabharata (S) A famous Indian epic, which tells the tale of the wars between the Pandavas and the Kauravas in their struggle for the kingdom of Hastinapura, but which also contains much philosophical and religious discussions, ancillary texts, etc. It is from the *Mahabharata* that Bhima, Arjuna, and many other personalities find their way into Javanese *wayang* performances and the bas-reliefs of the Tantric temples, the other influential text being the *Ramayana*.

Mahadevi (S) Lit. "Great Goddess."

Mahaguru (S) Lit. "Great Teacher." A form of Shiva.

maharasa (S) Lit. "great fluid." The commingling of the male and female essences in a Tantric ritual. See also the Javanese term *rasa*.

Mahavidya (S) Lit. "Great Wisdom." One of the ten aspects of the Great Goddess in Hinduism, of which Kali is one.

Mahayana (S) Lit. "Great Vehicle," one of the two major schools of Buddhism, the other being Theravada.

maithuna (S) Union, or intercourse. The last of the five tabus to be broken in the *pancatattva* ritual of the Five Ms.

Maitreya (S) The future Buddha, the Buddha to come.

Majapahit (J) The last non-Islamic dynasty of Java, which came to an end in the 15th century CE.

makar (S) Actually a Hindi word referring to a kind of fresh-water dolphin at one time found in the Ganges. The mount of the ocean god Varuna as well as of the goddess Ganga. It is also used to refer to the astrological sign Capricorn.

makara (S) A half-goat, half-serpentlike creature with a huge and ferocious mouth found carved into the entrances of Indian temples, most notably at Borobudur, Prambanan, and Sewu. They are also said to represent sexual desire.

mala (S) A string of beads, or rosary, in Indian religion.

mala mudra (S) A mudra in which the hand holds a mala, or rosary.

Malkuth (H) The lowest sphere on the Tree of Life, representing the created world.

Mami (B) The consort of Erra (q.v.).

mamsa (S) Meat, one of the five tabus to be broken during the *pancatattva* ritual.

mani (S) In Tantra, the glans of the penis.

Manis (J) One of the five days of the Javanese "week" in the formal *krama* style of Javanese. It is known as *Legi* in the less formal *ngoko* style of Javanese.

Manjusri (S) Lit. "Gentle Glory," an important bodhisattva in Mahayana Buddhism.

Manohara (S) A princess in the Buddhist Avadana texts, who was a kinnari (half woman, half bird) and who was rescued by Prince Sudhanakumara.

mantra (S) A word or phrase that is repeated over and over during meditation. Each Indian deity has its own mantra specific to it, and often mantras are used as magic incantations and invocations.

Marduk (B) From the Akkadian AMAR.UTU or "calf of the sun." One of the central deities of the Sumerian and Babylonian pantheons. The defeater of Tiamat, the serpent goddess, from whose body humanity was created.

Mataram (J) One of two Javanese dynasties. The first, Mataram I, was a Hindu kingdom of the ninth century CE. The second, Mataram II, was an Islamic sultanate that lasted from about the middle of the 16th century to the middle of the 18th century CE. The term Mataram refers more to the geographical area around the city of Yogyakarta than it does to a bloodline or genetic dynastic lineage (monarchical bloodlines as they are understood in the West did not obtain in Javanese culture or politics).

Matrikas (S) The Seven Mothers of early Tantric texts, fierce goddesses who help Durga in her fight against the demons.

Matronita (H) From an Aramaic word meaning "queen" or "mother," with its root in the Spanish word for mother or matron. It appears in the Zohar as a reference to the Shekinah, and was possibly borrowed from the Spanish by the Kabbalists who lived in Spain at the time the Zohar was written.

matsya (S) Fish. One of the five tabus to be broken during the *pancatattva* ritual of the Five Ms.

Merapi (J) Lit. "fire mountain." The active volcano to the north of the city of Yogyakarta, which erupted with devastating effect in October 2010.

Merkavah (H) Lit. "chariot." A word used to refer to a type of Jewish mystical practice known as the "Descent to the Chariot."

meru (S) Lit. "mountain"; in the context of Indian religion, it refers to the axis mundi, or the central pivot of the world. In Javanese, meru also means "mountain," as in Merapi or "mountain of fire."

mikvah (H) In Jewish religious practice, a ritual bath.

mudra (S) In Indian religion, a gesture with symbolic significance or one that generates spiritual power. Although usually made with the hands, in Tantra some mudras are dynamic and involve other parts of the body or even the whole body.

Muharram (A) The first month in the Islamic calendar.

muladhara chakra (S) Lit. "root place," the first or lowest of the seven chakras in Kundalini yoga. It is normally considered located at the base of the spine, or at the perineum.

Murwa Kala (J) A wayang performance that doubles as an exorcism or healing ritual.

Nagagini (J) A female form of the serpent spirit Naga. Also spelled Ngagagini.

Nagarakrtagama (J) A 14th-century text of the Majapahit dynasty, recounting the story of king Hayam Wuruk.

Nakula (J) The twin brother of Sadewa in the Sudamala epic.

Nandi (S) The mount of Shiva: an ox.

Naya Genggong (J) An advisor of King Brawijaya V, the last king of the Majapahit dynasty. Sometimes identified with Sabdapalon.

ngoko (J) A less formal form of Javanese speech.

notarikon (H) A numerological system in Kabbalah in which the individual letters of a single word are used to represent entire words, thus allowing a single word to produce a complete sentence. The word *notarikon* comes from Greek and Latin roots.

Nuit (E) The ancient Egyptian Goddess of the Sky. In Thelema, one of the three primary deities of the *Book of the Law*, the other two being Hadit and Ra-Hoor-Khuit (q.v.).

Nyai Agni (J) The name of the two guardians at the entrance to Candi Ceto.

Nyai Gemang Arum (J) The name of a stone figure at the entrance to Candi Ceto.

Nyai Lara Kidul (J) The name of the Goddess of the Southern Ocean.

orang (I) Person, human being.

Pahing (J) One of the days of the five-day Javanese "week."

palang (J) A penile insert, often precious stones inserted subcutaneously below the head of the penis, or a shaft running perpendicular to the head of the penis on which small balls or other ornaments are hung; designed to give greater pleasure to the female partner.

Paling (J) One of the days of the five-day Javanese "week," also known as Pahing.

pancamakara (S) An alternate name for the *pancatattva*, or "Five M" ritual of Tantra.

pancatattva (S) Lit. "five elements." A term used to refer to the Tantric ritual also known as the Five Ms.

Pandava (S) In the *Mahabharata*, one of the two major warring clans. Bhima and Arjuna were two of the five Pandavas.

Paramadibuddha Tantra (S) The root Tantra of the Kalachakra Tantra system.

Pararaton (J) The "Book of Kings," an ancient Javanese text.

Parvati (S) The consort of Shiva.

pasaran (I) The Javanese market calendar of five-day weeks.

pawukon (J) A 210-day lunar calendar used on Bali and Java.

Pendawa (J) See *Pandava*.

perwara (J) "Bridesmaid" or "ancillary": used to indicate the side temples at Prambanan.

pingala (S) One of the three main etheric arteries in the human body, the other two being *ida* and *sushumna* (q.v.).

Pon (J) One of the five days of the Javanese market calendar.

pranayama (S) In yoga, the practice of breath ("prana") control.

primbon (J) A type of diviner's almanac and spellbook.

priyayi (J) An elite class in Javanese society.

puja (S) Ritual.

Puranas (S) Creation epics of the Indian religion.

Pustakasala (S) Library. Also the name for the newly discovered temple in Yogyakarta on the grounds of the Islamic University.

Qudshu (E) Lit. "holiness." The name of a Semitic goddess in ancient Egypt associated with Hathor and with Asherah. The name Qudshu may be a variant of the Hebrew word for holiness, *Qadosh*.

Raden (J) Prince.

Ra-Hoor-Khuit (E) The third of the Thelemic deities who speaks in the Book of the Law, also known as the "Crowned and Conquering Child," and symbol of the New Aeon of Horus. A composite of Ra and Horus.

Rahu (S) In Indian religion, a monster who tried to steal the amrita and who was beheaded. His body died, but his head remained immortal as he had begun drinking the amrita. In Indian astrology, the point in space identical to the western Dragon's Head, used to calculate eclipses. See also dvarapala.

rajah (J) Javanese form of yantra (q.v.); a magical diagram.

rajas guna (S) One of the three gunas (q.v.), the principle of creation.

Ramalan Sabda Palon Naya Genggong (J) Lit. "The Prophecy of Sabda Palan Naya Genggong," an ancient Javanese text.

Ramayana (S) Ancient Indian epic concerning the life of Rama and Sita.

rasa (J) A word with many meanings and associations, usually understood to represent the inner self, sensitivity, awareness, etc. The cultivation of rasa is a goal of the *aliran kebatinan* (q.v.).

Rati (S) A goddess of lust and passion.

Ratnasambhava (S) A Tantric deity, one of the five Dhyani or meditation Buddhas.

Ravana (S) In the Ramayana, the name of the demon king of the island of Lanka who kidnaps Rama's wife, Sita.

rishis (S) One of the "Seven Sages" of Vedic Hinduism.

Rupadhatu (S) The World or Sphere of Forms.

Ruwatan (J) A Javanese purification ritual.

Sabdapalon (J) An advisor to King Brawijaya V, the last Majapahit king.

Sadewa (J) Also known as Sahadeva, one of the Pandavas who goes to the rescue of Uma, who has been turned into Durga by Shiva for having committed a transgression.

Sadhaka (S) The male co-performer or partner in a Tantric ritual.

Sahadeva (S) Same as Sadewa (q.v.).

Sahadharmini (S) A female co-performer (partner) in a Tantric ritual.

sahajoli mudra (S) The method of blocking the flow of semen in the urethra and redirecting it to the bladder, in order not to lose any of the vital essence. This can be done by pressing the heel of one foot against the perineum prior to, and during, ejaculation.

Sailendra (J) One of the famous Javanese kingdoms, which some believe to have been responsible for the building of Borobudur.

Saka (S) The Hindu calendar.

samadhi (S) A high state of consciousness, of control over all aspects of the mind. It is the goal of many Hindu and Buddhist esoteric practices, including yoga and meditation (*dhyana*).

samsara (S) Lit. "to flow on," meaning to wander endlessly through cycles of birth and rebirth. Sometimes used to refer to reality itself as a kind of prison or obstacle to enlightenment.

Samudra Manthan (S) The Churning of the Milk Ocean, which produced amrita.

sandhya bhasa (S) "Twilight language," a language where words have more than one meaning, usually esoteric. Analogous to the "green language" or the "language of the birds" in Western esotericism.

sandhya vandanam (S) Lit. "Union worship," it is a ritual performed by Hindu men who have been initiated by a guru. It is performed three times a day and includes quotations from the Vedas.

Sanjaya (J) One of the Javanese dynasties. Believed to have defeated the Sailendra dynasty in the ninth century CE.

Santero In the Caribbean religion of Santeria, a priest. From the Spanish word for "saint," *santo*.

santri (J) A devout or orthodox Muslim, as opposed to a nominal—*abangan*—Muslim.

Sapta Darma (J) An Indonesian esoteric group that mixes Hindu and Islamic elements with indigenous Javanese *kejawen* practices. Established in the 1950s, it has followers throughout Indonesia. One of its practices involves raising Kundalini (called *Nagatuhun* or "serpent of the soul" in Javanese) from the base of the spine. Sapta Darma also gives pride of place to Semar, the popular Javanese personality.

Sarasvati (S) In Hinduism, a goddess of the arts, music, and knowledge. In Buddhism, she is a protector deity who helps devotees uphold the Dharma. She is sometimes said to be the consort of Brahma.

sattva guna (S) The cosmic principle of preservation.

Sekhmet (E) The ancient Egyptian lion-goddess.

Semar (J) Considered to be the indigenous, guardian spirit of Java, his appearance is clownish—even cartoonish—but he is considered to be wise and the incarnation of a god. He is a popular character in wayang performances.

Shakti (S) A term meaning "ability," it is the divine feminine power emanating through the universe. Shakti is the "title" of the consort of Shiva; Shiva and Shakti together create the worlds. In Tantra, it can be used to refer to the female partner in the rituals.

Shekinah (H) From a Hebrew root meaning "to dwell," the concept of the dwelling of God within the Tabernacle. Usually characterized as feminine, and sometimes identified in a general way with the Indian concept of Shakti (q.v.) and with the Matronita (q.v.).

Shema (H) The name of the single most important invocation in Judaism, it is short for *Shema Yisrael Adonai Eloheinu Adonai Ehad*, or "Hear, Israel, the Lord is our God, the Lord is One."

Shem-ha-Mephorash (H) Lit. "The explicit Name," it is used to refer to the sacred four-lettered name of God in Judaism—YHVH—and also to a 72-letter name, a 42-letter name, or a 216-letter name, depending on the source consulted.

Shiva (S) One of the three primary gods in Indian religion—along with Brahma and Vishnu—Shiva represents the cosmic process of destruction. The Tantric texts are often in the form of a dialogue between Shiva and his consort; the method of Tantra often involves the gradual destruction of social conditioning through the confrontation with tabus and their transgression.

shunya (S) The Void.

shunyata (S) Emptiness.

siddhas (S) Occult powers.

siluman (J) The spirit of someone who has died a violent death, often appearing as a snake or as a water spirit.

Singhasari (J) A Javanese dynasty.

slematan (J) A ritual feast.

soma (S) See Homa.

Sri Devi (S) See Dewi Sri.

Sri Mariamman A mother goddess of South India who protects against disease.

Srivijaya (J) A once-powerful Javanese kingdom that spread from Java to Malaya, Cambodia, Thailand, and Vietnam from about the seventh century to the 13th century CE.

Subud (J) A Javanese esoteric society with followers worldwide.

Sudamala (J) Lit. "to remove evil," a wayang performance and myth cycle that is performed as an exorcism rite. The reliefs on the walls of Candi Sukuh depict scenes from the Sudamala.

Sudhana (S) The hero of the Buddhist Gandavyuha stories, a prince who goes on a quest to find wisdom.

sudra (S) A laborer. One of the lowest of the Indian castes.

Suhita (J) A Majapahit queen who was being manipulated by Islamic and Chinese influences that threatened to destroy the kingdom.

Suhunan (J) Lit. "His highness." A term used to refer to the ruler of Solo (Surakarta).

Sukerta (J) A person afflicted with bad luck, who must be cleansed during a Murwa Kala performance.

Sunan (J) Another title for the ruler of Solo, along with Suhunan (q.v.). It implies a lineage deriving from the saints who brought Islam to Indonesia.

sura (A) Chapter, usually used to refer to a chapter of the Quran.

sushumna (S) Of the three main etheric arteries in the human body, the sushumna is the "middle" channel, along with the ida and pingala (q.v.).

sutra (S) A type of literary construct that differs between Hindu and Buddhist usage. In Hinduism, it may be a series of brief, often cryptic or gnomic, statements connected by a common theme. In Buddhism, the term is generally used to refer to the scriptures that are the oral teachings of the Buddha himself.

sutta (P) The Pali form of the Sanskrit *sutra*.

Suvarnadvipa (S) Lit. "Golden Peninsula," the name of the Javanese kingdom where Atisha went to study in the 11th century CE.

Taman Sari (J) Lit. "flower garden," the name of the famous Water Palace in Yogyakarta, Indonesia.

tamas guna (S) The cosmic principle of destruction.

Tantra (S) A term used for texts structured around the dialogues of Shiva with his consort concerning the nature of reality, of creation, of certain esoteric practices, etc. It is a term widely used in the West to characterize a type of "sacred sexuality." There are both Buddhist and non-Buddhist forms of Tantric texts and practices. Tibetan Buddhism, for instance, is a form of Tantric Buddhism. One may say that Tantra is a magical approach to the world and to esotericism rather than a mystical, i.e., "passive," approach. Any simple definition of Tantra, however, is liable to be challenged as inadequate or in error.

Tantrika (S) A practitioner of Tantra.

tantroid A term coined by Bruce M. Sullivan to denote a practice that has fierce goddesses, transgressive sacrality, and identification with a deity.

tapa (J) Ascetism.

Tara (S) A goddess of uncertain origin, almost surely with roots in Indian religion, who became a bodhisattva and then a Buddha in Tibetan Buddhism. She takes many forms —as many as twenty-one— and these are often designated by color, such as the Green Tara and the Red Tara, among others. She represents compassion and salvation. The worship of Tara was said to be one of the elements brough to Tibet from Java by the Buddhist teacher Atisha.

Tarumanagara (J) The earliest known Javanese kingdom, of the fourth to seventh centuries CE.

Tathagata (S) A name meaning both "one who has gone" and "one who has come," i.e., a person who has escaped the field of samsara. It is a term the Buddha uses when referring to himself in the scriptures. The implication is that such a person is incapable of normal human categorization.

Tefnut (E) The ancient Egyptian goddess of rain and moisture, and one of the first to be created by Atum in an act of masturbation that also produced her brother, Shu, the God of the Air.

Tejomantri (J) See *Togog*.

temurah (H) A method of Kabbalistic numerology in which one Hebrew letter is replaced by another in a set series to produce new words and imply extended associations between those words. One example is the Atbash cypher, in which the first letter of the Hebrew alphabet—*alef*—is replaced by the last letter, *tau*; the second letter—*beth*—replaced by the next-to-last letter, *shin*, etc.

thalamus (G) From the Greek word for "room" or "chamber," in biology it refers to a region of the brain on top of the brain stem and midway between the cerebral cortex and the midbrain. It is believed to be essential to consciousness. All sensory functions except the sense of smell are controlled or linked to the thalamus.

Thelema (G) The Greek word for "will" and the name of a belief system created by the British magician Aleister Crowley as a vehicle for his received scripture, the *Book of the Law*.

Theraveda (S) Lit. "the ancient teaching," it is the oldest form of Buddhism and is the school most prominent in Sri Lanka and in most of Southeast Asia. Based on the Pali Canon it is growing in popularity in the West.

thrayi (S) A term meaning that words in the Vedas have three meanings: an exoteric one, an esoteric one, and a philosophical meaning as well. The basis for *sandhya bhasa* (q.v.).

Tiamat (B) The ancient serpent-dragon goddess who was slain by Marduk in the famous Sumerian creation epic, the Enuma Elish.

Togog (J) A famous character in Javanese wayang, Togog is sometimes considered the brother of Semar. Not as accomplished as Semar, Togog is Semar's "evil twin" who consorts with the Kauravas, the enemies of the Pandavas in the Mahabharata. Both Togog and Semar are brothers of Batara Guru, the Javanese form of Shiva.

Tong Len (T) Lit. "give and take," it is a form of meditation created by Atisha in which one breathes in the misery of others and breathes out happiness and well-being.

Trimurti (S) The trinity of important Hindu deities: Brahma, Shiva, and Vishnu.

Tung Shu (C) A Chinese almanac used for divination, Feng Shui (q.v.), etc.

Uma (S) The consort of Shiva. A mother goddess.

Upanishads (S) Hindu scriptures that date to the pre-Buddhist era but that are newer than the Vedas. They form some of the core philosophical teachings of the Indian religion.

Vaastu (S) The Indian science of architecture and construction, in harmony with the five elements (earth, air, water, fire, and ether). Similar to the Chinese system known as Feng Shui (q.v.).

Vairochana (S) A sect of Buddhism that emphasizes Emptiness, or shunyata (q.v.). In Tibet, the Vairochana Buddha is associated with his consort, the White Tara. He is one of the five "Wisdom" Buddhas and is considered to represent the body of Buddha after Enlightenment. The statue of Buddha in Candi Mendut is a Vairochana Buddha.

vaishya (S) The merchant caste in the Indian caste system.

vajra (S) Lit. "thunderbolt," and the name of a school of Buddhism, Vajrayana or the Way of the Thunderbolt.

Vajrayana (S) The Way of the Thunderbolt; the school of Tantric Buddhism practiced in Tibet.

vajroli mudra (S) The practice of either inhibiting the flow of semen during a Tantric ritual by exerting pressure on the perineum, or of using the penis to gather the ejaculate back into the Tantrika's body.

Vama Marg (S) The "left-turning path," a designation for those practices and groups that permit actual physical and/or sexual contact between partners during Tantric ritual rather than using sexuality as a metaphor. The term has sometimes been thought to derive from the placement of the female partner to the left of the male partner, but this interpretation has been challenged.

vara mudra (S) The gesture of charity, a mudra associated with the Tantric deity Ratnasambhava.

varna (S) The social order or caste system of India.

Varuna (S) A god of the ocean and of the Milky Way.

Vastuvidya (S) The science of Vastu. See *Vaastu*.

Vayu (S) The Lord of the Wind and father of Bhima.

Vedas (S) Lit. "knowledge." The root scriptures of the Brahmanic religions of India. They consist of four main collections, the Rig Veda, the Yajur Veda, the Sama Veda, and the Atharva Veda. These are considered revealed texts as opposed to those created by human knowledge and understanding, and are thus divine in origin.

vesica piscis A Latin phrase meaning "fish bladder," it is a shape with mystical significance. Made from the intersection of two circles, it is thought to represent the yoni. It is a significant element in sacred architecture and geometry, at least since the time of Vitruvius, and is also a common feature in Masonic lodges.

Vishnu (S) One member of the Trimurti, along with Brahma and Shiva. Vishnu represents the property of preservation, as opposed to creation (Brahma) and destruction (Shiva).

VOC (D) An acronym for *Vereenigde Oost-Indische Compagnie*, or Dutch East India Company. The VOC was responsible for the Dutch colonization of what is today Indonesia.

Wagi (J) One of the five days in the Javanese *pasaran* calendar.

wayang kulit (J) The shadow puppet theater of Java. In this case, the puppets are made from pieces of flat leather (*kulit*). Wayang kulit is more than a form of entertainment; it also re-enacts famous scenes of Javanese and Hindu mythology and religion. It can also be used as a type of occult ritual, such as an exorcism. The puppeteer—the *dalang* (q.v.)—is often also a shaman or ritual practitioner or healer.

Wesak (S) A festival celebrating the birth, death, and enlightenment of the Buddha.

wetonan (J) A calendar composed of the five-day-week pasaran calendar plus the seven-day-week Islamic calendar, giving a "month" of thirty-five days (5 x 7).

windu (J) A Javanese cycle of eight lunar years.

Yama (S) The Lord of Death in Buddhist and Hindu religion.

yantra (S) An occult or mystical diagram associated with a god or other source of occult power.

yogin (S) A male practitioner of yoga.

yogini (S) A female practitioner of yoga.

yoni (S) The female genital organ, often represented by a stone vessel in Hindu temples.

List of Illustrations

List of Illustrations by Temple

Borobudur:

Candi Ceto:

Candi Ijo:

26. Another of the many temples in a state of ruin at Candi Ijo (p. 228).
27. A view of the rear of the main temple at Candi Ijo (p. 229).

Candi Kimpulan (The White Temple):

1. The main and ancillary buildings at Candi Kimpulan, the White Temple (p. 231).
2. A view of the archaeological site of Candi Kimpulan in the spring of 2010, with a mosque in the background (p. 232).
3. A close-up of the main building of the White Temple showing some damage to the yoni. The statue of Ganesha was found on the pedestal to the right of the lingga-yoni (p. 233).
4. A closer view of the main temple showing dvarapala heads at various intervals along the top of the wall (p. 234).
5. The smaller building at Candi Kimpulan showing two pedestals in front of the lingga-yoni (p. 234).
6. A closer view of the smaller temple. The pit at right may have been a fire pit or used for the storage of water (p. 235).
7. Another angle of the small building showing the circle placements (p. 235).
8. Another view of the larger temple building (p. 236).
9. View of the two buildings (p. 236).
10. A close-up of the lingga-yoni (p. 237).
11. Another angle showing the high walls (p. 237).
12. One of two reliefs on either side of the entrance to the main temple, with a sitting figure next to what appears to be a lotus plant (p. 240).

Candi Mendut:

1. The dharma chakra mudra, which represents the turning of the Wheel of the Dharma, or Law, and is associated with the Buddha Vairochana (p. 93).

Candi Sewu:

1. Rahu relief at Candi Sewu over the entrance to the main temple (p. 131).
2. An image of a boddhisattva with a Rahu overhead (p. 132).
3. Gigantic dvarapalas at Candi Sewu (p. 133).

Candi Sukuh:

1. A statue of Garuda at Candi Sukh (p. 151).
2. The temple at Candi Sukuh (p. 160).
3. Close-up of a headless man grasping an em-palanged phallus (p. 161).
4. One of the wooden gates erected by the temple custodians at Candi Sukuh, with a close-up of the guardian above the gate (p. 163).
5. View of the other side of the shrine, with another set of wooden gates and a guardian at the top (p. 163).
6. A figure with exposed penis and another serpentine motif (p. 164).
7. Dramatic lingga-yoni on the floor of the inner shrine at Candi Sukuh (p. 165).

Kemukus:

Prambanan:

Taman Sari:

Other images:

Bibliography

While this is a book that cites other books, articles, etc., we should not limit our concept of what constitutes a text to the written word only. The temples are texts themselves, and are meant to be read as such. The Indian temples were always intended to be instructive, and those of Java are no different. What my book hopes to accomplish—in tandem with the other writers and scholars I have cited in these pages—is to help decode these texts or, at the very least, provide a means to allow the interested reader to do the same. Along those lines, then, I can heartily recommend a direct, close, and personal reading of each of these temples by the reader. Indonesia is not that far away any more. The land is lovely, the people are friendly, tolerant, and helpful, and the temples themselves will speak to you if you have the time or the inclination to listen.

Antara. "Merapi Evacuees Yet To Take Advantage of Stress-Busting Sex Shacks," *Jakarta Globe*, Nov. 24, 2010.

Arnold, Edward A., editor. *As Long as Space Endures: Essays on the Kalachakra Tantra in Honor of H.H. the Dalai Lama*. Ithaca NY: Snow Lion Publications, 2009.

Bakker, J. L. (Hans). "The Hindu-Javanese World View in Java: The Structural Roots of the Pancasila State," in *Managing Change in Southeast Asia: Local Identities, Global Connections. Proceedings of the 21st Meetings of the Canadian Council for Southeast Asian Studies*. Alberta: University of Alberta Press, October 15–17, 1993. Ed. by Jean DeBernardi, Gregory Forth, and Sandra Niessen.

Barborka, Geoffrey A. *H. P. Blavatsky, Tibet and Tulku*. Wheaton IL: Quest Books, 1986.

Basu, Srischandra (Sris Chandra Vasu). *The Esoteric Philosophy of the Tantras Shiva Sanhita*. Calcutta: Heeralal Dhole, 1887.

Bataille, Georges. *Erotism: Death and Sensuality*. San Francisco: City Lights Books, (1957) 1986.

———. *The Story of the Eye*. San Francisco: City Lights Books, (1928) 1986.

Beatty, Andrew. *Varieties of Javanese Religion: An Anthropological Account*. Cambridge: Cambridge University Press, 1999.

Behrend, Timothy E. "Kraton and Cosmos in Traditional Java," *Archipel*. Volume 37, 1989, pp. 173–187.

Benton, Catherine. *God of Desire: Tales of Kamadeva in Sanskrit Story Literature*. New York: State University of New York Press, 2005.

Bergreen, Laurence. *Over the Edge of the World: Magellan's Terrifying Circumnavigation of the Globe*. New York: HarperCollins, 2004.

Bertrand, Romain. "Penser le Java mystique de l'âge moderne avec Foucault: peut-on écrire une histoire "non-intentionaliste" du politique?" *Sociétés politiques comparées*, no. 2, February 2008.

Black, J. A., G. Cunningham, E. Fluckiger-Hawker, E. Robson, and G. Zólyomi. The Electronic Text Corpus of Sumerian Literature (http://www-etcsl.orient.ox.ac.uk/), Oxford 1998.

Booth, Martin. *A Magick Life*. London: Hodder & Stoughton, 2000.

Brakel, Clara. "*Sandhang-pangan* for the Goddess: Offerings to Sang Hyang Bathari Durga and Nyai Lara Kidul," *Asian Folklore Studies*, Volume 56, 1997: pp. 253–283.

Brown, Donald E., James W. Edwards, and Ruth P. Moore. "The penis inserts of Southeast Asia: an annotated bibliography with an overview and comparative perspectives," occasional paper No.15, Centre for South and Southeast Asian Studies, University of California at Berkeley, 1988.

Brown, Iem. "The Revival of Buddhism in Modern Indonesia," in Martin Ramstedt, ed. *Hinduism in Modern Indonesia: a minority religion between local, national and global interests.* London: Routledge Curzon, 2005.

Brown, Robert L. "Introduction," *The Roots of Tantra,* Brown and Harper, eds. Albany, State University of New York, 2002.

Bruno, Giordano. *De vinculis in genere,* translated as "A general account of bonding," in Richard J. Blackwell and Robert de Lucca. *Giordano Bruno: Cause, Principle and Unity, and Essays on Magic.* Cambridge: Cambridge University Press, 1998.

Bubandt, Nils. "Sorcery, corruption and the dangers of democracy in Indonesia," *Journal of the Royal Anthropological Institute (N.S.),* 2006, **12**, p. 413.

Burton, Sir Richard, trans. *The Kama Sutra of Vatsyayana.* Kama Shastra Society, 1883.

Cakraningrat, H.H. Prince Harya. *Kitab Primbon Betaljemur Adammakna.* Yogyakarta: Penerbit CV Buana Raya, 1994.

Chalmers, Robert. *The Jataka, Volume 1,* Oxford, 1895.

Cheong, Seong-Joon. "Formation of the Practice System of Anuttarayoga-tantra, with Special Reference to the Accomplishment of Physical Body," *International Journal of Buddhist Thought and Culture,* February 2003, Vol.2, pp. 347–356.

Cohen, Mark E. *The Cultic Calendars of the Ancient Near East.* Bethesda: CDL Press, 1993.

Couliano, Ioan P. *Eros and Magic in the Renaissance.* Chicago: University of Chicago Press, 1987.

Couperus, L. *The Hidden Force.* Alexander Teixeira de Mattos, trans. Amherst: University of Massachusetts Press, (1900) 1985.

Crawfurd, John. *History of the Indonesian Archipelago,* vol. 2. Edinburgh: Archibald Constable & Co., 1820.

Crovetto, Helen. "Bhairavi Cakra: Goddess Mandalas/Rituals in Contemporary Tantra's Nondualism," *Pacific World: Journal of the Institute of Buddhist Studies,* Third Series, Number 8, Fall 2006.

Crowley, Aleister. *The Cephaloedium Working.* (n.d., n.p.).

———. *De Arte Magica.* Edmonds WA: Sure Fire Press, 1988.

———. *The Confessions of Aleister Crowley.* John Symonds and Kenneth Grant, eds. New York: Penguin, 1989.

———. *The Book of the Law.* New York: Magickal Childe Publishing, 1990.

Dalai Lama, H.H. *Kalachakra Tantra: Rite of Initiation.* Jeffrey Hopkins, ed. Boston: Wisdom Publications, 1999.

Davidson, Ronald M. *Indian Esoteric Buddhism: A Social History of the Tantric Movement.* New York: Columbia University Press, 2002.

Damono, Sapardi Djoko. *Mantra Orang Jawa.* Magelang: IndonesiaTera, n.d.

Danielou, Alain. *The Gods of India: Hindu Polytheism.* New York: Inner Traditions, 1985.

Day, John. "Asherah in the Hebrew Bible and Northwest Semitic Literature," *Journal of Biblical Literature,* Vol. 105, No. 3 (September 1986), pp. 385–408.

De Alchimia opuscula complura veterum philosophorum. Unpublished manuscript, Frankfurt, 1550.

De Tollenaere, H. A. O. *The Politics of Divine Wisdom: Theosophy and Labour and Women's National Movements in Indonesia and South Asia 1875-1947.* Leiden: Uitgeverij Katholieke Universiteit Nijmegen, 1996.

Deveney, John Patrick. *Paschal Beverly Randolph: a Nineteenth Century Black American Spiritualist, Rosicrucian, and Sex Magician.* Albany: State University of New York Press, 1997.

Dever, William G. "Asherah, Consort of Yahweh? New Evidence from Kuntillet 'Ajrud," *Bulletin of the American Schools of Oriental Research,* No. 255, Summer 1984, pp. 21–37.

Dimock, Edward C., Jr. *The Place of the Hidden Moon: Erotic Mysticism in the Vaisnava Sahajiya Cult of Bengal* Chicago: University of Chicago Press, 1989.

Doniger O'Flaherty, Wendy. *Śiva: The Erotic Ascetic*. Oxford: Oxford University Press, 1973, 1981.

Douglas, Mary. *Purity and Danger: An analysis of concept of pollution and taboo*. New York: Routledge, 1996, 2008.

Duijker, Marijke. *The Worship of Bhima: the representations of Bhima on Java during the Majapahit Period.* Amsterdam: EON Pers Amstelveen, 2010.

Dumarçay, Jacques. *Candi Sewu: and Buddhist architecture of Central Java*. Jakarta: Kepustakaan Populer Gramedia, 2007.

Eliade, Mircea. *The Forge and the Crucible*. Chicago: University of Chicago Press, 1962, 1978.

Feuerstein, Georg. *Tantra: The Path of Ecstasy*. Boston: Shambhala, 1998.

Fic, Victor M. *The Tantra: Its Origins, Theories, Art and Diffusion From India to Nepal, Tibet, Mongolia, China, Japan and Indonesia*. New Delhi: Abhinav Publications, 2003.

Foucault, Michel. "The Repressive Hypothesis," in *The Foucault Reader*. Paul Rabinow, ed. New York: Pantheon, 1984.

Fulcanelli. *Les mystere des Cathedrales*. Las Vegas: Brotherhood of Life, 2000.

Gardner, Gerald B. "Notes on Two Uncommon Varieties of the Malay Keris," in *The Keris and Other Malay Weapons*. Kuala Lumpur(?): MBRAS Reprint Number 16, n.d., reprinted from *The Malaysian Branch of the Royal Asiatic Society* (MBRAS), December 1933.

Geertz, Clifford. *The Religion of Java*. Chicago: University of Chicago Press, 1960, 1976.

Ginsburg, Elliot Kiba. *The Sabbath in the Classical Kabbalah*. Albany: State University of New York Press, 1989.

Godwin, Joscelyn and Adam McLean. *The Chemical Wedding of Christian Rosenkreutz*. Grand Rapids: Phanes Press, 1991.

Godwin, Joscelyn, Christian Chanel, and John P. Deveney. *The Hermetic Brotherhood of Luxor*. York Beach ME: Samuel Weiser, 1995.

Grant, Kenneth. *The Magickal Revival*. London: Frederick Muller, 1972.

———. *Aleister Crowley and the Hidden God*. London: Frederick Muller, 1973.

———. *Cults of the Shadow*. London: Frederick Muller, 1975.

———. *Nightside of Eden*. London: Frederick Muller, 1977.

———. *Outside the Circles of Time*. London: Frederick Muller, 1980.

———. *Remembering Aleister Crowley*. London: Skoob Books, 1991.

———. *Hecate's Fountain*. London: Skoob Books, 1992.

Greenfield, T. Allen. *The Story of the Hermetic Brotherhood of Light*. Beverly Hills: Looking Glass Press, 1997.

Guillot, Claude. "The Tembayat hill: clergy and royal power in Central Java from the 15th to the 17th century," in Henri Chambert-Loir and Anthony Reid, eds. *The Potent Dead: Ancestors, Saints and Heroes in Contemporary Indonesia*. Honolulu: University of Hawaii Press, 2002.

Hall, Kenneth R. "Ritual Networks and Royal Power in Majapahit Java," *Archipel*. Volume 52, 1996.

Hasani, Asip A. "Taman Sari shows foreign architectural touches," *Jakarta Post*, April 27, 2002.

Headley, Stephen C. *From Cosmogony to Exorcism in a Javanese Genesis: the Spilt Seed*. New York: Oxford University Press, 2000.

Hellner-Eshed, Melila. *A River Flows from Eden: the Language of Mystical Experience in the Zohar*. Stanford: Stanford University Press, 2009.

Hooykaas, Jacoba. "The rainbow in ancient Indonesian religion," *Bijdragen tot de Taal-, Land- enVolkenkunde* 112: 291–322.

Hostetler, Jan. "Bedhaya Semang: the Sacred Dance of Yogyakarta," *Archipel*. Volume 24, 1982, pp. 127–142

Hull, Terence H. "Penis enhancements: popular with sailors and miners, but not necessarily with their women," *Inside Indonesia*, Vol. 68, Oct–Dec 2001.

Hull, Terence H. and Meiwita Budiharsana. "Male Circumcision and Penis Enhancement in Southeast Asia: Matters of Pain and Pleasure," *Reproductive Health Matters*, Vol. 9, No. 18, Nov. 2010, pp. 60–67.

Hummel, Siegbert. "Der Goettliche Shmied in Tibet," *Folklore Studies* Vol. 19, (1960) pp. 251–272.

Huysmans, J. K. *Là-Bas*. Paris: Tresse & Stock, 1891.

Idel, Moshe. *Kabbalah: New Perspectives.* New Haven: Yale University Press, 1988.

———. *Kabbalah and Eros*. New Haven: Yale University Press, 2005.

Isaacson, Harunaga. "Tantric Buddhism in India (From c. A.D. 800 to c. A.D. 1200)," *Buddhismus in Geschichte und Gegenwart*. Band II. Hamburg, pp.23–49.

Johnson, Allen W. and Douglass Richard-Price Williams. *Oedipus Ubiquitous: the family complex in world literature*. Stanford: Stanford University Press, 1996.

Jordaan, Roy E. "Tara and Nyai Lara Kidul: images of the divine feminine in Java," *Asian Folklore Studies*, Vol. 56, No. 2, October 1997, pp. 285–312.

Jordaan, Roy E. and Robert Wessing. "Human Sacrifice of Prambanan," *Bijdragen tot de Taal-, Land-, en Volkenkunde*, (1996) 152:45–73.

———. "Construction Sacrifice in India: 'seen from the east'" in Jan E.M. Houben and Karel R. van Kooij, eds. *Violence Denied: Violence, non-violence, and the rationalization of violence in South Asian cultural history*. Leiden: Brill, DATE.

———. "Death at the building-site: Construction sacrifice in Southeast Asia," *History of Religions*, 37:101–121.

Kali, Devadatta. *In Praise of the Goddess: the Devimahatmya and Its Meaning*. Berwick ME: Nicolas-Hays, 2003.

Kaczynski, Richard. *Perdurabo: The Life of Aleister Crowley*. Berkeley: North Atlantic Books, 2010.

King, Francis. *Tantra: the Way of Action*. Rochester VT: Destiny Books, 1990.

Kinney, Ann R. *Worshipping Siva and Buddha: The temple art of East Java*. Honolulu: University of Hawaii Press, 2003.

Kinsley, David. *Tantric Visions of the Divine Feminine: the Ten Mahavidyas*. Berkeley: University of California Press, 1997.

Klokke, Marijke J. *Art of Southeast Asia*. New York: Harry N. Abrams, 1998.

Kramer, Samuel Noah. *The Sacred Marriage Rite: Aspects of Faith, Myth and Ritual in Ancient Sumer*. Bloomington IN: Indiana University Press, 1969.

———. *The Sumerians: Their History, Culture, and Character*. Chicago: University of Chicago Press, 1971.

Leadbeater, C. W. *The Occult History of Java*. Adyar: Theosophical Press, 1951.

Levenda, Peter. *Sinister Forces, Vol. 3: The Manson Secret*. Walterville OR: Trine Day, 2006.

———. *Stairway to Heaven*. New York: Continuum, 2008.

Long, Mark and Cesar Voute. *Borobudur: Pyramid of the Cosmic Buddha*. New Delhi: DK Print World, 2008.

Lorenzen, David N. "Early Evidence for Tantric Religion," in *The Roots of Tantra*. Albany: State University of New York Press, 2002.

Loseries-Leick, Andrea. *Tibetan Mahayoga Tantra: An Ethno-Historical Study of Skulls, Bones and Relics*, Delhi: B. R. Publishing Corp., 2008.

Lohuizen-de Leeuw, J. van. "The Dhyani-Buddhas of Barabudur," *Bijdragen tot de Taal-, Land- en Volkenkunde 121* (1965), no: 4, Leiden, 389–416.

Magee, Michael, trans. *The Yoni Tantra.* Worldwide Tantra Project, Vol. II, 1995.

————. *The Magic of Kali: Inner Secrets of a Tantrik Goddess.* Sothis Weirdglow, 1995.

Makin, Al. "Mythical perceptions of nature and survival," *Jakarta Post*, Nov. 8, 2010.

Mallinson, James, trans. *The Shiva Samhita: A Critical Edition.* Woodstock NY: YogaVidya.com, 2007.

Mangunsuwito, S. A. *Kamus Lengkap Bahasa Jawa* [Complete Dictionary of the Javanese Language]. Bandung: Yrama Widya, 2006.

Martinez, Florentino Garcia. *The Dead Sea Scrolls Translated.* New York: E. J. Brill, 1994, 1996.

Mastin, B. A. "Yahweh's Asherah, Inclusive Monotheism, and the Question of Dating," in John Day, ed. *In Search of Pre-Exilic Israel.* New York: Continuum, 2006.

Matt, Daniel. *The Zohar: Pritzker Edition*, Volume 5. Stanford: Stanford University Press, 2009.

Mauss, Marcel. *Sociology and Psychology: Essays.* London: Routledge, 1979.

Meade, Marion. *Madame Blavatsky: the Woman Behind the Myth.* New York: Putnam, 1980.

Miksic, John, Marcello Tranchini, and Anita Tranchini. *Borobudur: Golden Tales of the Buddhas.* Jakarta: Periplus Editions Ltd., 1991, 2004.

Mylius, Johan Daniel. *Philosophia Reformata.* Unpublished manuscript, 1622.

Moens, J. L. "Barabadur, Mendut en Pawon en hun onderlinge samenhang," *Tijdschrift voor Indische Taal-, Land-, en Volkenkunde uitgegeven door het Bataviasch Genootschap van Kunsten en Wetenschappen*, LXXXVI, 1951. [In English translation as "Borobudur, Mendut and Pawon and their mutual relationship," translated by Mark Long. www.borobudur.tv, accessed November 18, 2010.

Mookerjee, Ajit. *Kundalini: the Arousal of the Inner Energy.* Rochester VT: Destiny Books, (1982) 1986.

Mulder, Niels. *Mysticism in Java: Ideology in Indonesia.* Amsterdam: Pepin Press, 1998.

Newman, John R. "A Brief History of the Kalachakra," in Geshe Lhundub Sopa, Roger Jackson, and John Newman. *The Wheel of Time: the Kalachakra in Context.* Foreword by H.H. The Dalai Lama. Madison WI: Deer Park Books, 1985.

Nitibaskara, Ronny. "Observations on the Practice of Sorcery in Java," in C. W. Watson and Roy Ellen, eds. *Understanding Witchcraft and Sorcery in Southeast Asia.* Honolulu: University of Hawaii Press, 1993.

Noorduyn, J. "The Eastern Kings in Majapahit," *Bijdragen tot de Taal-, Land- en Volkenkunde* 131 (1975), no: 4, Leiden, 479–489.

Ovason, David. *The Secrets of Nostradamus.* New York: HarperCollins, 2002.

Padoux, Andre. "What Do We Mean By Tantrism?" in *The Roots of Tantra.* Albany: State University of New York Press, 2002.

Pamungkas, Ki Ageng. *Rahasia Supranatural Soeharto* [Suharto's Supernatural Secrets]. Yogyakarta: Penerbit NARASI, 2007.

Parker, R. C. and Lux. "Psychoactive Plants in Tantric Buddhism: Cannabis and Datura in Indo-Tibetan Esoteric Buddhism," *Erowid Extracts*, Number 14, June 2008, pp. 6–11.

Parker, R. C. "The Use of Entheogens in the Vajrayana Tradition: a brief summary of preliminary findings together with a partial bibliography," n.p., 2008.

Parpola, Simo. *Assyrian Prophecies.* Helsinki: Helsinki University Press, 1997.

Patai, Rafael. *The Hebrew Goddess.* Detroit: Wayne State University Press, 1990.

————. *The Jewish Mind.* Detroit: Wayne State University Press, 1996.

Payne, Richard K. "Tongues of Flame: Homologies in the Tantric *Homa*," in *The Roots of Tantra.* Harper & Brown, eds. Albany: State University of New York Press, 2002.

Purwadi, Dr. *Horoskop Jawa.* Yogyakarta: Penerbit Media Abadi, 2007.

Ramstedt, Martin. "Introduction," in Martin Ramstedt, ed. *Hinduism in Modern Indonesia: a minority religion between local, national and global interests*. London: Routledge Curzon, 2005.

Randolph, P. B. *Eulis! the History of Love: Its Wondrous Magic, Chemistry, Rules, Laws, Modes, Moods and Rationale; Being the Third Revelation of Soul and Sex*. Toledo: Randolph Publishing, 1874, 1896.

Redford, Donald B., ed. *The Ancient Gods Speak: A Guide to Egyptian Religion*. Oxford: Oxford University Press, DATE.

Regardie, Israel. *The Golden Dawn*. St. Paul: Llewellyn Publications, 1971, 1986.

Resnik, G. J. "Kanjeng Ratu Kidul: The Second Divine Spouse of the Sultans of Ngayogyakarta," *Asian Folklore Studies*, Volume 56, 1997, 313–316.

Robinson, James M., ed. *The Nag Hammadi Library in English*. New York: Harper and Row, 1977.

Ryan, C. J. "Boro-Budur: The Great Pyramid of Java," *The Theosophical Path*, Vol. XIII, No. 5, November 1917, pp. 482–486.

——————. "Scenes in Java," *The Theosophical Path*, Volume XXVI No. 2, February 1924, pp 120–128.

——————. "Great Temples in Java," *The Theosophical Path*, Volume XXVI No. 3, March 1924, p. 225–236.

Sanford, James H. "Wind, Waters, Stupas, Mandalas: Fetal Buddhahood in Shingon," *Japanese Journal of Religious Studies* 1997 24/1–2.

Santiko, Hariani. "The Goddess Durga in the East-Javanese Period," *Asian Folklore Studies*, Volume 56, 1997: 209–226.

Sari, Godeliva D. "The sexual wisdom of the Sukuh temple," *Jakarta Post*, October 26, 2008.

Sarkar, H. B. "A Note on Atisha Dipankara, Dharmakirti, and the Geographical Personality of Suvarnadvipa," n.p., n.d.

Sasono, M. Rizky and Jean-Pascal Elbaz. *Situs-Situs Marjinal*. Yogyakarta: Enrique Indonesia, 2002.

Scheltema, J. F. *Monumental Java*. London: Macmillan, 1912.

Schiffman, Lawrence H. *Reclaiming the Dead Sea Scrolls*. New York: Doubleday, 1995.

Sochaczewski, Paul Spencer. *The Sultan and the Mermaid Queen*. Singapore: Editions Didier Millet, 2007.

Soekmono, Dr. *Chandi Borobudur: A Monument of Mankind*. Amsterdam: Van Gorcum, 1976.

Steiner, R. "The Aramaic Text in Demotic Script: The Liturgy of a New Year's Festival Imported from Bethel to Syene by Exiles from Rash," *Journal of the American Oriental Society*, 111 (1991) pp. 362–363.

Stolcius, Daniel. *The Pleasure Garden of Chymistry*. Unpublished manuscript, 1624.

Sudardi, Prof. Dr. Bani. "Candi Sukuh Bukan Candi Porno," on the website of the Fakultas Sastra dan Seni Rupa Universitas Sebelas Maret (Faculty of Literature and Fine Arts at the March 11 University in Surakarta, Indonesia). http://www.fs.uns.ac.id.

Sudiarno, Tarko. "Bedhaya Harjunowijoyo: Portraying a Sultan," *Jakarta Post*, May 24, 2010.

Sullivan, Bruce M. "Tantroid Phenomena in Early Indic Literature: An Essay in Honor of Jim Sanford," *Pacific World Journal of the Institute of Buddhist Studies*, Third Series, Number 8, Fall 2006, pp. 9–20.

Sura, Ki, ed. *Buku Primbon Jawa: Lengkap* (Javanese Primbon, Complete). Solo: Ud. Mayasari, 1995.

Sutin, Lawrence. *Do What Thou Wilt: A Life of Aleister Crowley*. New York: St Martin's Griffin, 2002.

Symonds, John. *The Great Beast*. New York: Rider & Co., 1951.

Tachikawa, Babulkar and Kolhatkar. *Indian Fire Ritual*. New Delhi: Motilal Banarsidass, 2001.

Tanojo, R., ed. *Primbon Sabdo Pandito*. Surabaya: Penerbit Karya Utama, n.d.

Thurman, Robert F. *Essential Tibetan Buddhism*. New York: Castle Books, 1995.

Trismosin, Solomon. *Splendor Solis*. British Museum, Harley MS 3469, dated 1582.

Turner, Victor. *The Ritual Process: Structure and Anti-Structure*. Harmondsworth UK: Penguin, 1969.

Urban, Hugh B. *Tantra: Sex, Secrecy, Politics, and Power in the Study of Religion*. Berkeley: University of California Press, 2003.

Urban, Hugh B. "The Power of the Impure: Transgression, Violence and Secrecy in Bengali Sakta Tantra and Modern Western Magic," *Numen*, Vol. 50. (2003), Leiden: Brill, pp. 269–308.

Hugh B. Urban. *Magia Sexualis: Sex, Magic and Liberation in Modern Western Esotericism*. Berkeley: University of California Press, 2006.

Van Dijk, J., A. Goetze, and M. I. Hussey. *Early Mesopotamian Incantations and Rituals*. New Haven: Yale University Press, 1985.

Waite, Arthur Edward, ed. *The Works of Thomas Vaughan, Mystic and Alchemist*. New York: University Books, 1968.

Warren, William Fairfield. "Where was Sakadvipa in the Mythical World-View of India?" *Journal of the American Oriental Society*, Vol. 40. (1920), pp. 356–358.

Wessing, Robert. "Spirits of the Earth and Spirits of the Water: Chthonic Forces in the Mountains of West Java," *Asian Folklore Studies*, Vol. 47, 1988: 43–61.

————. "Sri and Sedana and Sita and Rama: Myths of Fertility and Generation," *Asian Folkore Studies*, Volume 49, 1990: 235–257.

————. "A Princess from Sunda: Some Aspects of Nyai Roro Kidul," *Asian Folklore Studies*, Volume 56, 1997: 317–353.

White, David Gordon. *The Alchemical Body*. Chicago: University of Chicago, 1996.

————. *Kiss of the Yogini*. Chicago: University of Chicago, 2003.

Winstedt, R. O. *Shaman, Saiva and Sufi: A Study of the Evolution of Malay Magic*. Singapore: PUB, 1924.

Wolfson, Elliot R. "Shekinah," in Margaret Schaus, ed. *Women and Gender in Medieval Europe: An Encyclopedia*. New York: Routledge, 2006.

————. *Through a Speculum That Shines: Vision and Imagination in Medieval Jewish Mysticism*. Princeton: Princeton University Press, 1997.

Woodroffe, Sir John [Arthur Avalon]. *The Serpent Power*. New York: Dover Publications, 1919, 1974.

————. *Shakti and Shakta*. London: Luzac, 3rd edition, 1929.

Wright, Astri. "Javanese Mysticism and Art: A Case of Iconography and Healing," *Indonesia*, Vol. 52. (Oct. 1991), pp. 85–104.

Index

About the Author

Peter Levenda is the author of many works on esoteric subjects. His *Unholy Alliance: A History of Nazi Involvement with the Occult* bears a foreword by Norman Mailer and has been translated into six languages. *Stairway to Heaven: Chinese Alchemists, Jewish Kabbalists, and the Art of Spiritual Transformation* is a classic study of *Merkavah* or Chariot mysticism. *The Secret Temple: Masons, Mysteries and the Founding of America* is an excellent introduction to the Masonic Brotherhood. He is also the author of the three-volume study of the influence of esoterica on American politics, *Sinister Forces: A Grimoire of American Political Witchcraft.* While searching through the jungles of Java in 2008, gathering material for *Tantric Temples,* Levenda came upon evidence of a Nazi escape route that led from Europe to Argentina, Tibet, and eventually Indonesia. This research forms the substance for his newest book, *Ratline: Soviet Spies, Nazi Priests, and the Disappearance of Adolph Hitler,* also published by Ibis Press.